ALLERTON PARK INSTITUTE

Number 32

Papers Presented at the Allerton Park Institute

Sponsored by

University of Illinois
Graduate School of Library and Information Science

held

October 28-30, 1990
Allerton Conference Center
Robert Allerton Park
Monticello, Illinois

Evaluation of Public Services
and
Public Services Personnel

BRYCE ALLEN

Editor

University of Illinois
Graduate School of Library and Information Science
Urbana-Champaign, Illinois

CONTENTS

Introduction

On three magnificent late fall days in October 1990, 150 librarians met at Allerton Park to grapple with the issues of evaluation of public services and public services personnel. These proceedings are the formal record of the 1990 Allerton Institute although, clearly, they cannot fully convey the experiences shared by the participants. The papers document the formal presentations, but they do not reflect the atmosphere of intense debate inside the Allerton conference buildings that contrasted so strongly with the lazy sunshine and the beauty of the late fall foliage outside.

Keynote speakers are supposed to start the debate by outlining the issues. James Rettig certainly was effective in starting the process of creative dialog. He reminded us that evaluation cannot begin until we have clearly understood goals and objectives. He then raised a number of objections to one of our more cherished ideals and objectives in reference work: that of providing bibliographic instruction. Reading his paper may provide a partial insight into the discussion that it generated.

After the keynote presentation, papers presented theories and practical examples, overviews and individual experiences. This range of coverage was planned, as was the balance between speakers from library education and from the practice of public service librarianship. Tom Childers gave an overview of the history and capabilities of unobtrusive evaluation; then Wilf Lancaster, Alan Nourie and Cheryl Elzy presented a specific instance of unobtrusive testing in which they expanded the boundaries of the method by evaluating individual service

1

providers. Charles Bunge spoke about a thoroughly tried-and-tested mechanism for evaluating what goes on in a reference encounter; following him, Prudence Dalrymple discussed ways in which information science research can point out new directions for evaluating information services. Mary Goulding's paper described a classic approach to objectives-based evaluation, while Betty Turock suggested six or seven additional kinds of evaluation that might be attempted. Finally, Rick Rubin gave a masterful survey of personnel evaluation for public service librarians, and Geraldine King provided a specific example of peer evaluation.

This constant juxtaposition of how things are being done now and how they might be done in the future provided the basis for a great deal of debate and discussion. In three planned discussion periods, and in dozens of informal encounters, real-life problems were discussed, ideas were generated, and librarians' commitment to public service evaluation was renewed.

I hope that readers of these proceedings will sense a bit of the heat of that debate from a distance, and that they will benefit from the stimulation and inspiration of those three days.

BRYCE ALLEN
Editor

JAMES RETTIG
Assistant University Librarian
Reference and Information Services
Swem Library
College of William and Mary
Williamsburg, Virginia

Can We Get There From Here?

ABSTRACT

To evaluate libraries' public services and public services personnel, the library profession as a whole must agree about the purpose and role of public services. The most problematic service is reference service, especially in academic libraries. The bibliographic instruction movement is examined as a factor that puts reference service in academic libraries out of step with other types of libraries. The flaws in the premises of the BI movement are examined, especially in light of changes being wrought by automation and opportunities presented by the emerging concept of information literacy. These are impelling reference service in all types of libraries towards information delivery rather than instruction in document identification and retrieval. Once consensus forms around this idea, a method or cluster of methods for evaluating services can be devised. Desiderata for the method(s) are stated.

INTRODUCTION

[Author's note: My apologies to the late Walker Percy, a genius whose work can well withstand the occasional frivolous expropriation such as the following introduction. In Percy's *Love in the Ruins: The Adventures of a Bad Catholic at a Time Near the End of the World* (New York: Farrar, Straus & Giroux, 1971), the central character, Dr. Thomas More, invents More's Qualitative-Quantitative Ontological Lapsometer, "the stethoscope of the spirit," (p. 62) to measure "angelism, abstraction of the self from itself, and . . . the Lucifer syndrome" (p. 236) in individuals—in short, a one-stop, simple device for measuring an individual's mental, spiritual, and moral well-being. A more refined version created in the course of the events related in the novel permits a physician to use the lapsometer not just for diagnostic work, but also to adjust ion levels and correct the patient's angelism, etc.]

The author is pleased to announce that he has here in hand the solution to the problem set forth at this conference! This instrument renders the rest of these Proceedings superfluous; instead of discussing the issue of evaluation of public services and public services personnel, conferees can spend their time enjoying the late October air and taking in the pleasures of Allerton Park [the Monticello, Illinois location of the conference]! This is the Qualitative-Quantitative Ontological Lapsometer (model MCTK), the instrument that with just one easy reading measures and evaluates all aspects of public service and personnel. Its use is so self-evident that few users will ever remove the manual from its shrinkwrap. It will tell if a librarian fully understands and comprehends a library user's need, if the librarian selects the appropriate information sources and employs the most effective strategies to satisfy that need, if the staff member treats the patron with proper courtesy and care, and if the user is fully satisfied with the results of the encounter. By simply extending the antenna and pointing it in the direction of the library staff member and the patron, not only can a researcher or supervisor measure each of these things, but can also receive a diagnostic printout that assigns numeric values to each of these areas and recommends strategies for improvement. A more advanced model of the lapsometer that will be available in the near future is fitted with two RJ-11 jacks for input and output so that it can be plugged into a telecommunications line and measure these same variables in encounters between library staff and patrons conducted over the telephone or through electronic mail.

The lapsometer has been tested in a variety of libraries of all types and sizes; these tests have unequivocally demonstrated the validity of its measurements, its diagnostic capabilities, and its reliability in recommending remedial measures. Whenever staff members have conscientiously followed these recommendations, they have in all subsequent tests registered perfect scores in all areas, including the patron's satisfaction level. The read-out of these measures is not unlike that of a slot machine. When the lapsometer's LCD window simultaneously registers the harmonic convergence of the ions for the right staff member, the right information source, the right patron, and the right time, then one knows that the public service encounter measured has attained the state of perfection. Work is underway on a much more compact model that can be worn inconspicuously under a library employee's clothing. This ultracompact model will, through continuous subliminal tactile electromagnetic ethereal feedback, provide staff members with information on their performance during an encounter with a patron rather than after the encounter's conclusion as with the present MCTK model. This should assure a perfect score in every instance, since the staff member will know immediately whether or not he or she is performing properly to meet a library user's needs. Given the proven capabilities of this instrument, there is really nothing left for anyone else to say about the why and how of evaluating public services and public services personnel in libraries. The lapsometer asks all the right questions, gives all the right answers, and provides all the needed solutions. This author recommends, therefore, that readers abandon the rest of these Proceedings and place orders for as many Qualitative-Quantitative Ontological Lapsometer model MCTK instruments as their libraries need.

EVALUATION: WHY, HOW, AND TO WHAT PURPOSE

Would that it were so easy! Alas, it is not, and that is why we librarians are involved in the worthy, challenging endeavor of exploring the questions of why and how and to what purpose we should evaluate library public services and public services personnel.

Why evaluate these things? The saying attributed to Socrates about the unexamined life not being worth living might in itself be reason enough. But that implies that the public service function of libraries is a matter of importance only to librarians. That is a very narrow, unconstructive view of the matter. We need to evaluate public services and public services personnel because these services also matter to the people who use and who, not just incidentally, support libraries through taxes, tuition payments, or philanthropy. If these services did not matter to these people, they would not use nor would they support them. They deserve good service; librarians have an obligation to deliver it.

The title of this paper poses the question, "Can we get there from here?" "Get where?" one must wonder, and from what "here"? Everyone is familiar with the quintessential bit of American folklore about a traveler lost in a strange place who asks a local for directions and receives the perplexing, unhelpful reply, "You can't get there from here." These Proceedings are unlikely to provide clear answers to all of the questions, explicit and implicit, about evaluation of public services and public services personnel, but even answers posed provisionally will be more helpful than that of the local's reply. But before we can reach our hoped-for destination, that is, before we can say how public services and public services personnel ought to be evaluated, we need to agree on what it is that is to be evaluated and what its purpose is. For only if we know that can we judge whether or not it achieves its purpose.

The existence of public services and public services personnel in libraries in the United States is a given, something taken for granted by librarians and library users. It has not always been so, as Rothstein (1955) has chronicled in his history of reference service's first six or seven decades, a very brief span in a history of institutions that proudly trace their roots back to Alexandria. The role and purpose of public services in libraries can be summarized by a century-old definition of just one aspect of public services, that part of it known as reference service. In 1891, William B. Child of the Columbia University reference department defined reference as "the assistance given by a librarian to readers in acquainting them with the intricacies of the catalogues, in answering questions, and, in short, doing anything and everything in his power to facilitate access to the resources of the library" (Child, 1891, p. 298). This definition, although it rarely peeks out from the pages of the *Library Journal,* remains as valid today as it was then. The problem is that the phrase, "doing anything and everything . . . to facilitate access to the resources of the library," includes some "weasel" words open to interpretation.

One of the undeniable strengths of this definition is its breadth and its ability to accommodate functions and techniques that Child could not possibly have imagined a century ago. Surely the creation of a catalog is one of the things librarians do to facilitate access to libraries' resources. Provision of remote access to these catalogs via telecommunications systems is another, but not one Child could have imagined. Open stacks and classification of materials are also means by which librarians facilitate access to library resources. Perhaps the most popular thing librarians do to facilitate access to resources is loan those resources to individual library users. So fundamental and so important is this service that it eventually expanded to permit the users of one library to borrow the resources of another library either through reciprocal borrowing agreements or through interlibrary loan. Some of the services libraries provide to their publics are much less ambiguous than others. Circulation, although always the subject of mild controversy because some users or groups of users want more generous policies, is probably the least ambiguous service; patrons borrow books and they return them.

Probably the most ambiguous service, and therefore the most difficult to evaluate, is reference service. Just what is it that a reference librarian ought to do? Just what is encompassed by "anything and everything" in the effort to "facilitate access to the resources of the library"? "Anything and everything" is admittedly an ideal, and that perhaps explains why Child's definition never became a standard; ideals, after all, are hard to live up to. Furthermore, the library world is not a monolith, as demonstrated by the existence of its various special-interest associations. Some types of libraries have more difficulty defining for themselves (and, therefore, for their unwitting users) what they mean by reference service. Special libraries, it appears, have the least difficulty in establishing the scope of their reference services; their practices show that they have embraced Child's definition and have little trouble accepting anything and everything that a situation calls for in order to find the information a client in the parent organization needs. Public libraries seem to have little doubt about what their reference services should do. Whereas librarians in the public library community have not resolved the controversy about whether the collections, particularly the fiction collections, they build should widely represent various genre, periods, nations, and styles or should be "give-'em-what-they-want" collections similar to an airport newsstand's paperback rack, they do not appear to have deep conflicts among themselves about the function of reference services, at least not for adults. Public libraries attempt to answer adult patrons' questions. The situation regarding students is murkier. Sometimes, the service children receive is indistinguishable from the service adults receive; sometimes, it is more similar to a mode of service most frequently found in academic libraries: the instructional mode.

It is in academic libraries that one finds the greatest ambiguity about reference service and the way in which it should be carried out. Representative statements from the past decade illustrate the problem. On the one hand are statements such as those from the Bibliographic Instruction Think Tank of the Association of College and Research Libraries. This group of six librarians from universities met in July 1981 and "rejected the traditional notion of the academic library as a mere adjunct to the education program, which led to the establishment of a type of reference service borrowed almost unconsciously from the public library model" (Think Tank, 1981, p. 394). This group "further rejected the notion of bibliographic instruction as a secondary activity of library reference departments, and instead viewed it as the very heart of the reference process" (p. 395). On the other hand, Joanne Bessler (1990) has recently argued that "it's time for librarians to stop trying to teach patrons and to focus more on listening" and declared that "it is time for librarians to raise a new banner. Service, not instruction, should be the hallmark of the profession" (p. 77).

These two views could hardly be more different, yet they describe the "here" where public services in academic libraries stand and demonstrate a division in the ranks of academic librarians; some see the *raison d'etre* of public services as service (meaning fulfilling clients' information needs) and others see it as bibliographic instruction.

The term *bibliographic instruction* has not always been with us. Before it came into vogue, *library instruction* was an important buzzword among academic librarians. This is a point well worth keeping in mind, for library instruction or, more properly, the term *library use instruction*, lest one think institutions or even buildings were being taught, is more accurately descriptive of instructional efforts during the past several decades than the fuzzier *bibliographic instruction*.

Library use instruction has been promoted vigorously, especially during the past two decades, as a response to some very real problems. The basic problem that it has addressed, whatever its professed aims, has been that of physical access to library materials. North American academic libraries' prevalent open stacks arrangement provides great convenience to users; once they have identified an item they want, they can retrieve it immediately and begin using it. Combined with the practice of classifying materials and shelving them by classification numbers, open stacks also permit browsing, a not-infrequently useful information search-and-retrieval technique that ought not be scorned. Open stacks also undeniably serve libraries' convenience since they do not have to hire pages to retrieve books for patrons. But before a library user can retrieve anything from open stacks, he or she first has to identify the item(s) to be retrieved.

The principal tool for identifying items is the library's catalog. However, because the students on whom library use instruction has been concentrated—freshmen and sophomores—do not have a strong knowledge base nor a strong bibliographic base in whatever discipline they need library resources for, periodical indexes are equally important. Taking these factors into consideration, library use instruction has devised a template for successful library use for students to follow.

This template, promoted as a one-process-fits-every-discipline tool, guides the student to a general-purpose encyclopedia or a subject-specific encyclopedia as a first step. The purpose of this step is to compensate for the student's lack of knowledge on the topic he or she has chosen to write about. The next step guides the student to the *Library of Congress Subject Headings* and then to the catalog to identify books on the topic. The next step guides the student to a periodical index to identify recent journal articles on the topic. This strategy culminates with a trip to the stacks to retrieve the books and articles identified in its various steps. In other words, it was designed largely to enable students to take advantage of the convenience the open stacks arrangement offers all users regardless of their level of sophistication.

This basic approach remains the foundation of bibliographic instruction (BI) programs in countless academic libraries. The pattern is repeated and promoted in classroom lectures, audiovisual programs, workbooks, and computer software. For example, the user's manual for *Research Assistant* (Bevilacqua, 1989), a bibliographic instruction program for the Macintosh computer, includes a generic "Library

Research Flow Chart" that suggests checking a subject encyclopedia for a general overview, checking the catalog for books, checking periodical indexes, and consulting other reference books such as almanacs and dictionaries (p. 3). This is also essentially the model promoted by Gemma DeVinney (1987, pp. 13-23).

Yet this template is seriously flawed, especially when one examines the claims and justifications often made on its behalf by BI advocates. BI has been promoted by some for its promise to turn callow, ignorant freshmen into independent lifelong learners. Nobody can argue that it is not one of the ideals of a college education, including the role the library plays in it, to teach students to become independent lifelong learners. The question then becomes, how can the library best play its role in that noble effort? BI as it has been practiced at most institutions has yet to prove that it has a significant contribution to make.

A truly independent lifelong learner must be able to make independent judgments about the value, the truth, and the accuracy of information regardless of how that person came into possession of that information. This applies to all types of information—to the editorial in the morning newspaper delivered to one's doorstep, to the articles in a magazine one subscribes to, to the direct mail appeals delivered to one's mailbox, to the news bulletin one hears on the car radio while driving to work, to correspondence one receives from a business associate, and to the diagnosis of an illness made by one's physician, as well as to books one borrows from a library. BI programs, especially those promoting a universally applicable search strategy, have been very weak instruments for instilling the critical thinking skills needed to judge all of these forms of information. Their emphasis, sadly, has been on the mechanics of retrieving documents. This is a necessary skill, but not one that makes those who possess it independent lifelong learners. Miriam Drake (1989) has noted that "Librarians continue to be more concerned with delivery of documents and have not focused on delivery of content or the data and information contained in the documents" (p. 523). This is a serious shortcoming.

Theoretical discussions of the purpose of BI and its foundations have for many years transcended the document retrieval level. However, the programs as practiced, by and large, have not transcended it. Instead, they have been judged successful if students in them have demonstrated mastery of the behavioral objectives of being able to find a citation in an index and retrieve the cited article or to identify a book through the catalog and retrieve that book from the stacks. This is far too little to settle for in return for all of the fiscal resources, time, effort, and energy librarians have invested in these programs. Furthermore, given the vagaries of organization and architectural design in libraries, it is questionable how transferrable these skills are from one library to another. Unless they can be transferred *in toto*, they make little or no contribution to independent lifelong learning skills.

Because many in the BI movement—and the BI Think Tank of 1981 declared itself "a political movement within academic librarianship"—(Think Tank, 1981, p. 395) have cited as one of its goals the development of independent lifelong learners, BI has been promoted as vital to *every* college student (Association of College and Research Libraries, 1987, p. 257). As a result, a favored structure has been to incorporate a library use instruction component in freshman English courses. These courses have been targeted because in the cafeteria-style curricula of American universities in recent decades, English composition has often been the only course every student takes. When these courses have taken as their purpose the teaching of writing skills, the library component has been largely superfluous. When these courses have taken as a part of their purpose teaching students how to write a research paper, the library component has been able to resonate sympathetically with the courses' broader purposes. If properly designed and taught, these composition courses have focused on critical thinking skills and the ways in which students can judge the validity of a text and its use of logic, its presentation of evidence, its rhetorical devices, etc. In comparison to this, instruction in the mechanics of document retrieval is insignificant in the long run. At their worst, these courses focus on the mechanics of a style manual and proper forms for citing documents. In comparison to this dull stuff, instruction in the mechanics of document retrieval is simply one more incentive for students to daydream or cut class. Perhaps one of the reasons the BI movement has not succeeded in carrying out its 1981 manifesto is that it has made poor choices in seeking political allies. Within any university, one can hardly think of a less politically powerful group than English composition teachers, frequently an assortment of a few junior, nontenured faculty; several adjunct instructors; and many graduate teaching assistants. That does not, however, explain the failure of the BI movement to make reference librarians the equals of faculty in shaping and carrying out the university's academic mission. The shortcomings of the bread-and-butter approach employed by most BI programs give a fuller explanation.

The universal search strategy is inherently flawed and its limitations have been made evident towards the conclusion of many a BI session when a student has asked a librarian what subject heading to search in the catalog or what specialized encyclopedia to consult for information on a topic that made headlines in that day's newspaper. Since reference works such as specialized encyclopedias are late products of the process by which knowledge is generated and spreads, they are useless as sources of information for some topics. This model assumes that students are seeking information on a topic that is well-established and has, therefore, become equally well-established in the bibliographic chain. But topic selections and needs are simply too individual for the cookie-cutter search strategy to work for every student in a class, much less for every freshman in every course.

The literature of every discipline has its own structure. Freshmen and sophomores generally take courses in many different disciplines simultaneously. To offer them one approach and to suggest that it will be equally useful in all courses in all disciplines is a gross oversimplification of the way information is stored in documents and can be retrieved. As Tom Eadie (1990) recently summarized it, "Information gathering made simple is information gathering made superficial" (p. 45). Furthermore, as Stephen K. Stoan (1984) has argued, efforts to introduce students to the library in the first two years are probably premature, for as Linda K. Rambler (1982) has shown, even in a research university, less than 10 percent of the courses require heavy library use and more than half require none. Furthermore, Rambler demonstrated that requirements for library use are lightest in introductory courses and most intense in graduate courses. Many courses in Rambler's study relied on lectures and textbooks to impart information to students. Some courses augmented these with reserve readings; few did much more. In most courses, then, even the minimal document retrieval skills conveyed in bibliographic instruction are not needed. And those students introduced to the search strategy model who remember it long enough to apply it when they begin upper-division courses in their major may be using a tool better suited to some other discipline. Why, then, attempt to instruct every student in library use techniques? And why, furthermore, focus those very labor-intensive efforts on lower division students whose need for library resources is minimal or less?

The model has run into additional problems in recent years with the introduction of nonprint information retrieval systems. So long as this process was something carried on online and carrying unpredictable costs, BI librarians could largely ignore it and omit it from the model since it was done not by the users but by the librarians. However, the introduction of optical disk information products with predictable fixed costs and software intended for use by the general public challenged that. Some librarians, so confirmed were they in their belief in the validity of the search strategy model, responded to these new systems, particularly those easiest to use, by rejecting them. They chose not to introduce "an attractive and easy-to-use, but limited, searching tool into an undergraduate environment" (even though students "were eager to use the automated system") rather than suffer the sight of "the undergraduate user who prints out whatever results from the search term [entered], circles the journals cited, finds the journals left on the shelves, and thinks that the topic has been fully researched" (Van Arsdale & Ostrye, p. 515). One cannot help but think of Macaulay's statement that "the Puritan hated bear-baiting, not because it gave pain to the bear, but because it gave pleasure to the spectators" (1899, Vol. 1, p. 159). Some librarians rejected InfoTrac not because it was initially ridiculously overpriced, but because it made the process of identifying relevant documents easy. However, a deeper problem indicated by the statement quoted above is that some librarians have equated research and the tried-but-not-always-true model search strategy.

Stoan (1984) has convincingly drawn the distinction between these two activities. Library use can be a part of the research process, but it is *not* the same as the research process. The way in which a researcher identifies library materials has little to do with the search strategy model. Yet nobody can deny that scholars are, if nothing else, independent lifelong learners. How, then, have these scholars managed to become independent lifelong learners and yet not use the library as outlined by the model search strategy? They succeed because they have developed a deep knowledge base of their discipline through extensive exploration of its literature. In the process, they have also developed a deep knowledge base of the discipline's bibliographic structure. That literature, as Stoan points out, indexes itself very effectively through citation chains. These, far more than secondary reference sources, enable scholars to identify documents relevant to their work. The search strategy model has thrived because its proponents have failed to understand that research is *not* the same as a prescribed pattern for library use; indeed, research thrives without following this pattern.

Another reason the goals of the BI manifesto have not been realized is that the agenda BI librarians have had for library users has not been the agenda these users have for themselves. As Robert Taylor observed in 1957, "Most librarians approach the library by way of the book (form) while the user, often unconsciously, approaches the library by way of *information* (content)" (p. 303). For the most part, BI programs have emphasized form over content and document retrieval over document use. People, whether they are faculty members, students, business people, homemakers, etc., approach the library looking for answers to questions, not for lessons in retrieving those documents that might answer their questions. Instruction in library use would unquestionably be a valid approach if all patrons used their library as many hours each week as librarians work in it. This is not the case (especially in academic libraries between semesters); library use by most people is intermittent.

BI programs have been an attempt to solve problems some librarians in academic libraries have perceived but have failed to convince library users they (i.e., the users) have.

All of these are reasons why the BI movement has been misdirected. However, two reasons stand out. The first is that its practice, in spite of BI's rhetoric and its theoretical discussions about teaching critical thinking skills and the like, has not progressed significantly beyond the teaching of a simple strategy to students who may or may not have any immediate or even long-term use for it. The second is that it is not what people want when they seek library service.

To get answers to questions from documents stored in libraries and organized for (relatively) easy retrieval, one must know how to identify those documents and how to find them in their storage locations. From this undeniable basic need sprung bibliographic instruction programs. Wedded to a simple model search strategy and a limited set of behavioral objectives, the practice has not changed dramatically even though the literature and discussions about BI have grown increasingly sophisticated.

Earlier, BI was likened to puritanism. There is, it seems, a strong streak of puritanism in some reference librarians, at least among some in academic libraries. Puritanism strongly distrusts personal freedom and individual judgment. It seeks, therefore, to impose uniform behavior on all members of a society so that all will conform to standards that the society's leaders have judged to be the best. Nothing illustrates this streak more dramatically than the strong reaction to and rejection of InfoTrac because it allegedly made the process of identifying documents too easy. Stoan (1984) notes that "the logic of using . . . access and synthetic sources seems so evident to librarians that they are alternately critical, bemused, or amused when they observe that faculty members fail to use them consistently" (p. 100). And Bessler (1990) notes that "while Katz claims that 'the user should have the option to learn how to use the library or not and still expect an answer,' many practicing librarians resent choosers of the second option" (p. 77). The effort to teach every student the model search strategy and the claims sometimes made for the model strategy's adaptability to any and every discipline are nothing less than a puritanical attempt to control behavior. The crucial question for evaluation of reference services and any other library public service is: Who judges? A puritanical approach says that only the librarians may judge, for only they know what is best for others. One of the things that is good for library users is conformity in their approach to library resources; hence the importance of bibliographic instruction programs designed "to build better users" (Bessler, 1990, p. 77). In contrast, a democratic or *laissez-faire* approach says that each individual user may judge for herself or himself. Applied to reference service, this means that not only can patrons choose whether to be instructed in library use or to have their questions answered, but also that they can decide how much information is enough for their purposes and which documents identified in a search are relevant and useful to them. Indeed, these are decisions that ultimately *only* the patron can make for himself or herself. This latter model emphasizes document *use* rather than document *retrieval*.

It was relatively easy to impose a single approach on users when all resources and all finding tools were paper-based. But the situation is changing. Several forces are (or at least should be) impelling academic librarianship towards a reassessment of the role and purpose of reference service and user instruction. The first is automation. Most academic libraries today have implemented or are on the brink of implementing an online catalog. In the wake of this, some have been able to go beyond closing their card catalogs to removing them. A common result of the implementation of an online catalog is an increase in circulation. While no OPAC (many given a variety of local "-CAT" names) is perfect and none is as user-friendly as one's own dog, all make it easy to identify cataloged documents.

In one library, circulation of its Dewey books, none of which initially were in the OPAC database, dropped dramatically after the OPAC was implemented while circulation of its LC books, most of which were initially in the database, soared. This correlated with the librarians' observations that use of the card catalog had dropped almost to none, whereas use of OPAC terminals was nearly constant. The patrons of that library used the OPAC because it was easier to use than the divided card catalog; the increase in circulation, greater than that which was expected as a part of a perennial trend, indicated that, through the OPAC, users were identifying more books than they had identified through the card catalog and were, therefore, borrowing more. (Incidentally, when records for the Dewey books were eventually loaded into the OPAC's database *en masse*, circulation of those books increased.)

One observation often heard from interlibrary loan librarians after InfoTrac was introduced was that it increased the number of interlibrary loan requests. At the same time, these librarians rightly complained about the lack of inclusive pagination in InfoTrac citations. The significant point, however, is that, thanks to the ease with which patrons were able to identify documents, they sought to use a greater number of documents. Whether or not these documents were the best possible for the users' various purposes is mostly a moot consideration; these users had judged them to be good enough.

Although they are more user-friendly than their printed counterparts, OPACs and CD-ROM systems have a long way to go before they are truly user-friendly. To be truly so, the next generation of these systems needs to develop hypermedia user interfaces that are conversational in nature. These need to offer users options and explain, perhaps even model, the implications of the options and then allow each user to choose the path he or she judges best. Advances in telecommunications necessitate progress in this direction. When OPACs were first installed in libraries, access to their contents was available only from dedicated terminals in the libraries. Users who needed assistance could always turn to a library staff member for personal help. OPACs are now accessible from outside the libraries. This means that conversational interfaces and help devices are badly needed to compensate for the absence of the library staff. The ideal would emulate a system that reportedly is already in service at Disney World. A Disney World visitor can turn to a computerized information system for advice on restaurants, lodging, or other area attractions. If the user asks the system questions that it cannot answer, it switches to real-time video to link the user to a real human for a real, face-to-face conversation.

Meanwhile, however, we have the systems we have and users are using them, often without formal training, to identify more documents than they identified when they had to rely exclusively on manual systems and laborious manual transcription of citations. These systems increasingly are stealing the thunder of the typical BI program. When the process of identifying a document has been simplified through automation, when keyword search capabilities in OPACs and CD-ROM databases make it easy to find *some* things, even if not the *best* things, there is no need for students to be taught the model search strategy process. When libraries mount additional databases searchable through their OPACs, there is even less reason to teach this process.

Students do, however, need to learn the very skills that the literature of BI has promoted but that its practice has rarely imparted—critical thinking and how to judge a document's validity and relevance. The experiment OCLC has announced for enhancing bibliographic records by including tables of contents of monographs illustrates the need to emphasize critical thinking skills rather than document retrieval skills. An ever-increasing number of libraries are offering access to additional bibliographic databases through the software used to drive their OPACs. Projects like this will give library users more access to more information; and they must make judgments about all of it lest, in the words of T. S. Eliot (1963), they be left to ask:

> Where is the wisdom we have lost in knowledge?
> Where is the knowledge we have lost in information? (p. 147)

Furthermore, as more and more users search OPACs and other databases from outside the library, pressure will build for document delivery systems more convenient than a trip by the user to the library. As these systems become common, the document retrieval skills emphasized in BI programs will become completely irrelevant. If the Leviathan automated book retrieval system scheduled to go into service at California State University at Northridge in 1991 is a success, document retrieval will be reduced to issuing a command from the same terminal or PC used to search the OPAC (Hirsch, 1990). If the Northridge installation is a success, it will be imitated widely and BI designed to teach students to retrieve books will be reduced to one tap on a function key. Progress in library automation is one of the forces necessitating a welcome reassessment of reference service.

Another is the development of computer-based information systems marketed directly to consumers, some of whom, of course, are students and faculty. While every computer system, like the organization of any library, makes demands upon its users to conform to certain protocols, there is no sign that system and software developers intend to arrest or reverse the trend towards making the use of their products more intuitively self-evident. The almost rabid loyalty of Macintosh microcomputer users to their machines and the Mac's graphic interface—despite, until October 1990, the machine's relatively high price—indicates how important these features are to people. Vendors promote systems such as PRODIGY as "your personal one-stop source for information" (personal communication, September 1990). Relatively few people in the country use these systems thus far, and none of them can offer access to the many information riches stored in libraries' vast collections of printed documents, but their convenience and increasing ease of use will gradually change library users' perceptions of how libraries ought to deliver their information services. If libraries ignore this, then users may well decide to make these systems their one-stop sources. In using these systems, of course, critical thinking skills and the ability to evaluate and make judgments, to find knowledge in information, are just as important as with any library system, automated or manual.

While automation is both enabling and forcing librarians to rethink the purpose of reference service, a relatively new concept may offer libraries an opportunity to revamp hollow instructional programs. In its search for a name for itself, the phenomenon now most commonly known as bibliographic instruction once flirted with the label *library literacy*. Fortunately, this did not catch on, for if it had there would almost certainly be confusion between library literacy and the newer, much more meaningful term *information literacy*. The American Library Association's Presidential Committee on Information Literacy (1989) defined information-literate people as people:

> who have learned how to learn. They know how knowledge is organized, how to find information, and how to use information in such a way that

others can learn from them. They are people prepared for lifelong learning, because they can always find the information needed for any task or decision at hand. (p. 1)

It is significant that this definition says the information literate "know how *knowledge* is organized," not that they know how *libraries* are organized. In other words, this is a quantum leap from the typical behavioral objectives of BI programs, objectives made increasingly obsolete by automation.

Miriam Drake (1989) has explained the implications of this:

When dealing with students, we have a large agenda that goes beyond traditional courses in library usage. We need to extend our programs to develop information awareness and instill the practices of information finding and lifelong learning. . . . While bibliographic instruction has helped students find books and articles for term papers, it has not increased information awareness or significantly changed general information skills. (p. 527)

Like Bessler, Drake calls upon academic libraries to shift their focus from teaching skills whose importance is being diminished by automation; she says they must begin by "shifting emphasis from product (book, journal, etc.) to process and from access to the provision of information" (p. 529). Until one has information in hand, it is impossible to judge its value. This is when one needs to apply critical thinking skills, the very skills used constantly by researchers in their information searches even though they rarely use the reference tools promoted in the search strategy model.

Despite prognostications, this is not a paperless society, although more and more information is becoming available in electronic media, some of it exclusively so. Automation efforts take time and involve transitional periods. Library users will still need to use some manual processes to identify documents. For example, a reference librarian responding to Bessler's call for a shift from the BI paradigm to a service paradigm for academic reference librarianship, while agreeing with her basic argument, notes:

I would love to have a self-explanatory serials list. But I don't, so I explain it over and over again; I teach it every chance I get, despite the fact that I have yet to find a way to make it the least bit interesting. My serials list is a public service problem that begs for a technical services solution. (Lewis, 1990, p. 80)

Unfortunately, not all reference librarians see it this way. Some see automation as merely another cause or reason to teach patrons the mechanics of various processes. Clark N. Hallman (1990), discussing reference librarians' need to master new computer hardware and software, says that

new and ever-changing information technologies . . . make it paramount that students, faculty, and staff, and others are taught to cope with the information environment. . . .It is not enough for reference librarians to passively respond to specific inquiries. Instead they must actively teach information skills and techniques. (p. 206)

And Rebecca Martin (1990), attempting to formulate librarians' proper response to the proliferation of information and information systems, says "we place a high priority in reference interactions on providing patrons not with the answers, but with the tools they will require to find the answers themselves" (p. 25). A final example comes from a discussion carried on during September 1990 by members of the BI-L *ad hoc* electronic community that gathers online thanks to the agency of Martin Raisch and a computer at the State University of New York at Binghamton. The question being discussed was how to teach OPAC users to search subjects by Library of Congress Subject Headings rather than by keyword. One participant, speaking of OPAC users, said, "Without the concepts of descriptors and controlled vocabularies, they cannot conceive of the need to search first for the right way to describe the topic they are interested in" (personal communication, September 1990). Puritanism lives! The discussion eventually included many explanations of how various librarians have tried to teach this. What was sadly lacking was any suggestion that, rather than building better users, what is really needed are better integrated systems that include the LC Subject Headings and all of their cross references or, better yet, systems that will translate a user's natural language command made in English into LC Subject Headings! (It is, after all, what library patrons use to communicate.)

It goes without saying that some users in many libraries use a language other than English. To the degree possible, these users ought to be accommodated just as are the speakers of English. The capability of the VTLS integrated system, for example, to display help screens in languages other than English is a promising sign. If librarians continue to think in old ways, new ways will not evolve and information literacy will become a meaningless term. The worst fate that could befall it would be a continuation of the old BI programs, renamed information literacy programs. The new wine of information literacy ought not to be put into the old skins of BI.

While it may be necessary to continue to teach dull, user-hostile serials lists until such time as these are integrated into local OPACs, it is no longer necessary to promote bibliographic instruction as it has been. Bessler's and Drake's calls for a shift from instruction to information provision is also a call for an end to puritanical programs that insist that users conform to a single way of seeking information. Automation offers both ease and options; the most important thing is that users be critical of the information they retrieve and make sound judgments when choosing among options. They must be the ones to make these judgments. But first, librarians have to help them get information. The concept of information literacy holds the promise of unifying reference service, for the skills of information literacy are the skills needed by users of every type of library if they are to make intelligent use of library resources. Reference service, regardless of type of library, can take as its unifying purpose the provision of the information people need so that they can judge its value regardless of how it was gathered.

Where we librarians are now, the "here" from which we need to proceed to "there," is in a position of confusion and disagreement about the purpose of reference service and the role of reference librarians. Until this is resolved, we won't know what it is that needs to be evaluated. The discussion has become tedious. It is time to recognize the opportunities information technology and the concept of information literacy offer and to give patrons what they want rather than what librarians have decided they should want. This vision is not new. Rothstein (1955) points out that in 1897,

> W. T. Harris, [United States] Commissioner of Education, had in mind the employment of a whole corps of subject specialists at the Library of Congress, a group of experts who would not only select the materials for their departments but would be competent to furnish information on a scale going well beyond the simple answering of factual inquiries and the indication of possible sources. (p. 31)

The vision is not new, but the opportunity to realize the vision is.

In fact, the Library of Congress today has just such a service: the Congressional Research Service (CRS). However, instead of serving the nation in the way Harris dreamed, it serves only the Congress. Nevertheless, the CRS offers a model for what reference service could be, given sufficient resources in every library. William Robinson, its deputy director, says that "The role of the Service is to inform the decision-making process, not to make the choice or to press for one set of values over another" (Dalrymple, 1990, p. 321). That statement can stand as a model for reference service in any type of library; it presupposes a commitment to information service rather than bibliographic instruction and it recognizes the importance of information-literate users, the ones who must make the decisions about the value of a piece of information.

Edna St. Vincent Millay (1956) wrote:

> Upon this gifted age. . .
> Rains from the sky a meteoric shower
> Of facts . . . they lie unquestioned, uncombined.
> Wisdom enough to leech us of our ill
> Is daily spun; but there exists no loom
> To weave it into fabric. (p. 697)

Not so. Every information-literate person is a loom who can weave fact and theory into knowledge. Facts and discussions of theories can be found in the myriad resources available in and through libraries; it is up to libraries to provide these resources to information-literate persons and to help others become information-literate. Not only must librarians be careful not to equate information literacy with bibliographic instruction, they also must not take entirely upon themselves the burden for producing information-literate adults. That is a responsibility of the entire educational system. However, because teachers at every level and librarians in every type of library have an equal stake in the development of information-literate people, all reference librarians have a common ground. They need to recognize that common ground in information services and the information literacy skills necessary to judge the information delivered by those services.

If all libraries would emphasize the provision of information services rather than bibliographic instruction that serves very limited purposes and that is not the response patrons expect or desire when they seek information—if, in other words, all libraries defined reference service's purpose in the same way as do special libraries—then a universal approach to evaluating public services would be easier to find. Before we librarians can get to the "there" we hope to arrive at, that is, to an agreed-upon system of evaluating library public services and public services personnel, we have to reach the intermediate station of an agreed-upon definition of the purpose and role of those services. Since it seems that the only service in dispute is reference service, the sooner everyone accepts Child's definition (with the modernizing modification that it include the entire network of libraries beyond one's own), the better; the sooner everyone sees the purpose of public services as the delivery of information, the better. Given a clear understanding of the purpose of the various public services libraries offer, ways can be devised to evaluate their success in fulfilling that purpose. At their annual meeting in October 1990, the directors of the member libraries of the Association of Research Libraries discussed "the changing nature of public services in research libraries in the context of advanced technology" (Public Services Focus, 1990, p. 2). It is hoped that these library directors will provide leadership in redefining public services as information delivery with as much concern for content as for form.

Others in these Proceedings know much more about the various methods and techniques that have been developed to evaluate various aspects of library service, and can analyze these and point out each method's strengths and weaknesses. What is clear is that no single method has yet been devised that adequately measures and assesses all aspects of library public services; perhaps one cannot be devised. While considering the various methods and what they can contribute, these methods should be examined for certain desiderata.

Since it is the individual user of information who ultimately judges the value of information, it follows that users must have a significant role in judging the service that provides that information to them. Giving users a role in evaluating library services is not without its pitfalls. Surveys that simply ask users their opinion of the quality of library service, Herbert White (1985) has pointed out, "pose no particular threat, because they always come out complimentary and positive, regardless of the level of library service provided" (p. 70). If they pose no threat, then neither do they offer much value. Nevertheless, the consumers of library services *must* be participants in the evaluation process.

This need to include users in evaluation of services is another reason why it is imperative that our society develop information-literate adults. The critical thinking skills needed to assess information can also be used to assess information services. There is no question that courteous treatment of library users is one of the expectations every library manager should have of every staff member who deals with the public. The danger of involving users in evaluation is that they may weight this consideration too heavily. In an unobtrusive test of services at the University of Minnesota libraries, Geraldine King and Rachel Berry (1973) discovered that 90 percent of the test's proxy patrons, even though they had received incorrect answers to their questions 40 percent of the time, expressed a willingness to use the service again. The pleasant conduct of the library staff who so often failed them was an overriding consideration, apparently blinding the proxies to the service's failure to fulfill its purpose. Information-literate adults will be able to judge the value of the service received, not just the manner in which it is rendered. Because public services involve interpersonal communication skills, any successful evaluation method will also assess these in the service provider. Both the form and the content of the service are important and need to be evaluated.

Not only are both important, they are inseparable. Any successful evaluation method will be able to assess not only the product of a service but also the process by which that product is derived. Inadequacy in the product results from inadequacy in one or more components of the process. The evaluation method should identify the source of the problem.

Every profession should police and evaluate itself because no one knows more about it than its own members. Librarians' assessments of the quality of library services need to be considered just as seriously as users' assessments. Standards for services do not exist. The closest approximation to standards available are stated in the ALA Reference and Adult Services Division's (RASD) recently adopted *Information Services for Information Consumers: Guidelines for Providers* (1990). These guidelines, in part the product of the political processes of ALA, state that a "library should provide instruction in the effective use of its resources" (p. 263). When viewed in the context of the rest of the guidelines and their consistent promotion of information provision as the ideal for services, this must be viewed, at most, as a tepid endorsement of BI. These guidelines, bearing as they do the imprimatur of RASD, come as close as any statement to defining librarians' expectations of the services they offer. Librarians need to consider the guidelines in any assessment of their services. Furthermore, both users' and librarians' assessments need to be integrated. The work Charles Bunge and Marjorie Murfin (1984) have done demonstrates the value of this.

Any successful method or combination of methods must address the whole of a service, not just one aspect of it. One evaluation method, unobtrusive testing of reference, has been faulted for not doing this. Unobtrusive tests have focused on fact and bibliographic information questions. Jo Bell Whitlatch (1989) has pointed out that in academic libraries, more than two-thirds of all reference questions are "requests for locating references on a subject and/or assistance in how to use library reference sources" (p. 182); both types of questions have been poorly represented in unobtrusive tests.

In addressing the whole, no service presents as complex a challenge as reference service. Just to break reference down in the grossest manner yields these areas for assessment: the librarian's ability to conduct an effective reference interview, the librarian's knowledge of print and nonprint sources, the librarian's ability to retrieve information from these sources, the librarian's manner in interacting with patrons, and the adequacy of local and accessible remote resources to meet users' information needs. All of these must be assessed to get an adequate picture of the quality of a reference librarian's performance and a reference department's adequacy.

Because library public services are inherently labor-intensive operations, it follows that there is a cause-and-effect relationship between the quality of performance of the personnel providing a service and the quality of performance of the service as a whole. Methods must be found whereby this relationship can be verified. These methods must allow managers to trace weaknesses or failures of the service to the individuals responsible for those weaknesses or failures. If, of course, a problem is systemic (e.g., a policy that makes good service difficult or impossible), then the personnel are every bit as much the victims as are the ill-served users of the service. In such cases, it doesn't matter who does what in their service role; their failure is guaranteed. However, when the service is established on a sound foundation, there needs to be a way to improve the service by improving individual performance.

Personnel evaluation is not a favorite activity of either supervisors or the supervised. It is viewed as a necessity for salary reviews and, since these generally come but once a year, personnel evaluation generally comes but once a year. Personnel work throughout the year and offer library services throughout the year. Ways must be found to make evaluation of both personnel and the services they offer an ongoing process, nearly as much a part of the work routine as unlocking the front door in the morning or turning off the lights in the evening. This is not to say that, from time to time, intensive measures of service cannot be taken; rather, assessing the quality of a service needs to become an integral part of the service. This will be challenging. Circulation desk work, for example, does not lend itself as readily to a day-end assessment as a stockbroker's advice to clients which can be measured in dollars lost or earned at the sound of the market's closing bell.

A successful method of evaluation of services and personnel will be one that is easy to apply. Considerable research has been conducted in search of valid methods. Many of these efforts have required time-consuming preparatory design work and equally time-consuming data collection and analysis. Perhaps practitioners would have done more than they have in developing evaluation methods were they not so busy and were existing methods not so demanding on a staff's time. In-house evaluations have tended to be impressionistic and anecdotal, more folk wisdom than science. Much of the work on more rigorous methods has been done by faculty in library schools. The Murfin-Bunge collaboration is important because it combines a library school researcher's detachment from the problem with the perspective of a practitioner who must deal with the problem day in and day out. Charles R. McClure and Peter Hernon (1983, p. 21), Marcia Myers (1983, p. 21), and Jassim M. Jirjees (1983, p. 172) have had practitioners verify the representative nature of the questions they have used in unobtrusive tests of reference accuracy. More collaboration between library school faculty and practitioners can be beneficial.

Library school faculty generally know more than most practitioners about testing methods. The overcrowded library school curriculum does not guarantee production of graduates who will be "research literate," in other words, librarians who can read statistical and other types of research reports and draw conclusions from them, much less librarians capable of designing or replicating research studies and producing such reports. Library school faculty working alone could overestimate practitioners' overall ability and/or willingness to deal with various instruments. Collaboration between these two groups within the profession should assure that any method devised will not only be one validated by research, but will also enjoy ease of use and receive use in the field rather than just lipservice.

It may prove that no single evaluation method can accommodate all of these desiderata. Hypertext and hypermedia information products are still in their infancy, yet they offer a useful analog for the sort of method needed to evaluate library public services. Like a hypermedia product, the method or cluster of interacting methods developed needs to show the relationships between all aspects of service and the ways in which change in one aspect affects others.

In Walker Percy's (1971) *Love Among the Ruins,* Dr. More's Qualitative-Quantitative Ontological Lapsometer is initially merely a diagnostic instrument. After linking the theory behind the instrument with an earlier discovery, More is able to modify it so that it can correct a patient's emotional and psychological state. It is too much to ask of an evaluation method that it not only identify problems but also prescribe solutions. Life is too complex for a Qualitative-Quantitative Ontological Lapsometer to exist in anything but fiction. Library public services are probably too complex for any method to be able to both find and fix problems. A method that is an effective tool for diagnosing strengths and weaknesses will surely be enough, at least initially.

The question of how best to evaluate library public services and the personnel who provide them is not an easy one to answer. Perhaps the answer will begin to emerge at this conference. This author regrets that he is not able to offer the reader a very concrete answer to the question, ideally in the form of a functioning, reliable Qualitative-Quantitative Ontological Lapsometer (model MCTK or any other). But, like any worthwhile endeavor in the library profession, this answer will be arrived at only through collective effort.

REFERENCES

American Library Association. (1989). *American Library Association Presidential Committee on Information Literacy, final report.* Chicago: Author.

Association of College and Research Libraries Bibliographic Instruction Task Force. (1987). Model statement of objectives for academic bibliographic instruction: Draft revision. *College & Research Libraries News, 48*(5), 256-261.

Bessler, J. (1990). Do library patrons know what's good for them? *Journal of Academic Librarianship, 16*(2), 76-77.

Bevilacqua, A. (1989). *Research assistant.* Manchester, CT: Upper Broadway Bodega.

Child, W. B. (1891). Reference work at the Columbia College Library. *Library Journal, 16*(10), 298.

Dalrymple, H. (1990). Congressional Research Service: Think tank, policy consultant and information factory. *Library of Congress Information Bulletin, 49*(19), 319-322.

DeVinney, G. (1987). Systematic literature searching as a conceptual framework for course related bibliographic instruction for college freshman. In M. Reichel and M. A. Ramey (Eds.), *Conceptual frameworks for bibliographic education: Theory into practice* (pp. 13-23). Littleton, CO: Libraries Unlimited.

Drake, M. (1989). Management of information. *College & Research Libraries, 50*(5), 521-531.

Eadie, T. (1990). Immodest proposals: User instruction for students does not work. *Library Journal, 115*(17), 42-45.

Eliot, T. S. (1963). Choruses from "The Rock." In *Collected poems, 1909-1962* (pp. 145-72). New York: Harcourt, Brace & World.

Hallman, C. N. (1990). Technology: Trigger for change in reference librarianship. *Journal of Academic Librarianship, 16*(4), 204-208.

Hirsch, J. (1990). California State University Northridge builds high tech storage facility. *Library Hi Tech, 8*(3), 90-91.

Jirjees, J. M. (1973). Telephone reference information services in selected Northeastern college libraries. In M. J. Myers and J. M. Jirjees (Eds.), *The accuracy of telephone reference information services in academic libraries* (pp. 143-265). Metuchen, NJ: Scarecrow Press.

King, G. B., & Berry, R. (1973). *Evaluation of the University of Minnesota Libraries Reference Department telephone information service, pilot study.* Minneapolis: Minnesota University Library School. (ERIC Document Reproduction Service No. ED 077 517).

Lewis, D. W. (1990). A matter of return on investment. *The Journal of Academic Librarianship, 16*(2), 79-80.

Macaulay, T. B. (1899). *History of England* (Vols. 1-10). Boston: Houghton Mifflin.

Martin, R. R. (1990). The paradox of public service: Where do we draw the line? *College and Research Libraries, 51*(1), 20-26.

McClure, C. R., & Hernon, P. (1983). *Improving the quality of reference service for government publications.* Chicago: ALA.

Millay, E. St. V. (1956). Sonnet cxxxvii. In *Collected poems* (p. 697). New York: Harper & Brothers.

Murfin, M., & Bunge, C. (1984). Evaluating reference service from the patron point of view: Some interim national survey results. *Reference Librarian, 11*, 175-182.

Myers, M. J. (1983). Telephone reference information services in academic libraries in the Southeast. In M. J. Myers and J. M. Jirjees (Eds.), *The accuracy of telephone reference information services in academic libraries* (pp. vii-141). Metuchen, NJ: Scarecrow Press.

Percy, W. (1971). *Love in the ruins: The adventures of a bad Catholic at a time near the end of the world.* New York: Farrar, Straus & Giroux.

Public services focus of ARL meeting. (1990). *ARL: A Bimonthly Newsletter of Research Library Issues and Actions, 152*(September 21), 2.

Rambler, L. K. (1982). Syllabus study: Key to a responsive academic library. *Journal of Academic Librarianship, 8*(3), 155-159.

Reference and Adult Services Division, ALA. (1990). Information services for information consumers: Guidelines for providers. *RQ, 30*(2), 262-265.

Rothstein, S. (1955). *The development of reference services through academic traditions, public library practice, and special librarianship* (ACRL Monograph No. 14). Chicago: Association of College and Research Libraries.

Stoan, S. K. (1984). Research and library skills: An analysis and interpretation. *College and Research Libraries, 45* (2), 99-109.

Taylor, R. S. (1957). A coordinated program of library instruction. *College and Research Libraries, 18*(4), 303-306.

Think Tank recommendations for bibliographic instruction. (1981). *College & Research Libraries News, 42*(11), 394-398.

Van Arsdale, W. O., & Ostrye, A. T. (1986). InfoTrac: A second opinion. *American Libraries, 17*(7), 514-515.

White, H. S. (1985). The use and misuse of library user studies. *Library Journal, 110*(20), 70-71.

Whitlatch, J. B. (1989). Unobtrusive studies and the quality of academic library reference services. *College and Research Libraries, 50*(2), 181-194.

THOMAS CHILDERS

Professor
College of Information Studies
Drexel University
Philadelphia, Pennsylvania

Scouting the Perimeters of Unobtrusive Study of Reference

ABSTRACT

This paper reviews the origins of the unobtrusive method of evaluating reference service in libraries, setting the method in a theoretical and organizational context. Drawing examples from the more than sixty studies performed in the past twenty years, limitations and strengths of the unobtrusive methods are explored. It is concluded that the technique, perhaps the most rigorous method of evaluating reference service, is useful for its client-centered perspective and its non-reactivity. It deserves not only continued use but continued development as a method of evaluation.

INTRODUCTION

The unobtrusive method, a.k.a. "unobtrusive testing," "hidden testing," and "contrived observation" was applied to reference service for the first time by Terence Crowley in 1967 (Crowley & Childers, 1971). By now, most reference librarians in American public and academic libraries should have heard of it in one way or another. They may not have experienced it directly, either as subject or perpetrator, but they have probably encountered writings or discussion about it. From a recent online search and recent printed bibliographies, it might be estimated that over forty publications and semi-publications that *report* unobtrusive studies of reference service have been produced, in addition to uncounted others that *discuss* unobtrusive studies to one degree or another. The basic theme of the unobtrusive study of reference has always been to (1) ask a library staff member a query, posing as a real client, and (2) judge the response. There have come to be several variations on the main theme, as will be pointed out below, but virtually all unobtrusive studies of reference service do this.

In the early days, the response was judged on the basis of its *correctness* and *completeness*. These criteria, sometimes blended into a single criterion of correctness-cum-completeness, have dominated the interest of researchers. Most studies have also observed the demeanor or behavior of the respondent in one way or another, and some have explored the personal reaction of the poser of the query.

The first true publication (not a thesis) reported two studies that were situated in public libraries (Crowley & Childers, 1971). Since then, unobtrusive studies of reference have been performed in academic libraries, the one is by Marcia J. Myers and Jassim M. Jirjees (1983) being the first two such; academic government document centers; law school depository libraries; and health sciences libraries (Hernon & McClure, 1982; Way, 1983; Paskoff, 1989).

From the first light of publication, both the method and the findings of unobtrusive study of reference attracted attention, and they seem to continue to do so. Not only is the method inherently sexy—a "cool medium," in Marshall McLuhan's old terminology, similar in its appeal to a television game show—but the findings have been sometimes as juicy and shocking to the professional psyche as the report of an ax murder or the more modestly thrilling columns of *Dear Abby*. With some divine inspiration from the first edition of *Unobtrusive Measures* (Webb et al., 1966) and led by his own passion to know if librarians were giving out correct information on current events, Crowley concocted a bombshell of a technique, as research techniques go.

Even in the early days, the technique was not unique to the library field. Eugene Webb's (1966) book, citing examples of unobtrusive study from many fields, testifies to the fact. Examples out of this author's own files include the titles "IRS Answers Tax Limits of Accuracy," "Information Provided by Police Over Phone Often is Found Wrong," and "Measuring City Agency Responsiveness: The Citizen-Surrogate Method" (Warden, 1969; Buder, 1979; International City Management Association, 1981). Studies of performance by Internal Revenue Service staff have become commonplace in recent years. Comparison shopping and consumer testing are unobtrusive techniques that are firmly rooted in the social landscape. And in June of 1990, the father of a victim of the bombing of an airliner over Lockerbie, Scotland, passed a dummy bomb in his suitcase through a security checkpoint to test the preparedness of the airport security system (Fineman, 1990).

Even within librarianship, the technique is not unique to reference service. In their 1966 book, Webb and others included several examples of unobtrusive study in libraries—but not the testing of reference quality. For example, the informativeness of hospital physicians was deduced from the number of books circulated on the topic of the patient's illness, and the community impact of television was studied by reviewing the changes in library circulation patterns (Webb et al., 1966). Moreover, virtually all studies of library circulation are done unobtrusively, without the client's knowing that his or her borrowing is being scrutinized. But it was the unobtrusive study of reference that brought the method to the fore.

THE PROMISE OF THE UNOBTRUSIVE METHOD

For a snapshot of the real world, one wants an unobtrusive camera. Known-testing situations generate unnatural reactions in those being tested. Thus, it is assumed that its subjects will behave abnormally and most often will try to behave abnormally *better*.

From the outset, the promise of the unobtrusive study of reference service was to provide a *nonreactive* study situation. To the extent that a respondent could be made to believe that a bona fide reference transaction was underway, the respondent would, by definition, *not react* to the testing. One could assume that the respondent was operating normally. This is the conceptual foundation of unobtrusive study.

The unobtrusive method promised to allow the evaluation of a service, a library or group of libraries, and individuals. It has, in fact, been so used. The method promised, too, to tell why there were less-than-perfect reference librarians or reference departments and how to fix them. The latter promises are still largely unfulfilled.

So Far, So What?

If one were to list the dominant results of the unobtrusive study of reference to date, a handful stand out:

- Depending on how the results were scored, the majority of the unobtrusive studies have concluded that the percentage of answers that are acceptable is in the area of 50 to 60 percent. This percentage may rise to as much as 75 percent when referrals to outside sources are counted as correct answers. For individual libraries or librarians, scores have ranged from 0 to 100 percent.
- Relatively few answers are wrong. The major failure of the reference system is in not attempting an answer—turning the query away for one reason or another ("The book is out in circulation," "I'm sure we don't answer that kind of query," "I'm sorry, you must have dialed incorrectly—this is the library.").

• When studied, the demeanor of library reference staff has usually been found to be pleasant, but several studies have found that librarians did not engage in enough query negotiation to know what the underlying query is in many cases, or that they did not employ sufficient feedback mechanisms in the reference transaction.

STUDY VARIABLES

Unobtrusive studies began in order to evaluate the institution or the service from the perspective of the client. It was thus natural that the study focus on the product which the client received at the end of the service activity: the response to a reference query. That is to say, it was natural for the early studies to concentrate on the *output* of the reference transaction, inasmuch as the studies were client-centered.

Moreover, the bulk of the early studies were conducted by phone. This further emphasized the output focus of the method, inasmuch as the respondent's activity (the reference *process*) was unseen. Reference service was viewed mainly as a "black box" which, when stimulated with a query, triggered a largely unobservable process of some sort and eventually resulted in an observable response.

However, close on the heels of the first reports of unobtrusive studies, the profession showed interest in observing the process of the reference transaction unobtrusively because, naturally, reports of shocking levels of performance stimulated managers and reference librarians to seek the reasons. And the reasons, or determinants, of performance were thought to lurk in the reference process. The variables of the reference process, such as titles used in answering queries, were increasingly opened to scrutiny. To a large degree, the desire to observe the reference process has required face-to-face posing of queries, so that a proxy may observe more than just the final answer.

Moreover, other aspects of the reference transaction and product were gradually scrutinized through unobtrusive spectacles, expanding the view of reference.

The Dependent Variables

The aspects of reference service of first and greatest interest have been those of reference output: the reference product. The reference product and its aspects are the logical dependent variables of reference study. They depend on other things for their quantity and quality, on such independent variables as the people posing the queries, the people answering the queries, the collections used, the institution in which the answering occurs, and on various interpersonal aspects of the reference process. Peter Hernon and Charles R. McClure (1987a) present a checklist of eighty-two dependent and independent variables, both simple and in combined form, for the reference function. Kenneth D. Crews (1988) has reviewed the variables that have been correlated with reference accuracy in obtrusive and unobtrusive studies.

The main dependent variables in unobtrusive studies have been, first, the accuracy of the response and second, its completeness. Some studies have used a composite variable that combines them, while others have used two separate variables of accuracy and completeness.

The most important area of expansion in unobtrusive study has been the dependent variables. Beyond accuracy and completeness, major dependent variables that have been used to date include:

- Was the query referred to a *likely* outside source, such as a government agency? A recent study at the Illinois State University Library by Lancaster, Nourie and Elzy (in these Proceedings) scores respondents on their referral to a source which might be expected to hold the answer.
- Was an appropriate referral made to an outside source that *actually gave* the correct answer? In a 1978 study, referred-to outside sources were asked the original test query, and the libraries were scored on the accuracy-cum-completeness of those responses (Childers, 1978).
- Was the query referred to a likely inside specialist? At Brigham Young University, a major interest in at least two unobtrusive reference studies was the extent to which paraprofessional and student assistant aides correctly referred queries to internal specialists (Christensen et al., 1989; Adams et al., 1989).
- Did the respondent handle a query on a sensitive subject with composure and apparent objectivity? The two most prominent such studies consisted of one query each applied to thirteen libraries: "Information for the construction of a small explosive device" (Hauptman, 1976, p. 626) and "I want to find out how to freebase cocaine" (Dowd, 1989, p. 486).
- Did the respondent handle proxies dressed to represent alternative cultures equitably (Kroll & Moren, 1977)?
- How willing is the inquirer to return to the same staff member with another query at another time? This approach to the dependent variable was developed by Joan C. Durrance (1989) as an alternative to the accuracy/completeness variable, in acknowledgement of the degree to which the total reference environment—setting and librarian behaviors—is embedded in the client's valuation of reference "success." Accuracy of answer (as perceived by the proxy) was in this case an *in*dependent variable. It was highly correlated with willingness-to-return, but was not the "single, crucial key to the success of the reference interview" (p. 35). This study is a breed apart.

It addresses success from the holistic and pragmatic vantage point of the client (in this case, a proxy) and that client's personal assessment, rather than from the more explicit and more commonplace vantage point of the accuracy-cum-completeness criterion—a vantage point that is both more objective and idealistic. Hers is primarily a study of *process* rather than *product* quality and thus is very different from the mass of unobtrusive studies of reference. In light of warnings in the research literature of social science and of the well-documented halo effect that crowns library institutions, and despite the apparent care of the researcher in training the library school proxies to be critical of the reference process, it would be rash to equate the findings of this study of proxy perceptions with the findings of more abstract studies of the quality of the reference product—even though the "would return" figure was 63 percent, disconcertingly close to the findings in accuracy studies.

• In the summer of 1984, this author attempted an exploratory unobtrusive study of the total reference system at Memphis and Shelby County Public Library and Information Center. Using what might be called a qualitative and action-research approach, each member of a staff committee was assigned the task of recruiting a friend who was not a library client and having that friend approach the library with a query of personal interest, and record the whole experience. (For instance, one friend wanted a recipe for Mississippi mud cake. She walked into the library, went to the card catalog, and looked under "cake." The transaction deteriorated from there, even with some limited intervention of library staff, and she left, confirmed never to try the library again.) The data of their friends' experiences were not tabulated. Rather, the committee shared them, and the friends' reports became the basis for understanding clients' potential barriers to using the information system of the library.

The Independent Variables

From the first unobtrusive studies, researchers have tried to identify the things that predict or determine performance on the dependent variables. What factors lead to high or low performance and, by implication, what can be changed to improve performance? The determinants, or independent variables, are many and wide-ranging. They have been grouped below, showing illustrative individual variables:

• Library characteristics, including size of staff; size of various collections (general, reference, serials); budget; physical environment of the reference desk; ambiance of the reference area (such as degree of activity)

- Staff behaviors, including length of searching time; degree of negotiation of query; use of sources
- Staff demeanor, including friendliness; openness; approachability; interest in the questions; and professionalism
- Query characteristics, including subject area; difficulty; type (e.g., bibliographic, nonbibliographic); time of day or day of week
- Individual staff characteristics, including education or certification; time in grade; sex; age; individual staff member
- Client characteristics, including education; age; occupation or student status

Furthermore, unobtrusive studies have focused on different *units of analysis* for reference performance: individual staff members; the library organization; the department of the library; the query itself; and the query type.

BRINGING PAST STUDIES INTO FOCUS

Time has enriched the settings and variables studied. But what do the studies mean? How much of the reference story are they telling? Over the last several years there have been assertions and rebuttals about the scope of unobtrusive studies of reference, and there are issues that have yet to be debated.

The following pages will scout the perimeters of unobtrusive studies of reference, probing issues of scope and limitation. Some of the issues have been broached in the literature, and others are new. The purpose is to put unobtrusive studies of reference into a realistic perspective so as to know what can and cannot be claimed for them and to know what territories have yet to be explored.

The Nature of the Queries Studied

The way queries have been chosen for study has seriously compromised the validity of unobtrusive study in several ways. That is, the studies are not as representative of the real world because of limits that have been imposed on them.

First, some have claimed that the findings of unobtrusive reference studies indicate that the quality of reference work, generally, is little better than at the 50 percent level; others have claimed that the studies were so limited in scope that such broad claims about reference work in general were misleading. As this author (Childers, 1987) claimed in rebuttal to Hernon and McClure (1987b), the unobtrusive study of reference has emphasized one type of reference product to the virtual exclusion of all others: the provision of the specific (not necessarily easy) answer to the short, factual, unambiguous query—the *sfu*. Bibliographic queries are often included in this type. This author estimated that one-eighth of all reference demands received at a public library reference desk are *sfus* (Childers, 1987). Diane M. Brown (1985) found by actual count that "short-answer/fill-in-the-blank" queries accounted for 54 percent of telephone queries in a public library. In her classic study, Caroline E. Heiber (1966) had found that 48 percent of walk-in queries were of this type. The *sfu* is not the only kind of reference service demanded; other services include end-client computation, online searches, community calendar, distribution of brochures, a community resource directory, preparation of lengthy bibliographies, bibliographic instruction, advice on search strategy, and advice on reading and learning.

From the first investigation, the *sfu* has been the natural kind of query to study, for it standardized the query so that all proxies could present it in roughly the same way; specified the query so that there would be little likelihood that the respondent would want to seek clarification of it (thus reducing extraneous variation in the transactions); and codified the acceptable response so as to reduce the ambiguity and inconsistency inherent in judging the goodness of response. But all of these efforts to improve the *reliability* of the unobtrusive instrument compromise its *validity*—the extent to which the queries or the transactional situation represent the real world. And most students of the unobtrusive method have wittingly or unwittingly accepted the compromise, and seem to have forgotten that they did so.

However, in at least two cases, some relatively ambiguous queries and nonspecific answers, such as "I'm looking for background information on Tolkien" and "I need as much material as I can get for a 10-page paper on participative management," were incorporated in the study (Van House & Childers, 1984; Lancaster et al., these Proceedings).

Second, in many libraries, telephone intake is much less than half of all reference intake and it is not equatable with the walk-in where (a) a given transaction can be an intermittent series of transactions and (b) the range of valid response is wider (for example, enlist the client; instruct client; provide a mix of answer and guidance). Conducting a study wholly by telephone further compromises its validity in terms of representing the whole reference service program.

Third, in a number of studies, researchers have deliberately limited the test queries to ones that can be answered with the resources on hand in the library (for example, Lancaster et al., these Proceedings; Thompson, 1987). This has the effect of creating a test of the librarian's skills in using in-house resources, inasmuch as it artificially constricts the query pool. Limiting queries to those whose answering is possible creates a test of the librarian's ability within the current collection limits of the institution, rather than of the institution's capacity to respond to clients' queries, which range from the possible to the impossible.

Finally, when judging the accuracy and completeness of responses to *sfus*, it is necessary to establish explicit criteria for judging if one is to be consistent and keep subjectivity to a minimum. In designing the criteria, one must necessarily be arbitrary. The researcher must assume the role of a particular client and imagine a desired response that would seem natural. For example, in asking for the post office abbreviation for Alaska, does the hypothetical client require that the respondent say "capital A, capital K, no space, no punctuation," or will "a,k" be sufficient? In view of the arbitrariness of such criteria, it seems appropriate in the study of a sensitive topic, such as human performance, to be generous both in setting the criteria (that is, establish minimal criteria) and in judging the responses against them (that is, give them the benefit of the doubt). Both forms of generosity distort the view of reference as it might be viewed by the client.

Nature of The Reference Product

In many years of working with reference librarians, this author has been impressed by a marked lack of clarity in the policies governing reference services, especially those policies that define precisely what is to be delivered to the client. There is no reason to insist that all libraries deliver the same type and quality of reference service. But there is reason to believe that individual libraries cannot operate at optimum effectiveness or efficiency without heeding Peter Drucker's (1973, chap. 6) age-old call to define what business they are in.

Lacking a sharp and universally accepted definition of the reference business, one might look for clues in what is studied about reference service for an implicit definition. What is immediately clear as one views the many unobtrusive studies is that a variety of definitions of the reference product are operative.

In any one study of reference, it is possible to score performance in several ways—for example, penalizing for non-answers or not penalizing for non-answers; giving credit for referrals or not giving credit. The earliest study to do this was by this author (Crowley & Childers, 1971). Recently, the study at Illinois State University (Lancaster et al., these Proceedings) evaluated performance on both a fifteen-point and a three-point scale. The variable scoring was important in permitting a variety of views of the objectives or desired products of reference service. It reflects the ambiguity in the business statement of most reference services.

Almost all unobtrusive studies of reference operate under the assumption that providing direct answers to clients' queries is a valid reference service. The direct answer is not necessarily viewed as the only reference service, as will be noted in the discussion below; but it does occur as a matter of course in the program of reference services. And it is often seen as the most valued reference service, if there is an array of levels of services.

Moreover, as noted above, there are various features of the answer that are assumed to constitute goodness of answer. In many cases, the accuracy of the answer and its completeness are often features that are scored. In some studies, the citing of a source is valued. Further, in the studies of answering performance, it is assumed that any of the studied libraries (branches) offers or should offer direct answers to clients' queries as a regular service. The small library outlet that has chosen to serve, say, as a popular materials center only, will fall outside a study of answering performance or will fail the test.

In a number of studies, direction within the library or instruction in the use of library resources has been accorded a positive score. The Illinois State University study accepted leading to an answering source, directing to an answering source, within-library referral, and instruction to be valid reference responses. At Brigham Young University, the appropriateness of referral—to in-library professionals, another floor or department, interlibrary loan, or outside the library—was studied, rather than the actual answer to the proxy's query.

A number of studies (for example, Childers, 1978; Lancaster et al., these Proceedings) have granted points to library performance scores for referring the client to a likely outside source, thus suggesting referral to a likely outside source as a valid reference response. To many reference librarians, referral without certainty is an abrogation of professional responsibility. In response, some studies have explored the quality of the answer received from the referred-to outside source and scored the library on the quality of that answer (Childers, 1978; Hernon & McClure, 1987a). Thus, they have affirmed referral to a *correct* outside source as a valid reference product.

In some studies, there has been an attempt to develop an explicit hierarchy of reference products. Following the James I. Wyer (1930) concept of "liberal," "moderate," and "conservative" continuum of service, these studies grant more points to liberal service (delivery of the answer *per se*) and decreasing points as the client is increasingly brought into the search process (e.g., instruction in using an index) or left with an uncertain outcome (referral to likely, but perhaps untested, outside source). Two hierarchies of the reference product are presented here for comparison. Note that the points on the two scales are quite different, and that the differences are not explained by the mere fact that one study takes place in a public library and the other in an academic library. It means that the way in which reference service, or reference product, is conceived is substantially different in the two study sites.

Gers and Seward, 1985

Correct answer and source
Correct answer but no source
Source where answer can be found
Partial answer and source
Partial answer but no source
Internal directions, lead to correct answer
Internal directions, do not lead to correct answer
No answers, external directions
Incorrect answer
No answer, no directions

Lancaster et al., these Proceedings

Complete and correct answer
Led to single source which provided complete and correct answer
Led to several sources, one of which held answer
Directed to single source which provided complete and correct answer
Appropriate referral to specific person or source which would provide complete and correct answer
Provided with partial answer
Appropriate referral to the card catalog or another floor
Did not find answer or suggest an answer or source
Inappropriate referral to catalog, floor, source, or librarian
Inappropriate sources
Incorrect answer

The Method Itself

Over the years, just as the scope of unobtrusive studies has expanded and the criteria by which performance is judged have developed complexity, there have been three major developments that have enriched the unobtrusive method itself.

First, most unobtrusive studies of reference have been single efforts to describe the state of reference service (or a portion thereof). In contrast to these, there have been few true experimental studies. The latter have been conducted in the classical, though simple, experimental form of test-treatment-retest, wherein the service was studied, an intervention—

usually training—was applied to the service providers, and the service was retested to see if there had been any change. Hernon and McClure's (1987a) study of documents and general reference departments is probably the most prominent example of the experimental approach, even though it showed no effect of the treatment (training). Situations will be found in which unobtrusive studies have been done more than once, over a period of time, but not in a formal experimental situation. An example is two studies at Brigham Young University (Christensen et al., 1989; Beck et al., 1989).

Second, the most significant variation in the technical elements of unobtrusive study revealed by the literature is found in the study of performance at the top level of the State of California's reference referral hierarchy. A random sample of actual queries received by and answers delivered to the requesting library systems was distributed to a national panel of reference experts for their evaluation. The major advantage of this variation is that one is dealing with actual queries and a sample of the full range of queries received by the library, so distortion based on query selection does not occur. The main disadvantages are that one must assemble an expert panel; and that the judgment of answers, especially to ambiguous queries, may vary from person to person (Van House & Childers, 1984).

Third, a substantial contribution to the managerial aspects of unobtrusive study was made by Eleanor Jo Rodger and Jane Goodwin (1987). Three contiguous public library systems in the Washington, D. C. area used the staff of each system to study another system, round-robin fashion, demonstrating the value of cooperation and the economy achievable by not having to hire proxies.

CONCLUSION

The unobtrusive method itself was tested and proved itself in 1984, when Terry L. Weech and Herbert Goldhor published their findings of the first and only comparative study of obtrusive and unobtrusive evaluation of reference. Using identical queries applied obtrusively and unobtrusively to the best public libraries in Illinois, they found that there was a significant, albeit not large, difference in performance on the obtrusive compared with the unobtrusive studies, in the correct direction. To the immense relief of researchers who had invested in the unobtrusive approach, there were fewer correct responses to the unobtrusive queries. Important as this may seem to the continued use of the unobtrusive method, most studies to date preceded that publication. Before Weech and Goldhor, the method had operated on its own intuited validity.

As unobtrusive studies of reference have accumulated, the idea has settled in. The method is rarely labeled an affront to personal privacy, for it has been argued and seems to have been agreed upon that a paid service professional is a public being and thereby relinquishes some of his or her individual privacy. The method seems to be less frequently charged with being an instrument of autocracy, for it has been used wisely and humanely in enough libraries that it has proven its innate innocence. The charge of wasting the time of professionals by causing them to spend time on artificial queries seems to have lessened; could it be that the power (shock) of the findings justifies the time and cost of the method? Alvin M. Schrader (1984) has said that the technique has not become firmly ensconced in the library management "bag of tricks." It has reached the age of majority and a certain level of respectability, however, if only by virtue of its stability and continued power to give the field new perspectives on itself.

Hernon and McClure (1987a) raise questions of the reliability, validity, and utility of the unobtrusive method of reference study. While they do not research the questions, they do propose a checklist of how to improve the quality of unobtrusive data in each of the three areas. However, despite real reservations about validity or reliability, many of which are raised in the paragraphs above, the method has shown that it can offer a healthful vantage point, a client-centered antidote to the institutional myopia that afflicts us all. In addition, the unobtrusive method offers what many—excepting, perhaps, Durrance (1989)—consider to be a more objective assessment than asking the client's opinion. Witness one study where unobtrusive evaluation found the library's performance on correctness to be 75 percent; yet proxy patrons were satisfied with the service they received in 90 percent and were ready to recommend the library to others 97 percent of those same instances (Hansel, 1987).

More subtly, designing an unobtrusive study may force a given library to state its reference business, declaring what is and what is not its reference product. The impression this author holds, based on personal involvement with a number of studies, is that the decision on how to score performance has been an *ad hoc* one. It has often been a decision prompted directly by the study's requirement for such definition, rather a decision that preceded the study, as service policy would naturally precede the delivery and then evaluation of service. This is probably not the best condition under which to reflect on an organization's business. Drucker would not approve.

The approach and results of the Durrance (1989) study, in the context of Patsy J. Hansel's (1987) findings, above, further torments the question of what *is* the reference objective? Is it a set of good feelings about the process plus a certain level of client satisfaction? Is it a level of effort expended by the answerer or institution? Is it some objective or abstract quality of the answer? Whose perspective is valued in making these judgments?

The dearth of experimental studies may say something about the use of the unobtrusive study of reference. It implies that it is used relatively little as a mechanism for ongoing review of program quality and subsequent adjustment. Otherwise, one would see reports of many more true experiments, or at least more follow-up studies. Does it also further imply that the method is sought more for its value as a catalyst in fomenting change, unfreezing behavior, and capturing the attention of staff—in short, as a strategic managerial and political strategy tool?

Few unobtrusive studies of a qualitative nature have been done. As has often been the case in this field, research has favored quantitative probabilistic studies, where the interest is in uncovering precise proportions of a phenomenon, such as the number of reference failures, or the statistical correlation of staff behavior to performance. This is useful when the dimensions to be explored are known and can be codified. But where the dimensions are unknown and complex, probing is needed, and qualitative study may be called for. A qualitative approach to unobtrusive study may teach more about nuances of the reference process, such as how a person's body language is used in the transaction; or how he or she uses words in negotiating a query; or the nature of errors of interpretation. Hansel's (1987) work and this author's work in Memphis (Childers, 1984) (discussed earlier) both had substantial qualitative aspects.

The unobtrusive study of reference has had it limits; some past applications and reporting have been flawed. It continues to have innate appeal to many and, to some extent, demonstrable research value, for it offers a unique perspective on the products and services that libraries deliver. And it continues to develop. While some argue that the method is not worthwhile and should be abandoned, doing so would strip the field of one of its most rigorous techniques of self-examination. Now, when self-examination and attention to quality are critical as libraries compete with other information services, is not the time to abandon a method of such power. Now is the time to tune and expand it— to apply it to new types of reference queries; to try new dependent and independent variables; to explore new unobtrusive methods, such as diaries, logs, and expert panels; to undertake qualitative as well as quantitative inquiries; and to increase the number of truly experimental studies.

REFERENCES

Adams, I.; Parkinson, D.; & Hirst, M. (1989). *Appropriateness of referrals in Harold B. Lee Library: An unobtrusive study.* Revised unpublished master's thesis, Brigham Young University, Provo, UT. (ERIC Document Reproduction Service No. ED 308 875).

Beck, L.; Carter, L; & Skousen, D. (1989). *Accuracy at the reference desk: An unobtrusive study.* Unpublished master's thesis, Brigham Young University, Provo, UT. (ERIC Document Reproduction Service No. ED 311 894).

Brown, D. M. (1985). Telephone reference questions: A characterization by subject, answer format, and level of complexity. *RQ, 24*(3), 290-303.

Buder, L. (1979, March 11). Police act to improve phone replies to trim errors found in study. *The New York Times,* p. 34.

Childers, T. (1978). *The effectiveness of information service in public libraries: Suffolk County, final report.* Philadelphia, PA: Drexel University School of Library and Information Science.

Childers, T. (1980). The test of reference. *Library Journal, 105*(8), 924-928.

Childers, T. (1987). The quality of reference: Still moot after 20 years. *The Journal of Academic Librarianship, 13*(2), 73-74.

Christensen, J. O.; Benson, L. D.; Butler, H. J.; Hall, B. H.; & Howard, D. H. (1989). An evaluation of reference desk service. *College and Research Libraries, 50*(4), 468-483.

Crews, K. D. (1988). The accuracy of reference service: Variables for research and implementation. *Library & Information Science Research, 10*(3), 331-355.

Crowley, T., & Childers, T. (1971). *Information service in public libraries: Two studies.* Metuchen, NJ: Scarecrow Press.

Douglas, I. (1988). Reducing failures in reference service. *RQ, 28*(1), 94-101.

Dowd, R. C. (1989). I want to find out how to freebase cocaine or yet another unobtrusive test of reference performance. *The Reference Librarian, 25/26,* 483-493.

Drucker, P. F. (1973). *Management: Task, responsibilities, practices.* NY: Harper & Row.

Durrance, J. C. (1989). Reference success: Does the 55 percent rule tell the whole story? *Library Journal, 114*(7), 31-36.

Fineman, M. (1990, July 7). How a man whose child was killed got fake bomb aboard a jetliner. *The Philadelphia Inquirer,* p. 2-A.

Gers, R., & Seward, L. J. (1985). Improving reference performance: Results of a statewide study. *Library Journal, 110*(18), 32-35.

Hansel, P. J. (1987). Unobtrusive evaluation: An administrative learning experience. *The Reference Librarian, 19,* 315-325.

Hauptman, R. (1976). Overdue: Professionalism or culpability? An experiment in ethics. *Wilson Library Bulletin, 50*(8), 626-627.

Heiber, C. E. (1966). *An analysis of questions and answers in libraries.* Unpublished master's thesis, Lehigh University, Bethlehem, PA.

Hernon, P., & McClure, C. R. (1982). Referral services in U.S. academic depository libraries: Findings, implications, and research needs. *RQ, 22*(2), 152-163.

Hernon, P., & McClure, C. R. (1987a). *Unobtrusive testing and library reference services.* Norwood, NJ: Ablex.

Hernon, P., & McClure, C. R. (1987b). Library reference service: An unrecognized crisis—A symposium. *The Journal of Academic Librarianship, 13*(2), 69-71.

Higgins, E. (1975, June 29). Information please: Highest, quickest, lowest, slowest. *Trenton Times,* Part 5, pp. 1-2.

International City Management Association. (1981, May). Measuring city agency responsiveness: The citizen-surrogate method. *Urban Data Service Report, 13*(5).

Kroll, H. W., & Moren, D. K. (1977). Effect of appearance on requests for help in libraries. *American Libraries, 8*(9), 489.

Maass, E. A. (1981). Research methodology [Letter to the editor]. *Bulletin of the Medical Library Association, 69*(4), 402-403.

Myers, M. J., & Jirjees, J. M. (1983). *The accuracy of telephone reference/information services in academic libraries: Two studies.* Metuchen, NJ: Scarecrow Press.

Paskoff, B. M. (1989). Unobtrusive evaluation of the accuracy of telephone reference services in health sciences libraries. *Dissertation Abstracts International, 50,* 565A.

Rodger, E. J., & Goodwin, J. (1987). To see ourselves as others see us: A cooperative, do-it-yourself reference accuracy study. *The Reference Librarian, 18*(Summer), 135-147.

Schrader, A. M. (1984). Performance standards for accuracy in reference and information services: The impact of unobtrusive measurement methodology. *The Reference Librarian, 11*(Fall/Winter), 197-214.

Thompson, J. (1987). Unobtrusive reference-service testing at Auckland Public Library. *New Zealand Libraries, 45*(6), 117-119.

Van House, N. A., & Childers, T. (1984). Unobtrusive evaluation of a reference referral network: The California experience. *Library & Information Science Research, 6*(3), 305-319.

Warden, R. (1969, February 17). IRS answers tax limits of accuracy. *Chicago Daily News,* pp. 1, 37.

Way, K. A. (1983). *Measurement and evaluation of telephone reference/information service in law school depository libraries in the Greater Los Angeles, California, area.* MLS specialization paper, University of California at Los Angeles, Graduate School of Library and Information Science.

Webb, E. J.; Campbell, D. T.; Schwartz, R. D.; & Sechrest, L. (1966). *Unobtrusive measures: Nonreactive research in the social sciences.* Chicago: Rand McNally.

Weech, T. L., & Goldhor, H. (1984). Reference clientele and the reference transaction in five Illinois public libraries. *Library & Information Science Research, 6*(1), 21-42.

Wyer, J. I. (1930). *Reference work: A textbook for students of library work and libraries.* Chicago: ALA.

Young, W. F. (1985). Methods for evaluating reference desk performance. *RQ, 25*(1), 69-75.

F. W. LANCASTER

Professor
Graduate School of Library and Information Science
University of Illinois at Urbana-Champaign

CHERYL ELZY

Head, Education/Psychology/Teaching
Materials Center Division

ALAN NOURIE

Associate University Librarian for Public Services
and Collection Development
Milner Library
Illinois State University
Normal, Illinois

The Diagnostic Evaluation of Reference Service in an Academic Library

ABSTRACT

An unobtrusive evaluation of the quality of reference service was performed at the Milner Library, Illinois State University, using both accuracy and attitudinal scales. The results are summarized and follow-up actions that have occurred since the study are described and discussed.

INTRODUCTION

The object of this paper is to discuss the methodology and results of an unobtrusive evaluation of reference service at Milner Library of Illinois State University.

The project was first conceived during informal discussions between two of the present authors relating to the possibility that reference service at Milner might not be as uniformly excellent as the librarians maintained. (On several occasions where the quality of service was introduced as a topic, discussion was circumvented by the librarians maintaining adamantly and immediately that "...while we may not be able to do or provide [something], *at least we give great service.*") The high service status was a given in discussions, unchallengeable and undiscussable for years—even decades, perhaps. It had gained credibility over the years by repetition. The authors had some misgivings (as well as some concrete experiences) that seemed to indicate that problems did exist: during service at the General Reference desk, one had experienced problems associated with referrals and another had been approached unofficially by a colleague who complained that one librarian's performance had reached a "level of incompetence that needs to be addressed." Clearly, all was not right in the reference world. Possible solutions were discussed, ranging from trying various forms of evaluation of reference service to in-house corrective sessions. Finally, a decision was made to apply to the Council on Library Resources for a grant under their program for cooperative research projects between librarians and teaching faculty. Our proposal was funded by the Council and the project was underway. The methodology and results of the study have been described in detail elsewhere (Elzy et al., in press). In this paper, these aspects are discussed only briefly; our main purpose here is to deal with what has taken place at Milner since the evaluation was completed.

The Environment

Illinois State University is a comprehensive university, one of the largest in the state, with over 22,000 students. One hundred ninety-one degree programs are offered in thirty-three departments organized into five colleges. Masters degrees are offered in most areas and the doctorate in eleven. Milner Library, completed in 1976, is a six-story central facility housing 1.3 million bound volumes, 1.7 million volumes in microformat, 350,000 government publications, 420,000 cartographic items, 25,000 audiovisuals, and 10,000 serial subscriptions. The annual materials budget is $1.7 million.

Milner is organized into five subject divisions with five separate reference service points: Education/Psychology, General Reference and Information, Social Sciences/Business, Science/Government Publications, and Humanities/Special Collections. The five divisions are staffed by twenty members of the library faculty, nineteen classified employees, and a complement of student assistants. Each floor or division also has attached to it one auxiliary "special" collection (e.g., music, maps). The building is open 105 hours a week, with professional assistance available for most of that time. The facility is heavily used, with turnstile counts of 1.3 million during the past year. During the time that the study was conducted, in excess of 10,000 reference questions were answered plus more than 16,000 directional questions. About 8,000 students now receive library instruction each year: 4,000 through the General Reference area in a basic program tied to the Freshman Composition sequence, and 4,000 more through subject-specific classes conducted by division librarians.

The library faculty is unusually stable and mature: 90 percent of the thirty-four are tenured and many have as much as fifteen to twenty years of service at ISU.

METHODS

It was decided to perform the study unobtrusively. Students would be trained to walk into the various divisional libraries, seeking a particular librarian by name (librarians are identified by nameplate and the students were given schedules of who would be working on which reference desk at which time), and to pose questions for which answers were already known by the project staff (but not by the students). They were to record what the librarian did for them and the answer supplied or found, and were to answer various questions about the librarian's behavior and attitude. The questions used were drawn from many sources: reference textbooks, earlier studies, and the knowledge and experience of the project staff. From a pool of several hundred candidates, fifty-eight were eventually selected. All were checked against the holdings of Milner Library to be sure that they could be answered there. The evaluation, then, was not of the library's resources but of the ability of the staff to exploit the resources available.

Students were recruited mainly from applications made for employment in Milner Library. Eighteen students from Illinois State University and two from Illinois Wesleyan University, a neighboring institution, were selected. All were undergraduates who exhibited a wide variety of academic backgrounds. A group session was used to explain the study, to give the students preliminary training in how to pose the questions, and to pass out the necessary schedules and forms. The students, who were paid for their participation in the investigation, were asked to keep details of the study completely confidential; they were not to discuss it with anyone until the project was completed. Individual interviews were scheduled later with each participant to give final instructions and to answer any questions they might have. Figure 1 shows the first page of the evaluation form designed for use in the study. It identifies questioner, question, librarian, time spent by the librarian, time question asked, answer provided, and source used. The rest of the eight-page form was taken up with a series of twenty-eight attitudinal questions, the first two of which appear on Figure 1, and space for student comments. As Figure 1 shows, the student judged the librarian for each attitudinal element on a ten-point scale.

Questioner: _____

Librarian/Floor: _____

Question: Number: _____   Short phrase: _____

Time question asked: Date: _____   Hour: _____

Time spent with Librarian in minutes: _____

Anwer (actual answer, directions given. Sources or floors provided by librarian): _____

_____

_____

_____

Source:
    Title: _____

    Date or edition: _____

    Volume: _____

    Page: _____

Attitude and Demeanor

    1. Looks approachable

Not at All	Seldom		Some of the time	Mostly		To a large Extent

1	2	3	4	5	6	7	8	9	10

      Comments:

_____

_____

_____

    2. Acknowledges user's approach to desk

Not at All	Seldom		Some of the time	Mostly		To a large Extent

1	2	3	4	5	6	7	8	9	10

Figure 1. First page of evaluation form

All questions were posed over a three-week period in April 1989, and few problems were encountered. Almost all were posed to more than one librarian, sometimes on different floors if appropriate to more than one. The students were conscientious and all forms were completed with very few missing data. Students attended a group debriefing session to share their experiences and observations on the study.

The study was designed so that each floor and each librarian could be evaluated on both attitude and accuracy of their responses to the students. The attitude score was easy to arrive at. For each of 190 "incidents" (the posing of a particular question to a particular librarian), the attitude score was the mean of the values earned on the ten-point scale for each of the twenty-eight attitudinal aspects.

The accuracy score was more of a problem. Scoring a question posed by telephone is relatively easy, at least for factual questions: either the correct response is given or it is not. (Actually, this is an oversimplification since some questions can be partially answered.) The situation is more complicated for a walk-in question, particularly in the case of an academic library, because a variety of responses are possible from the librarian—everything from providing the answer to pointing the questioner to some possible sources.

In actual fact, of course, one can score the response to a question in various ways depending on what one considers an appropriate response to be. In an academic setting, librarians frequently consider that the most important component of reference service is that of teaching students how to find information; librarians should direct students to appropriate sources rather than provide an answer for them. In our study, however, we deliberately decided to look at the activity from a student's more short-term view. In general, it was felt that a student would rather be given an answer than shown where to find it. The scoring scheme used (see Figure 2) reflects this. The best score for a reference incident was awarded when a student was given a complete and correct answer. Scores were reduced when the student was *led* to an appropriate source, and reduced further when *directed* to an appropriate source. The worst score—zero on a 15-point scale—was awarded for the case in which the student was given an incorrect answer, the assumption being that a wrong answer is worse than no answer at all.

The authors still feel that the ranking of responses, as reflected in Figure 2, is logical, although the numerical values and the intervals between them are rather arbitrary; in retrospect, it would have been more logical to assign a zero to the "no answer" situation and a minus value to an incorrect response.

Using the 15-point scale in Figure 2, it was possible to give an accuracy score to each incident and to average the accuracy scores to arrive at an overall accuracy score for each librarian and each floor.

	Points
Student <u>provided</u> with complete and correct answer	15
Student <u>led to a single source</u> which provided complete and correct answer	14
Student <u>led to several sources</u>, at least one of which provided complete and correct answer	13
Student <u>directed to a single source</u> which provided complete and correct answer	12
Student <u>directed to several sources</u>, at least one of which provided complete and correct answer	11
Student given an <u>appropriate referral to a specific person or source</u> which would provide complete and correct answer	10
Student provided with <u>partial answer</u>	9
Student is given an <u>appropriate referral to the card catalog or another floor</u>	8
Librarian <u>did not find an answer</u> or suggest an alternative source	5
Student given an <u>inappropriate referral</u> to catalog, floor, source, or librarian unlikely to provide complete and correct answer	3
Student is given <u>inappropriate sources</u>	2
Student is given <u>incorrect answer</u>	0

Figure 2. Scoring method used

Figure 3 shows the accuracy score for the first fifteen (of fifty-eight) questions, along with the mean time spent by the librarian with the student. As the data reveal, the scoring method was quite discriminating. For example, questions 4 and 14, each posed twice, received a maximum score of 15, while question 6, posed four times, received the very low score of 5.5.

Figure 4 shows the breakdown of scoring for the 190 reference incidents. The best possible score, 15, was awarded in almost one-third of all cases. Clearly, how many incidents are judged "satisfactory" is entirely dependent on what one is willing to accept in the way of service. If one is willing to accept any of the outcomes down to "appropriate referral" then any incident scoring 10 or above would be considered acceptable—about 58 percent of the incidents, according to Figure 4.

Question	Times posed	Accuracy	Mean # of minutes spent on question
1	2	12.0000	13.5
2	2	13.0000	5
3	2	7.5000	4
4	2(1)*	15.0000	3.25
5	2	14.0000	6.5
6	4(1)@	5.5000	6
7	-	----------	7
8	2	8.0000	9
9	5	10.2000	4.2
10	2	14.0000	3
11	4	9.7500	4.2
12	4	13.2500	8
13	2(1)*	14.0000	5
14	2	15.0000	3.5
15	2	11.5000	3

* Missing data in accuracy code.
@ Missing data in minutes spent.

Figure 3. Question by question results
(first 15 questions)

Answer Code	Frequency	Percent
15	58	30.5
14	24	12.6
13	13	6.8
12	5	2.6
11	8	4.2
10	3	1.6
9	7	3.7
8	10	5.3
5	18	9.5
3	10	5.3
2	16	8.4
0	10	5.3
Missing*	8	4.2
	190	100.0

*Some students failed to provide enough information upon which to base judgments, or asked the question in such a way as to change the expected response, thus invalidating the question.

Figure 4. Accuracy of answers provided

Figures 5 and 6 show that accuracy and attitude scores were quite discriminating in separating the performance of different divisions (floors) and of different librarians. A more complete analysis of these results can be found in Elzy et al. (in press).

Floor	Questions	Accuracy	Attitude
A	30(3)*	10.4074	8.2100
B	30	12.7333	8.2067
C	20(2)*	11.7778	8.5200
D	71(2)*	9.6377	7.7141
E	39(1)*	8.1053	7.1256
Mean	190(8)*	10.1538	7.8342

*Missing data for accuracy scores.

Figure 5. Accuracy and attitude scores by floor

Librarian	Number of Questions Asked	Attitude	Accuracy	Mean Minutes Spent
1	10(1)*	8.1900	10.3333	4.35
2	10	7.0000	7.6000	5.45
3	10	7.6300	7.5000	6.975
4	9(1)*	7.6000	7.1250	5.65
5	10(1)*	8.7500	13.8889	7.88
6	10	8.2100	13.0000	4.85
7	10	7.7200	11.8000	6.7
8	10	8.2300	10.8000	6.3
9	10(1)*	8.2900	9.6667	4.3
10	10	7.8000	9.5000	7.6
11	10(1)*	5.7400	7.2222	2.15
12	10(1)*	7.3600	11.8889	3.95
13	10(1)*	7.7800	11.2222	6.95
14	10	7.8700	8.6000	8.05
15	10	8.1800	9.7000	5.85
16	12	7.0750	8.5833	4.75
17	10	8.6900	13.4000	7.30
18	9	8.2444	10.2222	8.05
19	10(1)*	8.6600	9.6667	8.5
Mean	190(8)	7.8342	10.1538	

*Missing data for accuracy scores.

Figure 6. Accuracy and attitude scores for each librarian

Follow-up to the Study

After the study was completed—the answers verified, the results compiled, correlations made, and reports written—the really *tough* part of the project began: sharing the results with the librarians involved and trying to do something positive to improve the service based on the results.

Our first action was to invite the public service librarians to an optional open meeting at which the details of the study—methodology and results—were presented. No individuals were identified but floor performance was noted. Some scores were presented by question and some of the written comments on the evaluation forms, good and bad, were read. We tried to keep things as anonymous as possible. Discussion was opened up through asking whether various levels of accuracy— 50 percent, 60 percent, 70 percent—could be considered "good reference service?" There was not much response to this. Some questions were raised about the philosophy of reference service in an academic library. Many took issue with the scoring system used. Much of the discussion focused on the belief that academic librarians should teach students how to find answers rather than provide them with the answers. They felt that perhaps answers should have been judged on a scale of only two or three points: acceptable versus unacceptable, or acceptable, marginal, and unacceptable. A few librarians asked what we hoped to prove by the study and what we were going to do with the results. There was no groundswell of support for improving reference skills, for holding workshops on reference service, or for exchanging ideas and information on tools of the trade. In fact, we heard later through the library grapevine (perhaps the most accurate gauge of staff reaction) that each librarian felt, as long as his or her performance was satisfactory, no real problem existed. This may not reflect lack of concern for the quality of the service but, rather, the feeling that one librarian cannot control or affect the performance of others.

Alan Nourie and Cheryl Elzy, the ISU members of the research group, offered to meet with individuals or floors to discuss results in more detail and to let each of the librarians read his or her comment sheets. Several months later, they had met with only one floor and been asked to meet with only one other. Only six of the nineteen librarians had availed themselves of the opportunity to read their individual comments. This is not quite as bad as it sounds, since five had left or were leaving the staff through attrition. After reading what students had written about them, librarians reacted with anything from an offer to slit wrists to noting that one cannot please all of the people all of the time—and a variety of responses in between.

The one floor meeting to take place involved the floor with the largest staff. They took the study seriously. They asked that we come to the meeting with our interpretation of what went wrong with the questions that scored 5 or below. They also wanted to know which questions were asked on their floor. These librarians also wanted to discuss philosophy—how much time should be spent with each patron, should answers be given as opposed to teaching the student how to use the tools, how should busy desks be handled, and so on. The meeting at least seemed to create a heightened awareness of a variety of problems and perceptions regarding reference service in academic libraries.

Two additional concrete approaches to improving reference service have been undertaken so far. Several videos on various aspects of reference service, produced by the Library Video Network and the American Library Association, were scheduled to be shown at brown bag lunch sessions, followed by a discussion. The sessions were open to anyone who worked a reference desk—public services librarians, technical services librarians, civil service staff, and even administrators. Thirteen staff members attended the first session and fifteen the second.

The final activity that resulted, more or less, from the reference study was a two-day reference workshop designed and directed by Thomas Childers for the professional staff. While perhaps no horrendous failures had shown up in the study, and no patterns of service actually cried out for attention, it was felt that a certain complacency had set in among at least the older members of the faculty. So the workshop was designed to define the qualities that constitute good reference service and to determine how the staff thought they measured up to this definition. The workshop was definitely participatory, incorporating small and large group discussions and a very informal unobtrusive study on the spot. Participants came up with a list of over sixty-five aspects of good reference service—everything from having a non-intimidating security gate at the entrance to the library to reliable terminals and copiers to many aspects of putting the patron at ease. Some qualities injected humor into the discussion, e.g., a librarian's need for humility in admitting he or she could not answer a question or "What do you do when the librarian (as opposed to the computer) is down?" Some were very serious concerns: "How much administrative support exists for the librarian?", for example. The list of good qualities in a reference librarian suggests a picture of a reference desk covered by a person who is energetic, ingenious, positive, humble, secure, interested, friendly, open, knowledgeable, empathetic, efficient, available, and probably exceedingly hard to find!!

Toward the end of the workshop, the librarians were asked to vote on the qualities that Milner should focus on for improvement. Those that received the most votes were:

- Knowing resources (15)
  1) internal
  2) external
  3) new
- Adequate staffing of the reference desk (14)
- Appropriate choice of service (12)
  1) advice
  2) education
  3) retrieving a document
  4) retrieving an answer

- Follow-up to the total fulfillment of a patron's need (11)
- Appropriate referral (10)
  1) internal
  2) external

What significance is there to the fact that accuracy of response received only seven votes and completeness of response only two? Before and during the workshop, a certain amount of negativism surfaced regarding the study and the unobtrusive methodology in general. Several felt strongly that unobtrusive evaluation was unethical, because it asks people to lie and ties up a legitimately busy reference desk with bogus questions. Many said they felt uncomfortable, even foolish, in participating in such a method of study. People were allowed to talk this issue through but without letting the negativism swamp the session. Nothing was resolved, of course, since ethical issues are highly personal and emotionally charged, but participants were at least given the chance to express their concerns.

Workshop participants actually did go out and observe other librarians working at reference desks. As they reported on their experiences, it was interesting to note that by far the majority of their comments—good and not so good—involved non-librarian aspects of reference service. Things like finding the doors to the library or lack of signs and handouts elicited more discussion than the librarian's attitude or skill. Possibly as little as 10 percent of the discussion focused in any way on the person whose job it is to deliver the answer, which is perhaps indicative of the unwillingness of librarians to evaluate their colleagues. However, in an age when accountability for time and dollars spent and services rendered is becoming increasingly prevalent throughout society, the profession must find more reliable measures of performance than check marks on a transaction sheet or the personal impressions of professional colleagues.

It is very difficult to study one's own colleagues. First, it is not easy to keep everything unobtrusive. The vast amounts of time it takes to organize the study, hire and train the student proxies, select and verify the questions, and tabulate results makes it obvious that one is working on a major project. Second, one is liable to antagonize some colleagues, which may be one reason why so many of the previous studies were done by outside consultants and researchers. It may be easier to accept the results of a study like this if they come from someone not on staff. This seems odd, because an internal faculty member would be more likely to give the benefit of the doubt in scoring a question and would be inclined to want the best results possible and interpret them in the most favorable light.

It is difficult to tell whether this study and its results have had any impact on the quality of reference service at Milner Library, but it does seem to have made some staff members more sensitive to the issues associated with the quality of service.

Administrative Value of the Study

As full faculty members, ISU librarians are evaluated each year for the distribution of merit dollars. Three areas of performance are scrutinized: (1) the practice of librarianship (considered as the equivalent of teaching as performed by other faculty), (2) research/scholarly activity, and (3) service. Librarianship (the most heavily weighted component at 70 percent) is also the most difficult to evaluate in many instances—especially for public services librarians. In evaluating reference activity, impressionistic anecdotes or testimonials from colleagues often replace more objective data. Teaching faculty have traditionally been subjected to regular student evaluations. In a similar fashion, unobtrusive evaluations such as that reported here furnish a comparable examination of reference performance from several perspectives, accuracy and deportment among them. Such evaluations allow the quality and character of reference service to be discussed and evaluated at a level more concrete than opinion, conjecture, or speculation.

In considering the results of this study, a consensus must first be arrived at as to exactly what is an acceptable level of accuracy and of attitude. Is 70 percent accuracy acceptable? Is 50 percent? Is an attitudinal score of 7.8 on a 10-point scale what an institution should be aiming for? What level is unacceptable: 7, 6, 5? Is the fact that 15 percent of the questions answered are dealt with in less than two minutes significant? That 37 percent are dealt with in less than four minutes? On such questions it is difficult to reach complete agreement. In making use of the results, the librarians involved have been made familiar with the methodology of the project and the instrument used. It was hoped that, once the group recognized that there very well could be problems in the level of service furnished, ideas on how to address them could be solicited, or presented, and discussed in the context of an informal meeting. On one level, simply *recognizing* that one may be perceived in a certain way by a patron, or that two or three minutes may not be an appropriate amount of time to give all questions, or that one may have developed a tendency over the years to point students in the direction of sources rather than lead them, might be enough to solve the problem. With some librarians, the mere fact that they were reminded of possible problems or weaknesses in their performance was enough to create a self-correcting situation. However, this was not always the case, and other options either might have been or were explored, e.g.,

(1) personal interviews for the librarians falling at the lower end of the rating scales, (2) use of outside speakers to present a workshop on improving reference service and combatting and reducing the effects of "burnout," and (3) identification of the types of questions most likely to be dealt with inadequately.

In an ideal situation, an unobtrusive study of the type described can indicate that improvement in reference service should be addressed at several levels: personal, divisional, and institutional. If warranted, personal conferences with the librarians can be conducted to discuss, for example, undesirable elements of service. This might be a tendency to use inappropriate reference sources or to conduct peripheral business at the reference desk, or to give an undesirable impression of one's approachability or friendliness or willingness to help. At this personal level, one can simply run through the list of comments made by the surrogate users and discuss the individual questions with the librarian.

On the divisional or institutional levels, the collective consciousness relating to reference service can be heightened by broad, non-confrontational discussion of patterns detected. Traditional assumptions and platitudes about the excellence of service furnished can be challenged, and strengths and weaknesses pointed out. Ideally, librarians with an accuracy score below some selected level should be consulted privately. The pattern of time spent on questions may be worth discussion with some (one librarian spent one minute or less on half the questions received and less than three minutes on 80 percent of them) as would the attitudinal evaluations made by the student observers (about seven pages for each librarian).

At the divisional (floor) level, if the assessment of performance showed real excellence, as it did in some instances, this can be mentioned and serve as a morale-builder. On the other hand, if undesirable trends have been disclosed (e.g., reluctance to handle questions dealing with a certain collection located on the floor), they should be discussed and existing policy regarding them clarified and/or revised.

One unfortunate aspect of providing anonymity in such a project is that, while the identities of the underachievers are protected, the same situation applies to the "stars"—the librarians whose performance is truly exemplary and who should be used as role models.

After conducting personal interviews, general and divisional meetings, and an in-house developmental institute, a similar project could be implemented, after an appropriate amount of time has passed, to determine what changes, if any, have occurred as a result of the evaluation process.

CONCLUSION

Some of the benefits, insights, and uses that have accrued as a result of the study include an increased or at least heightened sense of accuracy or appropriateness with regard to internal personnel transfers, several of which have occurred since the study was completed. The luxury of actually having documentation to support decision-making when placing personnel in or out of a particular area is not inconsiderable, but it is uncommon. On the other hand, the experience of participating in a series of meetings to evaluate personnel performance for the prior year, while in possession of pertinent information regarding individual performance and not being able to use it, is an extremely frustrating experience; this is exactly what has happened at Milner. Nevertheless, armed with the information generated, one now has increased confidence about the level of service furnished as well as the attitudes projected over the reference desks.

In addition, some minor problem areas have been identified and addressed through non-confrontational discussions. These included the case of one librarian who was surprised to find that she was in the habit of conducting peripheral business at the reference desk while students waited on several occasions. In another case, a floor was found to have a tendency to avoid serving users who required help with one of the auxiliary collections.

The library faculty seems now to be operating at a heightened level of consciousness regarding reference performance. They took the top five issues generated by the Childers workshop, published them in the library newsletter, and urged that the issues not be allowed to disappear. Finally, the librarian with the worst scores on attitude and second worst on accuracy has been motivated to improve performance to an acceptable level.

Although the study required a lot of work, and did cause conflict with some members of the faculty, the authors feel it was well worthwhile. It is exciting to study the inner workings of an organization in this way, particularly when the organization is one's own.

Considerable interest has been expressed in the methodology and results of the study since its completion, and one library director in Illinois has expressed an interest in our performing a similar study in that library. This raises an important question. If reference services are considered an important library activity, and if library directors are concerned with the quality of this service, why are studies of this kind not performed more often?

REFERENCE

Elzy, C.; Nourie, A.; Lancaster, F. W.; & Joseph, K. (in press). Evaluating reference service in a large academic library. *College and Research Libraries.*

CHARLES A. BUNGE

Professor
School of Library and Information Studies
University of Wisconsin-Madison

Gathering and Using Patron and Librarian Perceptions of Question-Answering Success

ABSTRACT

This paper discusses the strengths and weaknesses of patrons and reference librarians as sources of data for the evaluation of reference question-answering effectiveness, along with ways to enhance the usefulness of data from each source. It describes the Wisconsin-Ohio Reference Evaluation Program and discusses some illustrative statistics from the project, including data on relationships between patron-perceived answering success and factors such as staffing patterns, effort spent on answering questions, types and sources of questions, and collection size.

INTRODUCTION

The two most frequently used sources of data on reference question-answering success are the librarian who answers the question and the patron who asks it. Both *Output Measures for Public Libraries* (Van House et al., 1987, pp. 65-71) and *Measuring Academic Library Performance* (Van House et al., 1990, pp. 95-108) suggest these as basic sources. This paper will discuss briefly the strengths and weaknesses of each of these sources, as well as ways to enhance the usefulness of each. Within this context, the Wisconsin-Ohio Reference Evaluation Program will be described, and some illustrative statistics from the project will be discussed.

The Reference Librarian as Data Source

Undoubtedly, the most widely used measure of reference effectiveness is the librarian's perception of how successfully questions are answered. Many reference staffs record such perceptions, albeit often quite informally. Public libraries that follow the recommendations of *Output Measures for Public Libraries* (pp. 69-71) record the number of questions for which the users receive requested information on the same day they are asked, and staffs in various types of libraries record unanswered reference questions in one way or another.

One advantage of librarians as a source of data for reference evaluation is ease of data collection. Recording librarian perceptions of answering success can be fit into the normal work flow of the reference desk, without the additional staffing or special efforts required for patron surveys and other approaches. Using staff perceptions can be considerably less costly than hiring outside observers or proxy patrons. Staff motivation to provide full and accurate data can be higher than that of patrons, due to the staff's desire to improve service, or to pressure from peers and administrators.

Librarians can be a unique or especially valuable source of certain types of data. For example, librarians can provide information on factors that might be related to question-answering success, such as the number and type of sources consulted or collection weaknesses.

On the other hand, serious reservations have been raised regarding data from reference librarians. Librarians usually report a higher success rate than do independent observers or researchers. It is difficult for a librarian to report a reference encounter as unsuccessful when he or she has given it the best possible effort and when the information produced seems at least partially responsive to the question. Also, the librarian may not understand the real information need represented by the question and may feel that this need has been met when it has not. Gathering data on reference transactions can be intrusive to the reference process, causing reference librarians to be selective regarding the questions on which data is gathered, thereby raising concerns about the reliability and validity of the data produced.

Rather than reject the reference librarian as a source of data on question-answering success because of such reservations, reference evaluators should attempt to overcome or reduce the problems while taking advantage of the strengths. For example, one way to reduce the inflation of reported success is to avoid forcing a choice between "answered" and "not answered." Librarians are more likely to report less-than-complete success if they are allowed to choose options such as "partially answered" and "don't know." Librarians are also more likely to report less-than-successful results if they are given an opportunity to record reasons for lack of success. Providing such an opportunity also takes advantage of one of the potential strengths of the librarian as data source and provides fuller information for use in evaluation. The problems caused by the intrusiveness of data gathering can be addressed through sampling and by simplifying the data recording process.

The Reference Patron As Data Source

Like the librarian, the patron as a source of data on answering effectiveness has both strengths and weaknesses. Obviously, patrons are the most important source of data on their satisfaction with the information and service they receive. Because patron perceptions play a crucial role in their decision to use the information they receive and their inclination to use the reference service again, data on their perceptions are of great importance to reference evaluation.

On the other hand, patrons, too, have a tendency to report higher levels of satisfaction than the success rates found using outside observers or unobtrusive approaches. Conventional wisdom holds that, because patrons appreciate any attention and help they receive, they will report satisfaction even when the information they receive is less than completely useful. Also, patrons often are not knowledgeable about the information that could and should be provided to answer their questions and will report satisfaction with information that is inaccurate, incomplete, or out-of-date.

While reference patrons are an easily available source of data, they are frequently in a hurry and may be unwilling to be interviewed or to fill out survey forms to record their perceptions. Patrons who feel most strongly might be most likely to take the time and effort to respond, raising concerns about the reliability of the data gathered in this approach.

Patrons are too valuable as a source of evaluative data to reject because of potential reliability and validity problems, and steps can be taken to reduce these problems. For example, the problem of low response rate and patron reluctance to report perceptions can be addressed by making the survey forms as simple and quick to complete as possible. Patron response rate can be improved by having reference staff members exhibit a positive, upbeat attitude as the forms are handed to patrons, by emphasizing the survey's potential for improving service, and by using attractive signs to remind patrons to complete and return forms.

Patrons' tendency to overrate answering success can be addressed in a number of ways (Murfin & Gugelchuk, 1987, pp. 317-19). First, not forcing a choice between "answered" and "not answered" (or some equivalent dichotomy) is important. Patrons, like librarians, are more likely to report less than completely useful answers if options like "partially" are provided. Also, allowing patrons to report their reactions to particular aspects of the answer can increase validity and the richness of the data. Examples include the amount of information provided, the depth or complexity of the information, and the point of view or approach of the information in relation to the patron's need.

The conventional wisdom regarding reference patrons' inability to distinguish between the usefulness of the information they receive and the quality and extent of the service they receive is not necessarily true. If these two important aspects are carefully separated and addressed with focus, users can report one level of satisfaction with the information or materials received and another for the extent and nature of the service provided by staff members.

To summarize, reference librarians and their clients can provide valuable and unique data for the evaluation of question-answering effectiveness. It is important that evaluators take advantage of the strengths of such data, while recognizing their limitations and the need to take care to reduce problems with validity and reliability. It is most important to recognize that librarians and patrons can provide only their perceptions. The degree to which these perceptions accurately reflect reality is an issue to be addressed in the design and use of data-gathering instruments and in the interpretation of data. One way to address this issue is to use data from a variety of sources, including both librarians and patrons, to check, balance, and reinforce each other.

THE WISCONSIN-OHIO REFERENCE EVALUATION PROGRAM

Concerns such as these led Marjorie Murfin and this author to develop forms and associated computer programs for gathering and analyzing data from reference librarians and their patrons. The researchers' intent was to develop and provide a service that could be used by reference staffs to evaluate their question-answering effectiveness and to provide information that would suggest ways in which such effectiveness could be improved. It was also expected that the data gathered by participating libraries would accumulate into a national database that could be used for research and for the establishment of national norms that would be useful for various purposes. The result of these efforts is the Wisconsin-Ohio Reference Evaluation Program.

Several objectives guided the development of the data-gathering forms for the program. The first was to provide a means by which reference staffs could gather reliable and valid data from librarians and patrons regarding the degree to which reference questions are answered effectively. Second, data should be gathered from patrons and librarians on various environmental or situational factors that might be related to or used to explain answering success. Third, data from the two sources should relate to each other at the question-by-question level. Fourth, the data should be gathered and analyzed in the least intrusive and time-consuming manner possible.

The result of addressing these objectives is a set of forms that are called Reference Transaction Assessment Instruments (RTAI) (see Appendices A-F). Basic to the accomplishment of several of the researchers' objectives is a set of forms that are computer readable and the generation of data that can be analyzed by computer. The forms can be completed by librarians and patrons by simply filling in small circles with a pencil, thereby making them easy and quick to complete. Librarian and patron data can be related question-by-question through the use of computer-readable coding that allows the data from the patron's form and the librarian's form for each question to be brought together by the computer for comparison and analysis. To make sure that correctly coded forms are completed by librarian and patron for each question, the two forms for each question are attached to each other until they are torn apart at the time the question is asked.

It was anticipated that most libraries using the RTAI would sample their reference questions using cluster samples based on selected periods of time. Within a sample period, every question asked at the service point by walk-in patrons should be included in the sample, thus cutting down on choices and decisions that might affect the representativeness of the sample. This meant that directional questions should be included, as well as reference questions, even though data on answering success and environmental factors are not as important for directional questions. Very brief directional-question forms for patrons and librarians were designed that gather data on question type and patron characteristics (see Appendices D-F).

The patron form for reference questions asks for information about the patron (academic status and area of study or teaching for academic library patrons; occupation, age, gender, and source of the question for public library patrons). A group of questions at the top of the patron form asks about the patron's satisfaction with the information or materials that were provided or suggested in answer to the question. A group of questions on the bottom portion of the form asks about the patron's perception of the librarian and the service received. Other questions ask whether or not the patron feels that he or she learned about reference sources or library use (see Appendices B and C).

The librarian form for reference questions (Appendix A) gathers data about the type of information or materials that the question asks for, including its subject area. The librarian's perception of answering success is recorded, as are several items concerning how the librarian went about answering the question. These include whether the librarian searched with the patron or only directed or suggested sources, the amount of time taken, and the number and type of sources consulted or recommended. The librarian is also asked to indicate factors about the patron, the question, and the situation that apply to the encounter. These include, for example, indications that the patron had special characteristics such as difficulty communicating, that the collection was weak in the area of the question, or that the librarian was busy at the time the question was asked. The staff member is asked to indicate whether he or she is a professional or paraprofessional.

Guided by the objectives mentioned above, several drafts of the RTAI were prepared and were reviewed by practicing reference librarians and managers. A penultimate draft of the academic library version was field tested in the reference departments of fifteen academic libraries of various sizes in the fall of 1983, using a sample of fifty questions in each library.

A primary purpose for consultation with practicing librarians and for field testing was to improve the reliability and validity of the data gathered with the forms. The reference librarians who reviewed the forms attested to their high face validity. Using statistical cluster analysis on the field test data, it was determined that the questions relating to patron satisfaction with the information received and those related to satisfaction with the quality of the service do measure two different factors, further adding to the researchers' confidence in the validity of the form. Data from the field test were also used to assess the reliability of the forms, using Cronbach's alpha and an extension of this estimator, the theta statistic (Murfin & Gugelchuk, 1987, pp. 323-29).

Questions regarding patron and question-source categories for the public library version of the patron form were developed and field tested with the cooperation of reference librarians. Thus, the RTAI set consists of librarian forms for directional and reference questions that are used in both academic and public libraries (Appendices A and D) and patron forms for directional and reference questions that have different patron categories for academic and public libraries (Appendices B, C, E, and F).

Libraries that wish to use the service obtain copies of the RTAI from the project office for samples ranging from 100 reference questions upward (and for an equal member of directional questions), along with instructions regarding the use of the forms. For each question in the sample, the librarian quickly ascertains the patron's willingness to participate (participating libraries have experienced nearly 100 percent willingness), and the question is answered in the normal fashion. At the end of the encounter, the librarian and patron forms for the question are detached from each other, the patron is handed his or her form for completion, and the librarian completes the librarian form (or at least enough of it to allow completion later).

At the end of the survey, completed forms are returned to the project office for reading and analysis of the data. The response rate from patrons (i.e., the percentage of sample reference questions for which both patron and librarian forms are available for analysis) averages 93 percent for public libraries and 85 percent for academic libraries.

The data from each library is analyzed using a complex program on an IBM mainframe computer, and a detailed report is prepared and sent to the library. The report provides information on the library's question-answering success, as perceived by reference librarians and patrons, on the question-answering behavior of answering librarians, and on factors present in the reference situation at the time the questions were asked. The report compares the library's data with data from other participating libraries (either public or academic) of similar size, with all public or academic libraries that have used the service, and with the most successful participating public or academic library so far.

The data are also accumulating in a continually growing database, from which national norms and other useful information can be obtained. Other researchers can have access to this database for their own analysis as well. The participating libraries are a self-selected sample rather than a random sample. However, there is no reason to believe that they are unrepresentative of academic and public libraries in general.

The data on directional questions have not received much analysis. Participating libraries receive frequency counts and percentages for patron categories and types of directional questions. The data on patron categories, taken together with those from reference questions, can give a library a pretty good picture of who is asking questions at the reference desk.

Demographic Information

The forty-two public libraries that have participated in the program through September 1990 include libraries in six states. While there is a concentration of suburban libraries, there are also large urban libraries and libraries serving rural populations. Library collections range from 23,000 volumes to over 2,000,000 volumes, and populations served range from 7,500 to over 600,000. For purposes of comparison, libraries have been categorized as small (twelve libraries of under 50,000 volumes), medium (fifteen libraries of 50,000-99,999 volumes), and large (fifteen libraries of 100,000 volumes or more). There are data on some 6,000 reference questions from these libraries.

Table 1 shows the proportion of various patron categories and question sources for reference questions in the public libraries. In interpreting these figures, readers should be aware that some patrons marked responses in both the occupation and student categories and some in only one or the other. Figures for occupation categories are percentages of only those patrons who marked an occupation, while figures for student categories represent percentages for all patrons.

TABLE 1

PERCENTAGE OF PUBLIC LIBRARY PATRONS AND
QUESTIONS BY CATEGORY

Category	Percentage of Questions
OCCUPATION (% of total responses for occupation)	
Homemaker	22.79
Skilled labor/	14.97
trades/services	
Secretarial/	10.30
clerical/office	
Sales/marketing	10.74
Professional/	27.71
technical/management	
Unemployed	10.77
Retired	7.00
AGE (% of total responses for age)	
Under 18	21.79
18-40	45.76
41-64	26.96
65+	5.69
GENDER (% of total responses for gender)	
Male	39.74
Female	60.35
STUDENTS (% of total patrons)	
High School	19.61
College	20.67
Graduate School	7.74
Continuing Education	7.21
SOURCE OF QUESTION (% of total responses for source)	
Work related	19.66
School/education related	40.82
Recreation related	10.75
Other personal project	33.34

General reference departments in forty-eight public and private academic libraries in twenty-five states and Canada have participated in the Wisconsin-Ohio program through September 1990, and have provided data on over 5,000 reference questions. Participating libraries include twenty-three with collections of fewer than 500,000, thirteen with between 500,000 and 1,000,000 volumes, and twelve with collections of over 1,000,000 volumes. Table 2 shows the proportion of various patron categories among those who asked reference questions in the academic libraries. In interpreting these figures, readers should be aware that a few patrons marked responses for more than one "status" or "major" category, so that the figures add up to slightly over 100 percent.

TABLE 2
PERCENTAGE OF ACADEMIC LIBRARY PATRONS BY
STATUS AND SUBJECT AREA

Status or Subject	Percentage of Questions
STATUS	
Freshman	18.80
Sophomore	17.61
Junior	17.13
Senior	21.16
Graduate student	12.82
Continuing education/nondegree	2.82
Faculty	3.05
Alumna/us	1.35
Unaffiliated with college	5.45
MAJOR OR TEACHING/RESEARCH AREA	
Arts or Humanities	18.29
Business/Management	24.73
Education	7.98
Law	1.76
Other Social Sciences	11.50
Agriculture/Biological Science	5.49
Medicine/Health	7.78
Mathematics/Physical Sciences	2.79
Technology/Engineering	7.12
Interdisciplinary/Other	6.40
Major not declared	6.91

Reference Question-Answering Success

The main figure used to indicate question-answering success, and the figure in which reference librarians and managers seem most interested, is the patrons' perception of whether or not their questions were answered. A stringent criterion for patron-perceived answering success has been established. In order to be counted as successful transactions, the patrons must have reported that they obtained just what was wanted and that they were completely satisfied with the information or materials found or suggested. When the terms *success score* or *success rate* are used for a library or group of libraries, the terms refer to the percentage of questions on which patron responses meet this criterion. By a "significant" relationship is meant that the relationship has been tested statistically (usually with the chi square test for independence) using the .05 probability level to indicate significance.

The success rate across all forty-two public libraries is 60.01 percent. When patrons reporting finding approximately what was wanted are added, the percentage is 71.00. Comparable figures for the forty-eight academic libraries are 56.25 and 67.85. (The success rate in public libraries for higher education students with school-related questions is 61.57 percent.) While the difference between public and academic libraries is small (though statistically significant), one is tempted to look for reasons for it. Two factors on which the two types of libraries differ and that are related to patron-perceived success might be partial explanations. One is the percentage of questions for which the librarians reported simply directing the patron to a potential answering source, rather than searching with the patron. For academic libraries, the percentage of such responses is 22.02, while for public libraries it is 15.24. Also, in academic libraries the percentage of questions on which the librarian reported being busy when the question was asked is 25.72, while in public libraries the percentage is 21.25.

Because data on librarian-perceived answering success is easier to collect than that for patron-perceived success, it is interesting to know how close these perceptions are to each other when both are measured for the same questions (so that one might judge the usefulness of substituting the easier measure for the harder one). In most participating libraries, the librarians reported that the answer was found for a higher percentage of questions than that reported by patrons. The average librarian-perceived success rate across the forty-two public libraries is 72.05 (compared to a patron-perceived success rate of 60.01). For the forty-eight academic libraries, the librarian-perceived success rate is 68.45 (compared to a patron-perceived success rate of 56.25). The overall agreement between librarians and their patrons on "found," "partly found," and "not found" responses is 67.68 percent for public libraries and 64.98 percent for academic libraries.

Factors Associated with Success or Failure

In order for reference staffs and managers to make wise decisions to improve reference question-answering success, they need information on factors that are related to variations in success. Such relationships have been looked at across the participants in the Wisconsin-Ohio program.

Staffing

One important set of factors in the reference situation is staffing patterns. In this area, one factor that is consistently associated with question-answering success is whether or not the librarian is busy at the time the question is asked. On average, the public libraries lost 6.11 percentage points in their success scores when the librarians reported being busy when questions were asked, as compared to when they were not busy. For academic libraries, there was a loss of 4.82 percentage points on average.

Another staffing issue is the involvement of paraprofessional staff in answering reference questions. Analysis of data from twenty academic libraries that used both paraprofessionals and professionals to answer reference questions (among the first thirty-three academic library participants) showed that, overall, professional staff members were more successful (Murfin & Bunge, 1988). However, the same analysis showed that, with appropriate training and effective policy and procedure backup, paraprofessionals can effectively answer reference questions. While the public library data has not been analyzed with the same detail, the data indicates that, across all public library reference questions, paraprofessionals have been just as successful as professionals. However, some participating libraries have paraprofessionals answer only simple or apparently easy questions, while others have them answer the full range of questions, so that overall findings here must be interpreted with caution.

Time and Effort Spent on Questions

Another group of factors relates to the time and effort spent on questions by reference librarians. The RTAI collects data on whether the librarian searches for information with the patron or merely directs or suggests a strategy. For the public libraries, success scores are on average 9.45 points lower for questions where the librarian directed patrons to a potential source, rather than searching with the patron. For the academic libraries, this difference averages 18.05 percent.

To help reference staffs assess their potential for answering reference questions successfully, the report form that is sent to participating libraries includes the patron-perceived success rate for questions on which the patron was served by a professional staff member who was not busy and who searched with the patron. This allows the staff to see how its success under various conditions compares with its success under these "ideal" conditions (what is called the "potential" success rate). For the forty-two public libraries, this potential success rate averages 66.61 percent (compared with 60.01 overall); for the forty-eight academic libraries, it is 67.79 percent (compared with 56.25 overall).

The number of sources used or suggested in answering a question is of interest, as well. In academic libraries, the data indicates that there is a positive relationship between the number of sources consulted or suggested and patron-perceived answering success (at least up to a point of diminishing return). For example, Table 3 shows the average figures for all academic libraries and those for the library with the highest success rate (65.63 percent) among the forty-eight libraries. This relationship does not show up in the same way for public library participants. However, analysis of the data on time spent per reference question in the first thirty-six public library participants showed that, in the nine most successful libraries, the proportion of questions on which librarians reported spending less than three minutes (26.38) is significantly lower than for the nine least successful ones (31.47 percent) (Bunge, 1990).

As an aid to reference staffs in interpreting their data from the Wisconsin-Ohio program, Marjorie Murfin has constructed some indexes based on similar factors. Comparative figures for these indexes are reported to participating libraries. For example, she analyzed the data from the thirty-three earliest participating academic libraries to see if patron-perceived success is related to the amount of time and effort that is provided by the answering librarian. An "effort index" for a given library is based on the percentage of questions for which the librarians direct or suggest only (rather than search with the patron), the percentage of questions on which the librarians report working for under three minutes, and the percentage of questions for which only one source was used or suggested. Table 4 shows the percentage of such questions for the eleven libraries with the highest success rates and the eleven with the lowest success rates, along with a column combining what might be called the "negative effort" factors. From this table it is clear that library staffs who spend more effort on questions have higher patron-perceived success rates.

TABLE 3

NUMBER OF SOURCES CONSULTED OR SUGGESTED PER
QUESTION ANSWERED

| | Percentage of Questions | |
Number of Sources	All Academic Libraries	Most Successful Academic Library
1 Source	37.90	25.00
2 Sources	30.12	17.86
3 Sources	17.68	32.14
4 Sources	7.40	14.29
5 or More Sources	6.90	10.71

These "effort" factors are related to how busy the reference staff is, of course. It is interesting to note, however, that the percentage of reference questions on which the librarian searched with the patron, even though busy (again, based on data from the thirty-three earliest participating academic libraries), is 73.85 for the most successful eleven libraries, 47.06 for the least successful eleven libraries, and 63.52 for those in the middle range.

TABLE 4

ANSWERING EFFORT RELATED TO ANSWERING SUCCESS

Success Rate (%)	Percentage of Questions			Average: 1,2,3
	1 Directed Only	*2* Under 3 Min.	*3* Used 1 Source	
MOST SUCCESSFUL				
69.74	18.42	37.33	37.50	31.08
69.59	14.62	15.79	21.74	17.38
68.75	6.25	16.67	23.53	15.48
68.52	11.11	26.32	33.33	23.59
65.63	9.38	38.71	25.00	24.36
63.51	27.03	30.14	33.93	30.37
61.54	15.38	18.42	38.46	24.09
60.78	12.42	20.39	22.38	18.40
60.53	31.58	36.84	47.06	38.49
60.53	28.95	32.43	40.00	33.79
60.26	13.46	34.67	30.28	26.14
Average	17.15	27.97	31.11	25.74
LEAST SUCCESSFUL				
53.08	25.38	46.51	45.00	38.96
52.05	38.36	51.05	50.00	46.47
51.43	22.86	48.57	37.14	36.19
51.35	37.84	37.84	53.84	43.17
50.00	22.22	33.33	50.00	35.18
49.28	26.09	32.84	46.97	35.30
47.17	18.87	48.08	52.00	39.65
45.00	20.00	48.72	32.35	33.69
44.83	27.59	35.71	52.00	38.43
41.67	16.67	44.44	45.71	35.61
34.48	25.86	45.28	24.53	31.89
Average	25.61	42.94	44.32	37.62

Communication

Effective communication between the reference librarian and the patron is crucial to question-answering success. One measure of communication effectiveness is the percentage of questions on which the librarian and the patron agree in their assessment of whether or not the question was answered. For example, across all forty-eight academic libraries, this agreement rate is 64.98 percent, while in the library with the highest patron-perceived success rate it is 77.42 percent.

An analysis of the data from the earliest thirty-three participating public libraries shows that in the nine most successful libraries the agreement rate is 78.95 percent, while in the nine least successful libraries it is 63.77 percent. These and other data from the RTAI indicate that there is a greater communication gap between librarians and patrons in less successful libraries.

Type and Source of Questions

One of the most frequently studied sets of factors is the type and source of reference questions. Data on success rates for patrons and questions in various categories are provided in Tables 5 and 6. These figures might be used by individual libraries as norms against which to compare local results. For example, participants in the Wisconsin-Ohio program can use such comparison to identify areas for collection and staff development attention.

The librarian portion of the RTAI asks librarians to categorize questions using some fifteen categories. Table 7 shows the percentage of questions recorded in the most frequently used categories (based on all transactions and adjusted by choosing one category per transaction). Some interesting differences between academic and public libraries appear in Table 7. Types of questions that have been hardest for public libraries to answer to their patrons' satisfaction are ones asking for criticism and reviews (51.78 percent success), ones asking for trends, pro and con, how-to-do-it, etc. (51.86 percent), and explanation of the library, its catalog, or another tool (56.46 percent). For academic libraries, types of questions where patron-perceived success has been lowest are ones asking for trends, pro and con, how-to-do-it, etc. (46.85 percent success), for just something or anything on a topic (48.80 percent), and for facts or statistics (49.08 percent).

The data on the "just something or anything" on a topic type of question are interesting. Such questions have been much more prevalent in public libraries (23.43 percent of all reference questions, versus 14.02 percent in academic libraries). Public librarians seem to have been more successful at ascertaining the real information needs behind these questions and at providing satisfactory answers, achieving a 59.60 percent success rate. In academic libraries, significantly more patron-librarian communication difficulty is associated with these questions than is true for public librarians, and the success rate on them is only 48.80 percent.

TABLE 5

PUBLIC LIBRARY SUCCESS RATE BY CATEGORY OF PATRONS
AND QUESTIONS

Category	Patron-perceived Success Rate (%)
ALL QUESTIONS*	60.01
OCCUPATION	
Homemaker	59.90
Skilled labor/trades/services	63.72
Secretarial/clerical/office	63.01
Sales/marketing	49.15
Professional/technical/management	60.92
Unemployed	59.54
Retired	63.47
AGE	
Under 18	56.07
18-40	59.74
41-64	61.98
65+	64.42
GENDER	
Male	58.10
Female	60.80
STUDENTS	
High School	54.55
College	58.16
Graduate School	64.88
Continuing Education	59.11
SOURCE OF QUESTION	
Work related	58.75
School/education related	59.68
Recreation related	60.60
Other personal project	61.34

*Excluding questions asking for a specific book, serial, etc.

TABLE 6

ACADEMIC LIBRARY SUCCESS RATE BY PATRON STATUS AND
QUESTION SUBJECT

Status and Subject	Patron-perceived Success Rate (%)
ALL QUESTIONS*	56.25
STATUS	
Freshman/Sophomore	56.55
Junior/Senior	54.76
Graduate Student	51.74
SUBJECT AREA OF QUESTIONS	
Arts and Humanities	58.84
Social Sciences	51.94
Science and Technology	52.25

* Excluding questions asking for a specific book, serial, etc.

TABLE 7
TYPES OF QUESTIONS ASKED

Type of question	Percentage (of all questions)	
	Public Libraries	Academic Libraries
Specific book, serial, etc.	19.09	14.09
Smaller item in larger publication	1.78	2.46
Anything by a particular author	2.36	0.78
Short answer, verification, etc.	4.49	9.71
Facts or statistics	13.42	12.41
Explanation of library, catalog, or particular source	2.28	9.29
Something/anything on a topic	22.43	14.02
Certain type of format of material	7.90	11.35
Criticism, reviews, interpretation, etc.	2.45	6.05
Analysis, trends, how-to, pro/con	3.73	5.37

Collection Size

Collection size is another factor of interest. Simple correlation indicates no significant difference in patron-perceived success rate by collection-size category in either public or academic libraries. More detailed analysis of the data does indicate that there is a positive relationship between library collection size and success rate. However, this relationship is obscured by the fact that larger libraries tend to be busier and to receive more complex questions, both of which are associated with lower success rates. For example, when one looks at questions for which the librarian does not report being busy, the larger libraries have a much higher success rate than smaller libraries. This and other evidence suggest that larger collections have a greater potential for success, but that this success can be negated by being overly busy.

The size of the reference collection seems to have a curvilinear relationship to answering success. Not all libraries can provide accurate data on reference collection size, and the research team's analysis and interpretation of the data on this relationship have been somewhat impressionistic. However, success rate does seem to go up as reference collection size increases, up to an optimum size (around 4,000 volumes for public libraries and around 15,000-20,000 volumes for academic libraries), after which success rate seems to fall off. Evidence on other factors leads to the speculation that larger collections invite (or require) relatively more directing (rather than going with the patron to the shelves) and that it is harder for reference staff members to gain the mastery over larger collections that is required for quick and effective access to the information in them.

Bibliographic Instruction

One measure of the success of a reference encounter might be whether or not the patron learns anything about information sources as a result of it. The patron RTAI asks patrons whether they became acquainted with any reference sources that had not previously been known as a result of consulting the reference librarian. In academic libraries, 37.41 percent of the patrons who asked reference questions reported learning about two or more sources, 48.54 percent learned about one source, and 14.05 percent reported "No, none." For public library patrons, the figures are 30.04 percent, 44.16 percent, and 25.81 percent, respectively, indicating that more one-to-one bibliographic instruction is occurring in academic libraries than in public libraries. Likewise, when asked if they learned something about the use of the library or reference sources as the result of consulting the reference librarian, academic library patrons responded "Yes" more frequently (76.93 percent) and "No" less frequently (6.76 percent) than did public library patrons (70.01 percent and 12.45 percent).

CONCLUSION

This paper has tried to show that the reference librarian and the patron can both be valuable sources of data on which to base evaluation of question-answering effectiveness if appropriate care is taken in gathering and interpreting this data. Each of these sources is especially valuable for certain perceptions, including perceptions regarding important environmental or situational factors that are related to reference effectiveness. Each also has real or potential weaknesses that need to be minimized in the data collection process and accounted for in interpretation of the data.

The paper discusses the ways in which the Wisconsin-Ohio Reference Evaluation Program has addressed these concerns, including the development and use of the Reference Transaction Assessment Instruments. Data from forty-two public libraries and forty-eight academic libraries that have participated in the program are presented and discussed, including data on relationships between patron-perceived answering success and factors such as staffing patterns, effort spent answering questions, types and sources of questions, and collection size.

The long-range intent of the Wisconsin-Ohio Reference Evaluation Program is to improve the reference services that library patrons receive. This paper is presented in the hope that it will be of value to reference librarians and managers who have the same intent and who wish to evaluate their success at answering reference questions.

ACKNOWLEDGMENTS

    Grateful acknowledgment is made to Ohio State University, which provided
Marjorie Murfin a seed money grant for this project and whose Instructional
and Research Computer Center has provided extensive computer support; to
the University of Wisconsin-Madison Graduate School, which provided Charles
Bunge research funds to support the project; and to the Council on Library
Resources for financial support in the form of Faculty/Librarian Cooperative
Research Grants.

APPENDIX A

Librarian's RTAI for Reference Questions
Public and Academic Libraries

1. TYPE OF QUESTION Select <u>only</u> one category in A-D below that <u>best</u> fits type of answer wanted.	○ Librarian ○ Library Assistant ○ Other Assistant

A PARTICULAR TEXT(S) OR AUTHOR(S) WANTED
- ○ 1. Is particular book, serial, etc. in our collection?
- ○ 2. Smaller item in larger publication (<u>Particular</u> article, speech, quote, poem, law, etc.)
- ○ 3. Anything (or certain type of thing) <u>by particular</u> author

JOT DOWN QUESTION

○ **B** SHORT ANSWER WANTED (AND IS APPROPRIATE) (What, when, where, who, which, yes or no, etc.) (Answer of a few words. Includes verification and meaning of citations, bibliographical form, recommendations, etc., etc.,)

○ **C** GENERAL EXPL. OF CATALOG, LIBR., OR PRINTED REF. SOURCE WANTED (Rather than short answer)

D TYPE MATERIALS OR LONGER DESCRIPTIVE ANSWER WANTED (OR APPROPR.)
(Answer usually in the form of printed materials)

1. SUBJECT (Mark <u>one</u>)
- ○ a. Single subject(s)
- ○ b. Relate 2 subj. or concepts

2. ASPECTS (MARK ALL THAT APPLY)
- ○ a. Something, anything, everything
- ○ b. Must be cert. time period, currentness, place, country, lang., etc.
- ○ c. Must be cert. <u>type</u> ref. source, publ., materials, or format (map, pict., etc., etc., etc.)

- ○ d. Focus on aspect, biog., hist., other.
- ○ e. Requests factual inf. in general (or source containing it) (names, addr., definitions, statistics, ratings, rankings, etc., etc.)
- ○ f. Criticism, reviews, interpr., etc.
- ○ g. <u>Analysis</u>, trends, pro/con, cause/effect, how-to-do-it, how-it-works, & other
- ○ h. Requests that you compile list of references on a subject

2A RESULTS (MARK ONE)	**2B RESPONSE (MARK ONE)**	**2C TIME (MARK ONE)**
○ 1. Found	○ 1. Directed and suggested only	○ 1. 0-3 minutes (i.e. under 3 min.)
○ 2. Partly found	○ 2. Helped with or made search	○ 2. 3-5 minutes
○ 3. Not found	○ 3. Deferred	○ 3. 5-15 minutes
○ 4. Don't know	○ 4. Referred	○ 4. Over 15 minutes

3. SPECIAL FACTORS. DO NOT OMIT MARK ALL THAT APPLY

QUESTION AND PATRON	CONDITIONS
○ 1. Missing information or misinformation	○ 10. Difficult to think of source
○ 2. Concerned with foreign countr./lang.	○ 11. Difficult to find subj. headings
○ 3. Concerned with govt. docs.	○ 12. Books off shelf
○ 4. Inf. needed (or citat.) very recent	○ 13. Source difficult to consult
○ 5. Wants no. of things	○ 14A. Busy ○ 14B. Very busy
○ 6. Difficult citation	○ 15. Cataloging or tech. problem
○ 7. Patron in hurry	○ 16. Collection weak in that area or out-of-date
○ 8. Communic. diff. or confused question	○ 17. Need bks. in another area or location
○ 9A. Needs extra help ○ 9B. Returns freq.	

4. LIB. INSTRUCT. MARK ALL THAT APPLY
- ○ 1. Expl. sources, citations, search strat.
- ○ 2. Expl. cat., computer, holdings, locations

5. NUMBER OF SOURCES USED, REC., OR INTERP. ——   1 2 3 4 5+   ○○○○○

TYPE: MARK ALL THAT APPLY
- ○ 1. Indexes to period.
- ○ 2. Ref. books
- ○ 3. Cat. (card, online, etc.)
- ○ 4. OCLC, RLIN, etc.
- ○ 5. Comp. database srch. or CD-ROM
- ○ 6. Yr. own knowledge
- ○ 7. Inhouse prod. tools
- ○ 8. Phone bks., VF, Coll. cat.
- ○ 9. Circ. bks., period., newsp.
- ○ 10. Consult someone
- ○ 11. Refer

6. QUESTION DIFFICULTY (as perceived)	**7. ASPECT** (only if applicable)	**8.**	**SUBJECT**	
			1st	2nd (if applic)
		○ 0	○ 0	
○ Easy	○ Stat.	○ 1 ○ 1	○ 1 ○ 1	
	○ Biog.	○ 2 ○ 2	○ 2 ○ 2	
	○ Hist.	○ 3 ○ 3	○ 3 ○ 3	
○ Medium		○ 4 ○ 4	○ 4 ○ 4	
		○ 5 ○ 5	○ 5 ○ 5	
○ Hard		○ 6 ○ 6	○ 6 ○ 6	
		○ 7 ○ 7	○ 7 ○ 7	
		○ 8 ○ 8	○ 8 ○ 8	
		○ 9 ○ 9	○ 9 ○ 9	

Use separate guidesheet and select subj.
Mark boxes with no. of your subject.

	SUBJ. No. 2	SUBJ. No. 20
	○ 0	● 0
EXAMPLE	○ 1 ○ 1	○ 1 ○ 1
	● 2 ○ 2	● 2 ○ 2

▣■■○■■■○○○○●■■○○○○   **14454**

MAKE NO MARKS IN THIS AREA

FOR OFFICE USE ONLY
⓪①②③④⑤⑥⑦⑧⑨
⓪①②③④⑤⑥⑦⑧⑨
⓪①②③④⑤⑥⑦⑧⑨

APPENDIX B

Patron's RTAI for Reference Questions—Academic Libraries

FILL IN DOT LIKE THIS ⟶ ●

> The Reference Department is doing a survey of reference use and would appreciate it if you would mark the following brief checksheet. Thank you!
>
> (Deposit checksheet UNFOLDED in container on leaving this area or on leaving the library.)
> THANKS AGAIN FOR YOUR HELP!

◄ USE NO. 2 PENCIL ONLY

STATUS
- ○ Freshman
- ○ Sophomore
- ○ Junior
- ○ Senior
- ○ Graduate student or teaching assistant
- ○ Continuing education or nondegree student
- ○ Alumni
- ○ Faculty
- ○ Staff
- ○ Not affiliated with Univ.

MAJOR OR TEACHING/ RESEARCH AREA
- ○ Arts or Humanities
- ○ Education
- ○ Law
- ○ Business/Management
- ○ Other Social Sci.
- ○ Medicine/Health
- ○ Agric./Biological Sci.
- ○ Math./Physical Sci.
- ○ Technology/Engineering
- ○ Interdisciplinary/Other
- ○ Major not declared

1. Did you locate what you asked about at the reference desk?
   - ○ Yes, just what I wanted
   - ○ Yes, with limitations
   - ○ Yes, not what I asked for, but oth. information or materials that will be helpful
   - ○ Yes, but not really what I wanted
   - ○ Only partly
   - ○ No

2. If yes, how did you find the information or materials?
   - ○ Librarian found or helped find
   - ○ Followed suggestions and found on my own
   - ○ Didn't follow suggestions but found on my own

3. Were you satisfied with the information or materials found or suggested?
   - ○ Yes
   - ○ Partly
   - ○ No

4. If *partly* or *not* satisfied, why? **MARK ALL THAT APPLY.**
   - ○ Found nothing
   - ○ Not enough
   - ○ Need more simple
   - ○ Too much
   - ○ Need more in-depth
   - ○ Not relevant enough
   - ○ Want different viewpoint
   - ○ Couldn't find information in source
   - ○ Not sure if information given me is correct

5. How important was it to you to find what you asked about?
   - ○ Very important
   - ○ Important
   - ○ Moderately important
   - ○ Somewhat important
   - ○ Not important

	Yes	Partly	No
6. Was the librarian busy (e.g., phone ringing, others waiting)?	○	○	○
7. Did the librarian understand what you wanted?	○	○	○
8. Did you get enough help and explanation?	○	○	○
9. Were the explanations clear?	○	○	○
10. Did the librarian appear knowledgeable about your question?	○	○	○
11. Was the service you received courteous and considerate?	○	○	○
12. Did the librarian give you enough time?	○	○	○
13. Did you learn something about reference sources or use of the library as a result of consulting the reference librarian?	○	○	○

14. Did you become acquainted with any reference sources you hadn't previously known about, as a result of consulting the reference librarian?
   - ○ Yes, one
   - ○ Yes, more than one
   - ○ No, none

◻■○■○■○○○■■■■■○○○○   15914   MAKE NO MARKS IN THIS AREA

FOR OFFICE USE ONLY
⓪①②③④⑤⑥⑦⑧⑨
⓪①②③④⑤⑥⑦⑧⑨
⓪①②③④⑤⑥⑦⑧⑨

APPENDIX C

Patron's RTAI for Reference Questions—Public Libraries

FILL IN DOT LIKE THIS ─────────────► ●

> The Reference Department is doing a survey of reference use and would appreciate it if you would mark the following brief checksheet. Thank you!
>
> (Deposit checksheet UNFOLDED in container on leaving this area or on leaving the library.)
> **THANKS AGAIN FOR YOUR HELP!**

USE NO. 2 PENCIL ONLY

OCCUPATION
(Mark one)
- ○ Homemaker
- ○ Skilled labor/trades /services
- ○ Secretarial/clerical /office
- ○ Sales/marketing
- ○ Professional/technical /management
- ○ Unemployed at present
- ○ Retired

AGE
- ○ Under 18
- ○ 18-40
- ○ 41-64
- ○ 65+

SEX
- ○ Male
- ○ Female

STUDENT
- ○ High School
- ○ College
- ○ Graduate school
- ○ Continuing education

SOURCE OF QUESTION
- ○ Work related
- ○ School/education related
- ○ Recreation related
- ○ Other personal project (hobbies, self-development, curiosity, etc.)

1. Did you locate what you asked about at the reference desk?
   - ○ Yes, just what I wanted
   - ○ Yes, with limitations
   - ○ Yes, not what I asked for, but oth. information or materials that will be helpful
   - ○ Yes, but not really what I wanted
   - ○ Only partly
   - ○ No

2. If yes, how did you find the information or materials?
   - ○ Librarian found or helped find
   - ○ Followed suggestions and found on my own
   - ○ Didn't follow suggestions but found on my own

3. Were you satisfied with the information or materials found or suggested?
   - ○ Yes
   - ○ Partly
   - ○ No

4. If **partly** or **not** satisfied, why? MARK ALL THAT APPLY.
   - ○ Found nothing
   - ○ Not enough
   - ○ Need more simple
   - ○ Too much
   - ○ Need more in-depth
   - ○ Not relevant enough
   - ○ Want different viewpoint
   - ○ Couldn't find information in source
   - ○ Not sure if information given me is correct

5. How important was it to you to find what you asked about?
   - ○ Very important
   - ○ Important
   - ○ Moderately important
   - ○ Somewhat important
   - ○ Not important

	Yes	Partly	No
6. Was the librarian busy (e.g., phone ringing, others waiting)?	○	○	○
7. Did the librarian understand what you wanted?	○	○	○
8. Did you get enough help and explanation?	○	○	○
9. Were the explanations clear?	○	○	○
10. Did the librarian appear knowledgeable about your question?	○	○	○
11. Was the service you received courteous and considerate?	○	○	○
12. Did the librarian give you enough time?	○	○	○
13. Did you learn something about reference sources or use of the library as a result of consulting the reference librarian?	○	○	○

14. Did you become acquainted with any reference sources you hadn't previously known about, as a result of consulting the reference librarian?
   - ○ Yes, one
   - ○ Yes, more than one
   - ○ No, none

○●●○●●●○○○○●●●○○○○ **14454**   MAKE NO MARKS IN THIS AREA

FOR OFFICE USE ONLY
⓪①②③④⑤⑥⑦⑧⑨
⓪①②③④⑤⑥⑦⑧⑨
⓪①②③④⑤⑥⑦⑧⑨

APPENDIX D

Librarian's RTAI for Directional Questions
Public and Academic Libraries

MAKE NO MARKS IN THIS AREA

FOR OFFICE USE ONLY

○ Librarian

○ Library Assistant

○ Other Assistant

DIRECTIONAL QUESTIONS

○ 1. Location of Reader's Guide, Atlases, Dictionaries, Encyclopedias, College Catalogs, Phone Books, Zip Code Directory, City Directory, Periodical Directory

○ 2. Asks for book kept on ready reference and gives recognizable title

○ 3. Has call number and wants location

○ 4. Location of areas and collections within the building

○ 5. Request for use of supplies (stapler, phone, pencil, etc.)

○ 6. Location of persons within the building

○ 7. Library hours and rules

○ 8. Help with machines

○ 9. Locate periodical title in library's directory or union list

○ 10. Other

1746

APPENDIX E

Patron's RTAI for Directional Questions—Academic Libraries

FOR OFFICE USE ONLY

MAKE NO MARKS IN THIS AREA

USE NO. 2 PENCIL ONLY

FILL IN DOT LIKE THIS

The Reference Department is doing a survey of reference use and would appreciate it if you would mark this brief checksheet. Deposit sheet UNFOLDED in container. THANKS FOR YOUR HELP!

MAJOR OR TEACHING/RESEARCH AREA

- ○ Arts and Humanities
- ○ Education
- ○ Business Management
- ○ Law
- ○ Other Social Science
- ○ Engineering/Technology
- ○ Agriculture or Biological
- ○ Medical or Health
- ○ Math or Physical Science
- ○ Interdisciplinary or other
- ○ Major not declared

STATUS

- ○ Freshman
- ○ Sophomore
- ○ Junior
- ○ Senior
- ○ Graduate student or teaching assistant
- ○ Continuing education or nondegree student
- ○ Alumni
- ○ Faculty
- ○ Staff
- ○ Not affiliated with University

NCS Trans-Optic MP18-70176-3

APPENDIX F

Patron's RTAI for Directional Questions—Public Libraries

FOR OFFICE USE ONLY

MAKE NO MARKS IN THIS AREA

USE NO. 2 PENCIL ONLY

FILL IN DOT LIKE THIS

The Reference Department is doing a survey of reference use and would appreciate it if you would mark this brief checksheet. Deposit sheet UNFOLDED in container. THANKS FOR YOUR HELP!

OCCUPATION
Mark one

○ Homemaker

○ Skilled labor/trades/services

○ Secretarial/clerical/office

○ Sales/marketing

○ Professional/technical/management

○ Unemployed at present

○ Retired

AGE

○ Under 18

○ 18-40

○ 41-64

○ 65+

SEX

○ Male

○ Female

STUDENT

○ High School

○ College

○ Graduate school

○ Continuing education

SOURCE OF QUESTION

○ Work related

○ School/education related

○ Recreation related

○ Other personal project (hobbies, self-development, curiosity, etc.)

REFERENCES

Bunge, C. A. (1990). Factors related to output measures for reference services in public libraries: Data from thirty-six libraries. *Public Libraries, 29*(1), 42-47.

Murfin, M. E., & Bunge, C. A. (1988). Paraprofessionals at the reference desk. *The Journal of Academic Librarianship, 14*(1), 10-14.

Murfin, M. E., & Gugelchuk, G. M. (1987). Development and testing of a reference transaction assessment instrument. *College and Research Libraries, 48*(4), 314-338.

VanHouse, N. A.; Lynch, M. J.; McClure, C. R.; Zweizig, D. L.; & Rodger, E. J. (1987). *Output measures for public libraries.* Chicago: American Library Association.

VanHouse, N. A.; Weil, B. T.; & McClure, C. R. (1980). *Measuring academic library performance: A practical approach.* Chicago: American Library Association.

PRUDENCE WARD DALRYMPLE

Assistant Professor
Graduate School of Library and Information Science
University of Illinois at Urbana-Champaign

User-Centered Evaluation of Information Retrieval

ABSTRACT

This paper briefly summarizes the history of evaluation in information retrieval and describes both the strengths and limitations of traditional criteria for retrieval effectiveness such as precision, recall, cost, novelty, and satisfaction. It presents a continuum of approaches to studying the user in information retrieval, and suggests that because the situations in which information is sought and used are social situations, objective measures such as retrieval sets and transaction log data may have limited usefulness in determining retrieval effectiveness. Information retrieval evaluation has been locked into a rationalistic, empirical framework which is no longer adequate.

A different framework of analysis, design, and evaluation that is contextual in nature is needed. User-centered criteria employing affective measures such as user satisfaction and situational information retrieval must be incorporated into evaluation and design of new information retrieval systems. Qualitative methods such as case studies, focus groups, or in-depth interviews can be combined with objective measures to produce more effective information retrieval research and evaluation.

INTRODUCTION

Linking Information Retrieval and Libraries

The key to the future of information systems and searching processes ...lies not in increased sophistication of technology, but in increased understanding of human involvement with information. (Saracevic & Kantor, 1988, p. 162)

Librarians are committed to assisting the user in obtaining access to the best materials available quickly, easily and efficiently, yet when librarians step aside from the reference encounter and let users pursue the information needed "on their own," many users fail utterly, or at least fail to achieve optimal results. Because of limited understanding of the information search process and even less understanding of how to evaluate that process, librarians may well wonder, "What is it that we are supposed to be helping the user to do?" and "How will we know when we have succeeded?" When the information search process involves machines, the picture becomes even more complicated.

In many libraries today, the intermediary role of the reference librarian is substantially reduced or nonexistent. One response to the invasion of end-user search systems such as online catalogs, database gateways, and CD-ROMs is to increase the commitment of effort and resources to bibliographic instruction (BI). This renewed interest in BI is reflected in conference themes, in the literature, in job descriptions, and in library school curricula. Unfortunately, much of the BI that is being done today is one-to-one or small-group instruction which is exceedingly labor-intensive and expensive. And despite the widespread interest in BI, there is very little evaluative data about its effectiveness.

Another response is to design systems that can substitute for the librarian as either an intermediary or as an instructor. This response represents a challenge of a different sort, one that requires enormous capital outlay at the outset, and goes well beyond the "help" screens that assist the user in attaining a minimal level of competency with system mechanics. These systems must not only perform adequately as systems, they must also "stand in" for reference librarians, assisting with question negotiation and clarification, and providing the friendly support and helpfulness that is associated with reference work. Unfortunately, librarians have been reticent to demand a voice in the development and design of information retrieval systems; so reticent, in fact, that there is little agreement even on how to describe the features each system possesses. Obviously, librarians need to be intelligent consumers of these systems, yet there are few satisfactory criteria against which to evaluate them.

One logical place to look for criteria for information system evaluation is the information retrieval research, but this research has often been isolated from the library context and virtually inaccessible to most practicing librarians. In the past, reference librarians have mediated the gap between the information retrieval machines—the large search services such as Dialog and BRS—and library users. Today, library users interact with information retrieval machines directly, chiefly through CD-ROMs and OPACs. The recent growth in end-user searching of all types has resulted in a literature characterized by laments about the increased demand on the reference staff who feel called upon to instruct users individually or in classes, and by concerns that users are "not finding enough" or "not finding the best materials." But what is "enough?" And what are the "best materials?" These questions have usually been addressed in the context of reference service and mediated information retrieval, but when it comes to users' direct interaction with systems there is little information upon which to proceed.

Studies of end-user searching have focused on questions such as "Who is using the systems?" and "What are they finding?," or on management issues such as "How shall we select the best systems?" or "How shall we cope with the additional work load?" While there have been a few fine-grained analyses of the search experience of individual users, there have been even fewer studies that attempt to gauge users' success in fulfilling their actual information needs (Harter, 1990). Work done as prologue to expert system development has attempted to explicate the reference process in order to simulate and support reference tasks in an electronic environment. Also, some researchers are attempting to identify the core knowledge or expertise that should be incorporated into expert systems that could substitute for the assistance of a reference librarian in an information search (Fidel, 1986; Richardson, 1989). These are exciting and potentially productive research areas, but they are driven by a design perspective rather than an evaluation perspective. While it might be argued that until there are better information retrieval systems it is premature to be concerned with evaluation criteria, it is not too soon for librarians to articulate the criteria or goals of information retrieval systems. Furthermore, the design and development process is cyclical and iterative; what evaluation identifies as limitations in today's systems will lead to the innovations of tomorrow's systems.

These developments suggest that it would be useful and timely to look at the role of the user in evaluating the results of information retrieval. But in order to propose user-centered measures for information retrieval effectiveness, there must be a clear understanding of the goals of information retrieval so that appropriate evaluations can be performed. Some of the issues that must be addressed are:

- What are the implications of removing the intermediary from the information retrieval task?
- What does our knowledge of users' experience of information retrieval tell us about the goals of information search and retrieval, and how close we are to achieving them?
- How can the ways in which we ask our users about the services provided make the responses more useful?

USER, USE, AND USER-CENTERED STUDIES

User Studies

Most of the literature of the past three decades has focused on describing the characteristics of individuals and groups who use libraries or library information systems. Such studies answer questions like "Who is using the online catalog?," "Who are the users of MEDLINE CD-ROM?," and "Who are the end-users of Dialog?" They are generally descriptive, and examine variables such as profession, major, education, age, or sex. User surveys ask users to report their activities rather than directly observing their behavior. Little attention has been paid to defining what constituted a "use" and even less to understanding the nature of the interaction, and virtually no attention has been paid to non-users of libraries.

Use Studies

In the late 1970s, Brenda Dervin and Douglas Zweizig were some of the first to direct attention to the nature of users' interaction with libraries (Zweizig, 1977; Zweizig & Dervin, 1977). They found that information needs and uses were largely situation-bound and could not be generalized across all groups of users. While their work focused mostly on the use of libraries and information centers, other researchers, particularly in the 1980s, began to examine the process of searching (Markey, 1984; Kuhlthau, 1988). That is, they asked, "How and (sometimes) why is X system used?" "Was the search by author, subject, or title?" "Was the search for research, work, an assignment, or curiosity?" "How long was the search session?" "How many search statements were entered?" "How many modifications were made?" "What did the user do at the completion of the search?" Use studies often employ experimental designs or field research in which users are observed either directly or unobtrusively through transaction logs—the machine-readable record of the user's interaction with the computer (Nielsen, 1986). A recent book by David Bawden (1990) introduces a subcategory of use studies which he calls *user-oriented evaluation*. Bawden argues that in designing and testing information systems, one must move out of the laboratory and into the field, actually testing systems with real users. This may seem intuitively obvious, but unfortunately, it is often all too rarely done. Bawden also advocates the use of qualitative methods instead of or in addition to the experimental designs characteristic of information retrieval evaluations.

User-Centered Evaluation

User-centered evaluation goes one step beyond user-oriented evaluation. A user-centered study looks at the user in various settings—possibly not even library settings—to determine how the user behaves. The user-centered approach examines the information-seeking task in the context of human behavior in order to understand more completely the nature of user interaction with an information system. User-centered evaluation is based on the premise that understanding user behavior facilitates more effective system design and establishes criteria to use in evaluating the user's interaction with the system. These studies examine the user from a behavioral science perspective using methods common to psychology, sociology, and anthropology. While empirical methods such as experimentation are frequently employed, there has been an increased interest in qualitative methods that capture the complexity and diversity of human experience. In addition to observing behavior, a user-centered approach attempts to probe beneath the surface to get at subjective and affective factors.

Concern for the user and the context of information seeking and retrieval is not new, nor is it confined to library and information science. Donald Norman (1986) and Ben Shneiderman (1987) are well-known names in user-centered computer design. In library and information science, T. D. Wilson (1981) called for greater attention to the affective (or feeling) dimension of the user's situation nearly ten years ago. Wilson suggested that "qualitative research" leads to a "better understanding of the user" and "more effective information systems" (p. 11). For example, information may satisfy affective needs such as the need for security, for achievement, or for dominance. Qualitative methods are more appropriate to understanding the "humming, buzzing world" of the user than are the pure information science models derived from the communication theories of Shannon and Weaver (Shannon, 1948; Weaver, 1949).

The situations in which information is sought and used are social situations, where a whole host of factors—such as privacy or willingness to admit inadequacy and ask for help—impinge on the user and the information need. The context of the information-seeking task combined with the individual's personality structure, create affective states such as the need for achievement, and for self-expression and self-actualization (Wilson, 1981). Similarly, the subjective experience of the user can be examined in order to determine how it might be enhanced. For example, some studies have identified such affective dimensions of information retrieval as expectation, frustration, control, and fun (Dalrymple & Zweizig, 1990).

The user-centered approach, then, asks what the goals and needs of users are, what kind of tasks they wish to perform, and what methods they would prefer to use. Note that the user-centered approach starts with examining the user or the user's situation, and then goes about designing a system that will enable the user to achieve his or her goals. It does not start with the assumption that a certain objective amount of information is "appropriate" or "enough" for the task at hand. Having described the user-centered approach, the next section will summarize the history of evaluation in information retrieval and will describe the traditional criteria for retrieval effectiveness.

MEASURES OF EFFECTIVENESS IN INFORMATION RETRIEVAL

Precision and Recall

Ever since the Cranfield studies in the mid-1960s (Cleverdon, 1962; Cleverdon et al., 1966), the classic evaluative criteria of information retrieval system performance have been precision and recall, measures that were developed to evaluate the effectiveness of various types of indexing. *Precision* is defined as the proportion of documents retrieved that is relevant, while *recall* is defined as the proportion of the total relevant documents that is retrieved. These measures are expressed as a mathematical ratio, with precision generally inversely related to recall. That is, as recall increases, precision decreases, and vice versa. Despite their apparent simplicity, these are slippery concepts, depending for their definition on relevance judgements which are subjective at best. Because these criteria are document-based, they measure only the performance of the system in retrieving items predetermined to be "relevant" to the information need. They do not consider how the information will be used, or whether, in the judgment of the user, the documents fulfill the information need. These limitations of precision and recall have been acknowledged and the need for additional measures and different criteria for effectiveness has been identified. In addition to recognizing the limits of precision and recall, some of the basic assumptions underlying the study of information retrieval are being called into question by some information scientists (Winograd & Flores, 1987; Saracevic & Kantor, 1988). Thus, what appear at first to be objective quantitative measures depend, in part, on subjective judgments.

Relevance and Pertinence

> We are seriously misled if we consider the relevant space of alternatives
> to be the space of all **logical** possibilities. Relevance always comes from
> a pre-orientation within a background. (Winograd & Flores, 1987, p. 149;
> emphasis added)

Relevance is defined as the degree of match between the search statement and the document retrieved. This is distinguished from *pertinence* in that the latter is defined as the degree to which the document retrieved matches the information need. Note that the difference between the two is the relationship between the search statement and the information need. Here is where the role of the intermediary comes in, and also the role of the system in helping the user to develop a search strategy. Research has shown that most users (indeed, even most searchers) have difficulty with search strategy.

One of the problems associated with precision and recall is the relevance judgement. Indeed, one of the first indications that there were cracks forming in the wall of precision and recall was Tefko Saracevic's (1975) review of relevance, in which he pointed out that relevance was a subjective and therefore unstable variable that was situation-dependent.

In a major study published recently, Paul Kantor and Saracevic (1988) presented findings that further questioned these traditional measures of retrieval effectiveness, particularly recall. They found that different searchers found different items in response to the same query. A similar phenomenon was identified by the author in a study of searching in both online and card catalogs (Dalrymple, 1990).

Precision and recall need not be discarded as evaluative measures; they remain useful concepts, but they must be interpreted cautiously in terms of a variety of other factors. For example, when determining precision, is the user required to actually examine the documents that the citations refer to? If so, then another variable is being tested: the accuracy of indexing. If not, then what is being measured is the degree of fit between the user's search statement as entered into the system and the indexing terms assigned to the documents. The "fit" between the documents and the user's information need is not being considered. After all, it is the skill of the indexer in representing the contents of the document that is tested when the user compares the retrieved document to the original information need; the retrieved citation is merely an intermediary step. In fact, the Cranfield studies themselves were designed to do just that—test the accuracy of indexing, not evaluate the "success" or "value" of the information retrieval system or service.

If users are not required to examine the documents in order to make relevance judgements, then what shall be substituted? Users make evaluations simply on the retrieved citation. Brian Haynes (1990) found that more than half (60 percent) of the physicians observed made clinical decisions based on abstracts and citations retrieved from MEDLINE without actually examining the documents. Beth Sandore (1990) found in a recent study of a large Illinois public library that users employ various strategies in determining relevancy of retrieved items—"the most common appear to be arbitrary choice or cursory review" (p. 52). Several issues can be raised immediately. First, without evaluation studies in which users actually examine the documents—i.e., read the articles and absorb the information—then perhaps what is being evaluated is the ability of a bibliographic citation or abstract to catch the user's attention and to convey information. Second, how do relevance judgments change when users read the documents? Third, what other factors affect the user's selection of citations from a retrieved list?

Recall has also come under scrutiny as an effectiveness measure. Since it is virtually impossible to determine the proportion of relevant items in an information system except in a controlled laboratory study, it may be more useful to regard recall as approximating the answer to the question, "How much is enough?" Sandore found that "many patrons use—that is, follow up and obtain the document—much less information than they actually receive" (p. 51). In her provocatively titled article, "The Fallacy of the Perfect 30-Item Search," Marcia Bates (1984) grappled with the notion of an ideal retrieval set size, but these studies have focused on mediated information services. Little has been done to examine how much is enough for users when they access information systems directly. Stephen Wiberley and Robert Daugherty (1988) suggest that the optimum number of references for users may differ depending on whether they receive a printed bibliography from a mediated search (50) or search a system directly such as an OPAC (35). Although one limitation to recall as a measure is that it requires users to describe what they don't know or to estimate the magnitude of what might be missing, perhaps a more serious limitation is that it is not sensitive to the ever-increasing threat of information overload. As systems increase in size, users are more likely to receive too much rather than not enough; when retrieved documents are presented in reverse chronological order (as is the case in virtually all information retrieval systems), users may find themselves restricted to seeing only the most recent, rather than the most useful, items.

Other Measures of Information Retrieval Effectiveness

In addition to precision and recall, there are other evaluative measures that have enjoyed a long history in information retrieval research. Some of these dimensions are cost (in money, time, and labor), novelty, and satisfaction related to information need.

Cost

Cost of online retrieval is subject to external pressures of the marketplace. For example, in 1990, current pricing algorithms of major vendors were changing away from connect time charge and toward use charges, which may have the effect of reducing the incentive to create highly efficient searches. Access to optical disk systems, online catalogs, and local databases provided directly to the user with neither connect charges nor use charges creates an incentive toward greater use regardless of the efficiency of the search strategy or the size of the retrieval set.

F. W. Lancaster (1977) observed that precision can also be treated as a cost in that it is an indirect measure of the time and effort expended to refine a search and review results (p. 144-46). In direct access systems, precision may be achieved iteratively, much more so than with delegated searches. The user can decide where the effort is going to be expended—in doing a tutorial, in learning to be a so-called "power user," or in doggedly going through large retrieval sets.

Novelty

Novelty is defined as the proportion of the retrieved items not already known to the user (Lancaster, 1979, pp. 132-33). With mediated searches, novelty is usually measured by asking the user to indicate which of the items retrieved were previously known. Novelty, of course, is related to the degree of subject expertise possessed by the user. That is, a subject specialist is quite likely to be familiar with a great many of the items retrieved in an area of expertise; the only items that are truly novel are those recently published. For the subject specialist, presenting the most recent items first makes sense; but this design decision may not apply to all, or even most, users in nonspecialized libraries. For those users, it may make much more sense to present the most relevant items first; this can be done by assigning mathematical weights based on term frequency or location. Such systems currently exist on a small scale, but are not yet widely available. Regardless of which model is chosen (and ideally, both options should be available in any given system to accommodate various knowledge states in users), the point is that both approaches recognize that the effectiveness of the retrieval is affected by the user situation.

Information Need

In order to discuss satisfaction it is necessary to address the problem of information need. Some researchers sidestep the problematic area of information need, arguing that because these problems are abstract, unobservable, and subject to change, it is futile to include them in research and evaluation. Others, while admitting these problems, nevertheless call for increased efforts in trying to grapple with them. One of the most convincing statements of the importance of understanding information needs was made by Brenda Dervin and Michael Nilan (1986) in a review of information needs and uses. They call for a paradigm shift that:

> posits information as something constructed by human beings....It focuses
> on understanding information use in particular situations and is concerned
> with what leads up to and what follows intersections with systems. It focuses
> on the users. It examines the system only as seen by the user. It asks many
> "how" questions—e.g., how do people define needs in different situations,
> how do they present these needs to systems, and how do they make use
> of what system offer them. (p. 16)

Within this paradigm, information needs focus on "what is missing
for users (i.e., what gaps they face)" (p. 17) rather than on what the
information system possesses.

Focusing on the user's information need may lead to a reconsideration of the assumptions underlying library and information systems
and services. As an example, consider Karen Markey's (1984) research
in online catalogs. By observing what users actually do when searching
an online catalog, she discovered that a remarkable number of catalog
users were conducting subject or topical searches in the catalog, rather
than known-item searches. Her findings prompted a reconsideration
of how libraries approach the study of catalogs, and even how they
approach their evaluation and improvement. Catalogs are now seen
as subject access mechanisms, and there have been many proposals as
to how to go about improving subject access in online catalogs. Valuable
as this research is, it has proceeded without a thorough examination
of librarians' assumptions about the function of the catalog. That is,
there has been no attempt to ascertain what users need the catalog
for, what their purposes are in searching the catalog, what they expect
to find, what need prompts them to approach the catalog—or even
the library, for that matter—and how and whether it meets those needs.
Until these questions are asked and answers attempted, librarians shall
be bound within the old paradigm that defines an information need
as something that can be satisfied by what is available in information
systems.

USER-CENTERED MEASURES OF
INFORMATION RETRIEVAL

Satisfaction

> ....satisfaction is determined not by the world but by a declaration on the
> part of the requestor that a condition is satisfied. (Winograd & Flores, 1987,
> p. 171)

It has been suggested that the satisfaction of a human user rather
than the objective analysis of the technological power of a particular
system may be a criterion for evaluation. This is generally not the
position that has been taken by library and information researchers,

but the literature is by no means devoid of concern for user satisfaction. When one reviews two decades of library and information science research, a renewed interest in affective measures seems to be on the horizon. The waxing and waning of interest in affective measures in information retrieval may parallel the changing role of the intermediary in information retrieval. That is, affective measures have been attributed to the "human touch" in information service rather than to the machines that perform the information retrieval task.

The user's satisfaction with the outcome of the search when it is performed by an intermediary was investigated by Judith Tessier, Wayne Crouch and Pauline Atherton (1977). Carol Fenichel (1980) used both a semantic differential and a five-point rating scale to measure intermediaries' satisfaction with their own searches and found no evidence to support the contention that intermediary searchers are good evaluators of their searches. Sandore (1990) found that there was very little association between search satisfaction and search results as indicated by precision; patrons who were dissatisfied with the results still reported satisfaction with the service. In both of these studies, satisfaction with the search experience is separated from satisfaction with the retrieved results as measured by precision. Satisfaction is indeed a complex notion that may be affected by the point in time at which the measure is taken; it can be affected by the items that the user selects, the difficulty encountered in locating the documents, and the information contained in the documents.

Considering the context of the information retrieval experience, particularly for end-users, underscores both the importance and the multidimensionality of affective—that is, feeling—measures. Judith Tessier (1977) identified four distinct aspects of satisfaction with the information retrieval process: output, interaction with intermediary, service policies, and the library as a whole. She wrote: "Satisfaction is clearly a state of mind experienced (or not experienced) by the user...a state experienced inside the user's head..." (p. 383) that is both intellectual and emotional. She observed that the user's satisfaction is a function of how well the product fits his or her requirement (or need), that satisfaction is experienced in the framework of expectations, and that people seek a solution within an acceptable range rather than an ideal or perfect solution.

Tessier's work is insightful, but it has rarely been integrated into studies of end-user searching in today's environment. In most studies of end-user searching, satisfaction is treated as unidimensional: users are either satisfied or they are not. Furthermore, most studies depend on users' self-assessments, and most users are not adequately informed about the system's capabilities. Users have notoriously low expectations and are usually unimaginative in identifying additional features that would be desirable, nor are they presented with alternatives from which to select. While retaining a degree of skepticism when users respond on a questionnaire that they are "satisfied," it must be acknowledged that it is the users themselves that determine their response to systems. And while it would be desirable for users to be more discriminating, little has been done to provide alternatives or even simply to ask users to rank various features of a system or its output. Users are not asked, "Did the information make a difference?" or better yet, "How did it make a difference?" In general, users have not been asked to describe their experiences in any but the simplest terms.

Much of the interest in examining user responses that was begun in the 1970s, when systems were first made available for direct access, waned over the past two decades when most searching was done by intermediaries. Stimulated by the current interest in end-user searching, it is interesting to return to some of the approaches used twenty years ago. For example, Jeffrey Katzer (1972) used factor analysis with a semantic differential to identify three dimensions that were relevant to information retrieval systems: the evaluation of the system (slow-fast, active-passive, valuable-worthless), the desirability of the system (kind-cruel, beautiful-ugly, friendly-unfriendly), and the enormity of the system (complex-simple, big-small).

The author and Douglas L. Zweizig recently factor-analyzed data from a questionnaire designed to determine users' satisfaction with the catalog search process (Dalrymple & Zweizig, 1990). The data were collected at the conclusion of experimental search sessions in which users were randomly assigned to perform topical searches in either a card catalog or an online catalog. Interestingly, the objective measures of catalog performance failed to discriminate between the two catalogs' conditions, and simple descriptive comparisons of the two groups did not reflect differences, either. But when the questionnaire data were subjected to a factor analysis, two primary factors were identified: Benefits and Frustration. Frustration emerged from responses such as "it was difficult to find the right words, it was frustrating, and confusing to search" (p. 22). Additional factors were also identified, and the strength of each of the factors differed depending on the catalog setting—card or online—and the way in which these factors correlated with other aspects of the search differed, depending on the type of catalog. For example, in the OPAC, users who reformulated their searches often, scored high on the Benefits factor, but in the card catalog, the reverse was true. Intuitively, it makes sense that changing direction in an online search is easier than having to relocate into another section of the card catalog. Thus, in the card catalog, redirecting a search (reformulating) is perceived as frustrating and detracts from the user's perceived benefits, but reformulation is a natural part of the search activity in the OPAC and so correlates positively with the Benefits factor. Also, users were asked to assess the results they achieved on their searches. Subjects who enjoyed their experience searching in the OPAC viewed their results favorably, while in the card catalog, users viewed their search results favorably despite the frustration they experienced.

These examples indicate the complexity and multidimensional nature of affective measures, and show that they are sensitive to a variety of situational factors. In the next section, context as a factor in evaluating the impact of information retrieval will be discussed.

Context and Impact

Reference librarians are well aware of the importance of understanding the context of an information request, and the literature of the reference interview is replete with discussions of symbolic and nonverbal aspects of the communication between reference librarian and user. Much less attention has been paid to contextual aspects of end-user searching of electronic information systems, by either librarians or information scientists. Two studies (Saracevic & Kantor, 1988; Dalrymple, 1990) examined the sets of items retrieved by individual searchers and found that the overlap was relatively low, even though the databases searched were identical. That is, given the same questions, different searchers tended to select a few terms that were the same and a considerably larger number that were different. This finding held true both for experienced intermediaries and for end-users in both database searches and OPAC searches. In explaining these differences, both studies acknowledged the importance of the user's context in determining the direction of the search.

Because context is such a powerful element in retrieval effectiveness, looking only at "objective" measures such as retrieval sets and transaction log data may have limited usefulness in determining retrieval effectiveness. Rather, it may be better to look at human beings and the situations in which they find themselves, and to evaluate retrieval effectiveness in terms of the user's context (Dervin & Nilan, 1986).

Not only does context affect retrieval, but it also affects the progress of the search through system feedback. The psychological aspects of information retrieval are receiving a great deal of attention by information scientists, computer scientists, and cognitive scientists alike. Studies of computerized searches can often reveal much about the ways in which individuals interpret queries, pose questions, select terms, and understand and evaluate information. One might even say that the information search provides a kind of laboratory for understanding human information processing. By examining in detail the history of a search, both from the system's perspective (through the transaction log) and from the user's perspective (through "talking aloud" and in-depth interviews), insight can be gained into the factors that affect the search, and these can be used to articulate the criteria against which information systems will be evaluated.

Some of the models used to design information systems underscore the role of psychological understanding of the search process. One is a communication model in which information retrieval is seen as a conversation between user and information system; another is a memory model in which information retrieval is seen as analogous to retrieval from human long-term memory. In the conversational model, the user and the system engage in a "dialogue" in which each "participant" attempts to gain an understanding of the other. For example, an expert system embedded in an information retrieval system might prompt the user to provide more specific information about what is needed (Do you want books or articles?), to provide synonyms (What do you mean?), or to limit the retrieval in some way (Do you want materials only in English? Only in the last five years? Only available in this library?). By answering the questions and engaging in the dialogue, the user participates in the process.

In retrieving from long-term memory, the searcher is even more active. In this model, the user finds a context by entering terms into a file and displaying the results until the context that seems most likely to meet the information need is found. The user searches that context for other similar items until all probable useful items are found, and then "verifies" them by asking, "Will these meet my need? Is this what I am looking for? Does this make sense?" In both models, the user performs the evaluative judgment based on her or his situation in the world. Regardless of the particular model chosen, the point is that both models are iterative and interactive. That is, they assume that the user is an active participant in the information retrieval process, and that continuous feedback from both system and user, one to the other, enables the process to advance and to continually improve.

But how does this fit into evaluation of information retrieval systems and services in a library? Stepping back for just a moment, it is essential to ask what it is that information retrieval systems are designed to do. For example, should catalogs do as Patrick Wilson (1983) suggests and simply verify the existence of an item in a collection? Or shall they act as knowledge banks, capable of providing information that goes well beyond simply indicating probable shelf locations for relevant items? Shall databases provide "quality-filtered" information that can support decision-making in highly specific areas, or shall they simply indicate the existence of an article on a topic? Shall systems "stand in" for reference librarians, and if so, is it reasonable to use the same criteria in evaluating an information system as in evaluating reference personnel?

Definitive answers to these questions do not yet exist, nor will one set of answers apply to all systems, to all libraries, and to all users, all of the time. By placing users and their needs much closer to the center of evaluation, methodologies can be employed that are sensitive to situations and contexts of users. "Qualitative evaluation tells us how well we have met the patron's needs" (Westbrook, 1990, p. 73).

Exactly how one should begin to both answer and ask these questions suggests a methodological discussion. Increasingly, researchers in user studies call for applying qualitative methods—that is, in-depth investigations often using case study, which seek to study the behavior of individuals in all of the complexity of their real-life situations. Qualitative evaluation seeks to improve systems and services through a cyclical process, in which both quantitative (statistical) and qualitative methods are employed, each used to check and illuminate the other. Some methods such as observation and interviews are particularly well-suited to field studies to which librarians can contribute substantially. Gathering the data in qualitative studies is done over time, often by participant observers who possess a knowledge of the setting and who could be expected to have insight into the situation. While simply "being on the scene" is hardly enough to qualify one as a researcher/evaluator, cooperative research and evaluation projects in which librarians play a significant role can do much to enhance one's understanding of the issues and problems associated with satisfying information needs. What follows is a discussion of some of the dimensions of the user's experience with an assessment of information retrieval.

Although Bawden's work presents it, it is necessary to go one step further—to question librarianship's assumptions about users and the purpose of information retrieval, and then to move to an in-depth exploration of what it means to seek information in libraries today. Until answers to such questions as "What are the user's expectations for how a system functions?," "What needs does it meet?," and "What is the experience of searching really like for the user?" are found, criteria for evaluating retrieval effectiveness will not be improved.

CONCLUSION

...the involvement of the practitioner is a *sine qua non* for the success of user-oriented evaluation. (Bawden, 1990, p. 101)

Information retrieval has been locked into a rationalistic, empirical framework which is no longer adequate. A different framework of analysis, design, and evaluation that is contextual in nature is needed; such a framework is both interpretive and phenomenological. It implies that information retrieval tasks are embedded in everyday life, and that meanings arise from individuals and from situations and are not generalizable except in a very limited sense. Users are diverse, and their situations are diverse as well. Their needs differ depending on their situation in time and space.

Information systems may therefore differ, offering diverse capabilities—often simultaneously within the same system—which provide an array of options the user can select. For example, such systems may offer interfaces tailored to many skill and knowledge levels; they may allow users to customize their access by adding their own entry vocabularies or remembering preferred search parameters; or they may provide a variety of output and display options. In order to move beyond the present-day large, rather brittle systems which are designed to be evaluated on precision and recall, evaluation studies must be conducted that can be used in the design of new systems. By focusing on users as the basis for evaluative criteria, new systems that are more responsive and adaptive to diverse situations can be created.

User-centered criteria—affective measures such as user satisfaction and situational factors such as context—are beginning to be used in research and evaluation. But this is just a beginning. Librarians and researchers alike must retain and refine their powers of critical observation about user behavior and attempt to look at both the antecedents and the results of information retrieval.

The methods used to gain insight into these issues are frequently case studies, focus groups, or in-depth interviews which, when combined with objective measures, can afford effective methods of research and evaluation. When placing the user at the center of evaluations, it is important not to take behaviors at face value but to probe beneath the surface. In order to do this successfully, it can mean small scale, in-depth studies carried out by astute, thoughtful individuals—ideally, a combination of both practitioners and researchers.

REFERENCES

Bawden, D. (1990). *User-oriented evaluation of information systems and services.* Brookfield, VT: Gower.

Bates, M. J. (1984). The fallacy of the perfect thirty-item online search. *RQ, 24*(1), 43-50.

Cleverdon, C. W. (1962). *Report on testing and analysis of an investigation into the corporate efficiency of indexing systems.* Cranfield, England: College of Aeronautics.

Cleverdon, C. W., & Keen, M. (1966). *ASLIB Cranfield Research Project: Factors determining the performance of smaller type indexing systems: Vol. 2.* Bedford, England: Cyril Cleverdon.

Cleverdon, C. W.; Mills, J.; & Keen, M. (1966). *ASLIB Cranfield Research Project: Factors determining the performance of smaller type indexing systems: Vol. 1. Design.* Bedford, England: Cyril Cleverdon.

Dalrymple, P. W. (1990). Retrieval by reformulation in two university library catalogs: Toward a cognitive model of searching behavior. *Journal of the American Society for Information Science, 41*(4), 272-281.

Dalrymple, P. W., & Zweizig, D. L. (1990). Users' experience of information retrieval systems: A study of the relationship between affective measures and searching behavior. Unpublished manuscript.

Dervin, B., & Nilan, M. (1986). Information needs and information uses. In M. Williams (Ed.), *Annual review of information science and technology* (Vol. 21, pp. 3-33). White Plains, NY: Knowledge Industry.

Fenichel, C. H. (1980). Intermediary searchers' satisfaction with the results of their searches. In A. R. Benenfeld & E. J. Kazlauskas (Eds.), *American Society for Information Science Proceedings, Vol. 17: Communicating information* (Paper presented at the 43rd annual ASIS meeting, October 5-10, 1980) (pp. 58-60). White Plains, NY: Knowledge Industry.

Fenichel, C. H. (1980-81). The process of searching online bibliographic databases: A review of research. *Library Research, 2*(2), 107-127.

Fidel, R. (1986). Toward expert systems for the selection of search keys. *Journal of the American Society for Information Science, 37*(1), 37-44.

Harter, S. P. (1990). Search term combinations and retrieval overlap: A proposed methodology and case study. *Journal of the American Society for Information Science, 41*(2), 132-146.

Haynes, R. B.; McKibbon, K. A.; Walker, C. J.; Ryan, N.; Fitzgerald, D.; & Ramsden, M. F. (1990). Online access to MEDLINE in clinical settings. *Annals of Internal Medicine, 112*(1), 78-84.

Katzer, J. (1972). The development of a semantic differential to assess users' attitudes towards an on-line interactive reference retrieval system. *Journal of the American Society for Information Science, 23*(2), 122-128.

Katzer, J. (1987). User studies, information science, and communication. *The Canadian Journal of Information Science, 12*(3,4), 15-30.

Kuhlthau, C. C. (1988). Developing a model of the library search process: Cognitive and affective aspects. *RQ, 28*(2), 232-242.

Lancaster, F. W. (1977). *The measurement and evaluation of library services.* Washington, DC: Information Resources Press.

Lancaster, F. W. (1979). *Information retrieval systems: Characteristics, testing and evaluation* (2nd ed.). New York: John Wiley & Sons.

Markey, K. (1984). *Subject searching in library catalogs: Before and after the introduction of online catalogs.* Dublin, OH: OCLC.

Mick, C. K.; Lindsey, G. N.; & Callahan, D. (1980). Toward usable user studies. *Journal of the American Society for Information Science, 31*(5), 347-356.

Mischo, W. H., & Lee, J. (1987). End-user searching of bibliographic databases. In M. Williams (Ed.), *Annual review of information science and technology* (Vol. 22, pp. 227-63). Amsterdam: Elsevier.

Nielsen, B. (1986). What they say they do and what they do: Assessing online catalog use instruction through transaction monitoring. *Information Technology and Libraries, 5*(1), 28-34.

Norman, D. A., & Draper, S. W. (Eds.). (1986). *User-centered system design.* Hillsdale, NJ: Erlbaum.

Richardson, J., Jr. (1989). Toward an expert system for reference service: A research agenda for the 1990s. *College and Research Libraries, 50*(2), 231-248.

Sandore, B. (1990). Online searching: What measure satisfaction? *Library and Information Science Research, 12*(1), 33-54.

Saracevic, T. (1976). Relevance: A review of the literature and a framework for thinking on the notion in information science. In M. J. Voigt & M. H. Harris (Eds.), *Advances in librarianship* (Vol. 6, pp. 79-138). New York: Academic Press.

Saracevic, T., & Kantor, P. (1988). A study of information seeking and retrieving. *Journal of the American Society for Information Science, 39*(3), 177-216.

Shannon, C. E. (1948). *The mathematical theory of communication.* Urbana, IL: University of Illinois Press.

Shneiderman, B. (1987). *Designing the user interface: Strategies for effective human-computer interaction.* Reading, MA: Addison-Wesley.

Tessier, J. A.; Crouch, W. W.; & Atherton, P. (1977). New measures of user satisfaction with computer-based literature searches. *Special Libraries, 68*(11), 383-389.

Waern, Y. (1989). *Cognitive aspects of computer supported tasks.* New York: John Wiley & Sons.

Weaver, W. (1949). The mathematics of communication. *Scientific American, 181*(1), 11-15.

Westbrook, L. (1990). Evaluating reference: An introductory overview of qualitative methods. *Reference Services Review, 18*(1), 73-78.

Wiberley, S. E., Jr., & Daugherty, R. A. (1988). Users' persistence in scanning lists of references. *College and Research Libraries, 49*(2), 149-156.

Wilson, P. (1983). The catalog as access mechanism: Background and concepts. *Library Resources & Technical Services, 27*(1), 4-17.

Wilson, T. D. (1981). On user studies and information needs. *The Journal of Documentation, 37*(1), 3-15.

Winograd, T., & Flores, F. (1987). *Understanding computers and cognition: A new foundation for design.* Reading, MA: Addison-Wesley.

Zweizig, D. L. (1977). Measuring library use. *Drexel Library Quarterly, 13*(3), 3-15.

Zweizig, D. L., & Dervin, B. (1977). Public library use, users, and uses—Advances in knowledge of the characteristics and needs of the adult clientele of American public libraries. In M. J. Voigt & M. H. Harris (Eds.), *Advances in librarianship* (Vol. 7, pp. 231-55). New York: Academic Press.

MARY GOULDING

Director, Reference Service
Suburban Library System
Oak Lawn, Illinois 60453

Minimum Standards as a First Step Toward Evaluation of Reference Services in a Multitype System

ABSTRACT

In 1986, the Suburban Library System (SLS) adopted minimum reference standards for their eighty public libraries. Four years later, similar standards are in place for over 100 academic, school and special SLS members. In order to ensure that the standards are effective, a sanction of withdrawal of access to System Reference Service is invoked for those libraries where policy, staff training, or resources fall short of the required minimum. The development and implementation of the standards has been a cooperative effort of almost 200 libraries. The ramifications call for training workshops, core lists of resources, policy models, and evaluation instruments which can be used in the smallest member library. A basic evaluation manual for public libraries has been produced and is being tested as an effective method of introducing more sophisticated methods to libraries where evaluation has never been done before.

BACKGROUND

Technical Standards: An Introduction for Librarians (Crawford, 1986). Would you really want to spend an hour reading a paper with a title like that? Are you already sliding down in your chair? Groaning inside?

I was, when I saw the same title on a book I had to read. But— paycheck at risk—I opened it to Sandra Paul's foreword, read the first sentence, and was hooked. "Standards aren't sexy," Paul wrote (p. v.). Every ensuing page proved Paul's point. Standards, indeed, are not sexy.

Both Paul's foreword and Walt Crawford's text were surprisingly fascinating and even enlightening, especially when applied to our own long-standing debate on the practicality and the prudence of standards as a measure of effective library service.

This paper is not about technical standards, but borrows the philosophy woven throughout Crawford's book. Standards, it explains, are something we live with every day, every hour—electrical plugs that fit the outlets, untainted chickens at the grocery store, ALA forms that are recognized in interlibrary loan departments across the country. If they are good standards, they simply serve to make us secure in a particular environment. If they are good standards, individual developments will emerge from them. Good standards do not stamp out initiative, do not suppress a capitalistic society, nor do they stunt the growth of the unique personality of an individual library. Good standards should make us comfortable. That view has done a lot to make me comfortable during these past seven years, as the Suburban Library System bit the bullet and adopted minimum standards for reference service in seventy-nine public, eleven academic, thirty-nine special, and fifty-one high school libraries.

INTRODUCTION

A Volatile Decade at SLS

Back in the early 1980s, the System, referred to locally as SLS, was facing another budget crunch. Every service was examined and, where tolerable, cutbacks were made. When member libraries looked at backup reference service, someone made the observation that the System Agency's load might be lightened if members truly provided basic reference service at the local level, leaving backup staff free to deal with reference queries that called for more specialized expertise and collections. It was the member libraries—though they were loathe to admit it a few years later—who first asked, "Is it I, Lord?" The problem was that many SLS libraries didn't have a clear idea of what others expected in the way of basic reference service. "Tell us," they said. "Tell us what it is and we'll do it." There was no problem—or so it seemed.

The problems came later. First, there was the commitment. The libraries adopted the 1984-89 Long Range Plan, which included an objective charging System staff "to set, in conjunction with membership input, minimum standards for reference services in SLS libraries, and to work cooperatively with local library staff to meet these standards." So far, so good. But the statement continues: "...and to enforce implementation of mutually established levels of service by withdrawal of (backup) reference services from those not meeting minimum requirements."

Still, the voice of objectors was relatively faint. Standards, after all, are good. Every year there are new ones, from ALA committees, from education commissions, from state libraries. They describe what librarians do in lovely terms and, of course, we meet most of them anyway—well, we would meet them if we could just get that referendum passed, or if our director would just give us that extra staff person.

Perhaps they weren't listening. The committees which began to meet in 1984 were drawing up standards which were going to force those libraries to make decisions about their missions. This, it should be remembered, was long before PLA's role-setting guidelines. They were going to have to decide, "Are we going to provide full reference service for our patrons or not? If we can't answer a question in-house, will backup service be available to us?" This time, the standards had teeth.

By way of explanation to those readers who are not familiar with the Illinois library network: Our libraries are autonomous. Each library can choose to be a member of one of the eighteen Illinois systems and participate in the statewide network as well as receive system services, which are completely funded by the state. Even as members, however, they remain individual entities who control their own staffing, choose their own materials, and require or provide training as they see fit. There is no centralized purchasing and no centralized hiring. There are few centralized "rules," though in the past three years, we have seen more systems adopt requirements for membership. The philosophy that has always prevailed is that the members are the system; it is they who cooperatively develop and endorse system policies which will serve their best interests. That philosophy prevailed from the beginning in developing reference standards—but not everybody was listening.

The original Ad Hoc Committee on Reference Standards decided to address public libraries first. By September 1984, thirty-three libraries had volunteered committee members to serve with three separate working groups. One group would develop minimum standards on policies, another on staffing, a third on resources. Two persons from each group made up a coordinating committee which met with the SLS Reference Service Director.

The first task of the committees was a literature search. Frankly, although citations on standards were frequent enough, they could find nothing that indicated that any library group had been willing to set and enforce them. Existing standards were couched in terms general enough to allow interpretations that would ensure that everyone could stay comfortable. If specifics were mentioned, they were "guidelines," and those who needed them most had no tangible reason to reach for them.

The SLS committees knew that the Long-Range Plan had predetermined sanctions, and while there were still those who preferred the guidelines approach, others were strongly in favor of sanctions. One reason was the philosophy that if a library chose not to meet this minimum level, they chose not to provide basic reference service, at least as we were to define it, and so had no need of backup service; the sanction, then, was not a slap on the wrist but a logical result of the library's right to make choices in service. Another philosophy was the "carrot on the stick." Ronald Dubberly (1988), in his article on potential public library accreditation, makes a point about the carrot theory. The effort of working for accreditation, he says, assumes that it is worth the investment (p. 56). Many members agreed with his thinking, believing that, without sanctions, our standards would be just one more pretty document.

Sanctions intact, by Spring 1985, the committees were ready to present their working drafts to the membership.

All of a sudden, everybody heard. These were not lofty ideals, guidelines, goals, or "pies-in-the-skies." These were specific, measurable standards, and nowhere in the document could anyone find the words "appropriate to" or "sufficient for." And if libraries did not meet every single requirement within three years, they would lose access to backup reference service.

It was a summer of meetings: big system meetings, little zone meetings—undoubtedly some unscheduled meetings over coffee, tea, and more. After all the discussions and further work by the committees, the final document was prepared and submitted to the membership in Fall 1985. Public libraries, which were directly affected, were asked to cast an advisory vote on whether or not it should be adopted by the SLS Board. At that time, public library members numbered eighty. The vote was 39-31 in favor of adoption, with ten abstentions. This was not exactly a grassroots call to action, but enough to convince a courageous SLS Board of Directors to adopt SLS Minimum Reference Standards for Public Libraries in January 1986.

Plans were immediately begun to develop standards for special libraries, adopted in 1987, then for academics in 1988 and high schools in 1989. SLS elementary schools are still eagerly awaiting their turn. All the documents are written in the same format with the same basic elements: policies, staffing, and resources. All have the same sanctions and the same period of implementation for libraries to meet standards before sanctions are imposed: three years. There are, of course, important differences in specific requirements for different types of libraries, but consistency was a consideration where possible.

Because public library standards were the first to be adopted, these standards are the primary focus of this paper, although others will be mentioned. After five years, we have a better feel for how standards are working in the public libraries and—in some cases—how they are not working. In January 1989, when sanctions became effective, five of SLS' seventy-nine public libraries did not meet standards. By action of the SLS Board and after due process, they lost access to SLS Reference Service. This summer, halfway between the implementation date and the agreed-upon evaluation year of 1992, we did a survey of librarians' perceptions of the effectiveness of standards in their libraries. Those results are discussed later in this paper. What follows are some of the more important requirements of the standards and how they might affect future plans for evaluations. (Copies of SLS Minimum Reference Standards for all library types are available from SLS free of charge; they may be requested from SLS Reference Service, 9444 S. Cook Avenue, Oak Lawn, IL 60453.)

THE REQUIREMENTS

A Written Reference Policy

Without a written policy, the rest of the requirements would be empty efforts. We hoped, too, that emphasis on local policies would point up the complementary supports of regional standards and local service goals. Only nine SLS public libraries had written reference policies in 1985. Today, seventy-seven are on file in our office. They aren't all "model" policies; some are twenty pages long, some only one page. Clinics are offered on how to write policies, but no judgements on format or style are made once the policies have been submitted. The important point is that staff in every library have discussed what their service goals are, put them in writing, and had them approved or endorsed by their governing bodies. Such a process can only strengthen those unique personalities.

Each standards document calls for inclusion of policy statements on certain issues. Except for special libraries, the lists are quite similar, with an emphasis on primary and secondary clienteles in all but the publics. They ask for statements on such things as hours reference service is offered, trained staff, confidentiality, policies on special categories of questions—e.g., homework and criss-cross directories—and assurance of policy review and updating. They also call for periodic evaluation of local reference service, a particularly difficult standard for many libraries to meet, and one which merits more discussion in the pages to follow.

Not surprisingly, more than two-thirds of SLS' public libraries had never attempted reference evaluation of any kind. They have counted, but they have not evaluated. Those who had were often victims of what Mackay (1988) refers to as the "Ready? Fire! Aim" approach, and were uneasy with results (p. 37). Again, they turned to system staff to tell them how.

The need for help was fairly urgent and none of us at SLS was an expert in what we were to learn was a very complex field. We attacked the problem with the usual cure—a committee. At first, it was a small committee, just three other people with the author as facilitator. Like good librarians, we began with a literature search. We certainly found plenty to read on evaluation—and had full shopping bags to prove it. (During that time, the author was asked to be a member of RASD's Evaluation of Reference Services Committee, and may have accepted just to have something to do with those shopping bags!)

The committee was disappointed with its findings. Some of what we found was the work of some of the readers of this paper. It was impressive, admirable, even enviable. But very little of it could be useful in SLS' small public libraries.

These small public libraries wanted it simple. They wanted forms. They wanted it easy to administer. They wanted it non-threatening to both staff and patrons. They wanted it private. And they wanted it cost-free. Impossible? Maybe. But we were in a situation where impossible wasn't an option. The Suburban Library System had adopted standards which required every library to evaluate, and the System does not require anything without offering support needed to do it.

The committee of three generated themselves into a committee of fifteen. We would produce something to help those libraries do what they had to do. The result was the *Reference Evaluation Manual for Public Libraries* (Suburban Library System, 1989), an in-house publication which has since been requested by several hundred out-of-house people. While the manual won't win the Dartmouth Medal, it is doing the job it had to do: getting some public libraries to at least begin to recognize that reference activity is as important to consider as circulation figures and story-hour attendance.

The committee's first step was a survey asking the libraries what they would like to know about their reference services. Their task was defined by the questions the libraries most wanted answered. They were:

1. Are our patrons satisfied with the answers we provide?
2. What subjects do people ask about most and can we meet those information needs?

3. How can the output measures of "Reference Completion Rate" and "Reference Transactions Per Capita" be used as evaluative measures?
4. Are our patrons getting accurate and complete answers?

The fifteen divided into groups of three, enlisted help from colleagues, and went to work.

No one expected the manual to be more than it was meant to be: a starting point for libraries where "evaluation," in the true sense of the word, is perceived to have no place in their priorities. Only the threat of losing backup reference service has urged them to try these first steps. In years to come, we must build some bridges between the researchers and the practitioners—somewhere we must find valid methods of evaluation that are acceptable to all public, school and academic libraries.

Meanwhile, we at SLS are learning that standards are a first step in themselves. Since they have become effective, and libraries have indeed tried some simple "count and compare" methods, they are reaching for something better, e.g., one group is collecting feedback from those using the manual, already looking toward a second edition that can offer more valid models; another group is investigating the possibility of doing an unobtrusive study on accuracy, patron satisfaction, referrals, and has even committed themselves to spending some significant dollars to do it.

A few years ago, when on the lecture circuit trying to convince SLS administrators of the value of formal evaluation, this author used what she thought was a "sure sell" technique. If (the audience was told) you are willing to admit that some of you might be providing "average" public library reference service, you are giving your patrons right answers only about 52 percent of the time. Suppose that you discovered that 48 percent of your books had the wrong Dewey numbers on the spines, or that 48 percent of the people who came to pick up reserves got the wrong material? As administrators, you would be hitting the roof and willing to spend whatever the cost to identify and correct the problem. How can you go on accepting a 48 percent fail rate in the most expensive operation in your libraries—your reference departments?

But the idea didn't sell—at least not with many of the administrators. Maybe they had never evaluated, but they knew one thing: those figures didn't apply in their libraries. What finally sold them was standards. With standards in place, libraries had to *do* something. It was as simple as that—and in some cases, appetites have been whetted. A few administrators are already beginning to build bridges toward those

impressive studies in the literature, but they're not going to make it
all the way across without the help of the researchers who must meet
them in midstream.

Trained Reference Workers

All the standards include minimum formal education requirements
for the person with principal responsibility for reference service, and
a list of basic duties. Most of the controversy, however, arose over the
training requirements for any person doing reference work, even if it
were only for an hour on Wednesday nights.

Proceeding from the premise that *not* just anyone can answer
reference questions, the standards require that everyone who is assigned
that duty, professional and paraprofessional alike, attend a reference
interview workshop. That requirement is common to all standards except
specials, where CEOs are not friendly toward probing questioners. It
was not a popular requirement with many old-timers. They've done
it, though, and most have agreed that they gained from it. Since 1986,
874 SLS librarians have attended an interview workshop—some tailored
for those who work with children, with students and faculty, or with
the handicapped. As different sets of standards become effective,
interview workshops will be a part of our schedules for years to come,
and we continue to look for new approaches. For example, right now
a workshop is being developed specifically for people who claim they
"don't need an interview workshop." Because we know all reference
staff have been exposed to good interview techniques, future evaluations
of interpersonal skills will proceed from a common base.

Even more controversial than the interview requirement was the
standard for training in reference sources for paraprofessionals. For
purposes of the public libraries document, *paraprofessional* was defined
as anyone without an ALA-accredited MLS. This meant that hundreds
of circulation clerks, student helpers, part-time staff from the
community, library school students, and even a few non-degreed
administrators helping out at the reference desk had to attend at least
four workshops in addition to the reference interview. Though no one
believed that five workshops a reference librarian maketh, we did have
a consensus that this was the necessary minimum to work behind the
desk.

In 1985, many SLS libraries complained that they could not spare
desk staff to go off to some far-flung suburb for a half-day—that they
did not drive; that one or another had twenty years experience and
would be insulted; that, in short, the training requirement was an
impossible goal. As of this month, SLS has issued 385 certificates of
completion to public library reference staff. It was hard, it took some
effort, but it was not impossible after all.

In *Swim With the Sharks Without Being Eaten Alive*, Harvey Mackay (1988), referring to the four-minute mile, makes a point about the changing nature of the impossible. Some will remember that day when Roger Bannister shattered the centuries-old record and ran the mile in under four minutes—a feat runners had heretofore conceded could never be accomplished. One year after the Bannister miracle, thirty-seven people had run the mile in less than four minutes; two years later, 300 had done it (pp. 79-80).

Analogously, 385 reference librarians have broken our impossible "four-minute mile" training requirement. Judging from those attending their tenth or fifteenth workshop, the standard is a long-forgotten reason for coming.

Resources and Equipment

Standards for public, academic, and school libraries all include a core reference list, drawn up by a committee specific to the type of library. It is not a recommended reference collection, but a list of things that even the smallest reference service should not be without. Some are specific titles, but most are subject areas for which any title will suffice, though many have currency requirements. If a library had to buy everything on the public library core list, they could do it for under $3000. No one has had to spend even close to that, but 50 percent of SLS public libraries had to buy something in order to meet the standard. The lists are updated every two years, though we try hard not to give the libraries a moving target.

Not unexpectedly, the core lists differ significantly for the three types of libraries and not everyone agrees that every item is an absolute necessity. In one letter responding to the academic list, the librarian complained that he saw no need for a zip code directory in an academic library. His letter, however, got there too late to present to the committee—it was addressed to the wrong zip code!

Other resources requirements deal with local government documents, backruns of newspapers, voter information, and in-house access to a bibliographic database. Academic and special libraries also require in-house access to information databases, and all except public libraries call for a telefax machine. Some equipment standards have delighted librarians who have used them to finally get approval to add a photocopy machine, a fax, or (believe it or not) a telephone and authority to make outside telephone calls in pursuit of information.

Future evaluators will know that SLS libraries have a common core of resources and equipment that allows them to access a basic body of information. (Copies of core reference lists for each library type are available for $5, prepaid to Suburban Library System and mailed to SLS Reference Service, 9444 S. Cook Ave., Oak Lawn, IL 60453.)

HOW ARE STANDARDS AFFECTING LOCAL REFERENCE SERVICE?

The long-term effects of these standards on local reference service is not yet known. Some good things have come of them, there's no doubt about that, but in the end the good will have to be great enough to justify the continued effort. SLS has scheduled a time for the libraries themselves to make that decision.

As mentioned earlier, each library has three years to meet standards before sanctions become effective. Three years after that, they will decide—in 1992 for the public libraries, 1993 for special libraries, 1994 for academic libraries and 1995 for high school libraries. Meanwhile, each library files with SLS its written policy and an annual report which indicates if they continue to meet standards and if they have reviewed their policy and evaluated their reference service. We keep a record of staff training, policy reviews, and evaluations, though there is no requirement that they share results. Other than that, we believe what they tell us—and, truth be told, sometimes wish they weren't quite so honest about their failings!

In 1989, our mettle was tested when five public libraries lost access to SLS Reference Service. In at least some of those five, we feel the libraries made a responsible decision, recognizing that their major role in the community did not include reference service as we defined it. Unfortunately, we haven't found a way to make all of them feel so good about it. In any case, it happened, and the roof at SLS is still intact.

We are busy now gearing up for D-Day in academic libraries and are expecting fireworks. Some of the academic libraries were every bit as resistant as the public ones, and SLS will face a difficult problem in high schools where release time to attend workshops is not easy to come by. But high schools, too, are working hard, and will have their chance to re-evaluate three years down the road.

Only now are we discovering our own mistake in not planning for those evaluations when we began the process. We should have done some measuring of reference services in system libraries before standards went into effect. We didn't, and that will make SLS' job harder in those telling years to come—but it is too late to wish we had known what we didn't know about evaluation. Like our libraries, we are learning a lot from the standards.

An Interim Survey of Public Libraries

Perhaps to help make up for that omission, SLS has just recently done a halfway point survey of its public libraries, asking for their perceptions of how standards have affected their local services a year and a half after they became effective.

The surveys were sent to all libraries, including those which do not currently meet standards since, as members of SLS, they have a voice in their future. Return rate was 81 percent, quite good for members who have to make choices these days about how much more paperwork they can deal with.

The full results of the survey are in the Appendix to this paper. The most important are the answers to two basic questions:

IN GENERAL, DO YOU THINK SLS MINIMUM REFERENCE STANDARDS HAVE IMPROVED REFERENCE SERVICE IN YOUR LIBRARY?

Yes: 78%   No: 14%   Don't Know: 8%

WHETHER YOU ANSWERED YES OR NO TO THE ABOVE, WOULD YOU RECOMMEND SOME TYPE OF REFERENCE STANDARDS AS A GOOD IDEA?

Yes: 90%   No: 1%   Don't Know: 4%

Yes, but without sanctions: 5%

This response was from a group of libraries which, five years earlier, recommended standards by a majority vote of only 56 percent!

Survey results indicate that there are, indeed, a few requirements that, in practice, members do not consider either "vitally" or "very" important. Less than half consider the collection of local government documents worth the trouble and only 36 percent believe six-month retention of local newspapers is necessary to minimum standards. While more than 50 percent consider all other elements appropriate, not all are converts. Four percent think that a telephone has no effect on the quality of service; a few think formal education requirements and the Core Reference List have a negative effect because of costs involved.

CONCLUSION

It appears evident that for the majority of SLS members, the development and implementation of minimum reference standards has been and is a worthwhile process. SLS libraries made a courageous decision in 1985 and have stood by it.

Most communities or neighborhoods of communities are not so different from those in SLS. Our public libraries serve as many as 61,000 people and as few as 300. Some of our academic libraries are large four-year institutions, some are junior colleges, and some are small private ones. Our schools serve a few thousand or a few hundred. Among SLS special libraries, only the hospital libraries have similar missions. And not one of those 275 libraries feel they are anything like another. Each has its own unique community of users, its own unique personality. And yet we have found some common ground on which to measure ourselves, and have determined that we will not hide behind our individuality and lose an opportunity to examine, and hopefully improve, our reference services in SLS.

The mid-1990s may see SLS libraries with a dramatically different set of standards than we now have—or with no standards at all. But, come that time, we will have done what we set out to do: have the evidence on which to base a responsible choice.

In a recent article, Herbert S. White (1989), commenting on the library world's negative reaction to standards, said the response was too often "what we have 'meets the needs' because, after all, it is what we have" (p. 62). Not if we can help it, Herb White, not if we can help it!

APPENDIX

Effects of Reference Standards in SLS Public Libraries

Survey Results: Summer, 1990

In January of 1989, SLS Minimum Reference Standards for Public Libraries, adopted in January of 1986, became effective. Formal evaluation of the standards is scheduled for 1992. This informal survey is indicative of their impact at the half-way point in the process.

Surveys were distributed to 79 member public libraries. Return rate was 81%.

77 responses were received from 64 libraries.

6 libraries sent multiple responses from administrators and department heads responsible for different reference service points. Scores were tallied on a basis of either 64 or 77, as seemed appropriate, and as noted below.

2 of the 5 libraries which do not meet standards responded, and are included in the tally.

RESULTS

1. IN GENERAL, DO YOU THINK SLS REFERENCE STANDARDS HAVE IMPROVED REFERENCE SERVICE IN YOUR LIBRARY? (of 77)

    Yes: 60 (77.9%)   No: 11 (14.3%)   No Opinion: 6 (7.8%)

2. WHETHER YOU ANSWERED YES OR NO TO THE ABOVE, WOULD YOU RECOMMEND SOME TYPE OF REFERENCE STANDARDS AS A GOOD IDEA? (of 77)

    Yes: 69 (89.6%)   Yes, but without sanctions: 4 (5.2%)

    No: 1 (1.3%)   No Opinion: 3 (3.9%)

3. EVEN IF THERE WERE NO REFERENCE STANDARDS WHICH OF THE FOLLOWING SLS-PROVIDED REFERENCE AIDS WOULD YOU WANT CONTINUED? (of 77)

Reference interview workshops for new staff	64 (83.1%)
Other reference workshops for all staff	71 (92.2%)
Core Reference List for Public Libraries	67 (87%)
Manual: "Evaluation of Reference Services"	46 (59.7%)
Workshops/Samples of reference policies	40 (51.9%)
Regular visits to library by SLS staff	34 (44.2%)

4. IS THE CURRENT ANNUAL REPORT FORM CONVENIENT FOR YOU TO FILL OUT? (of 77)

    Yes: 62   No: 1   No Opinion: 14

APPENDIX *(Cont.)*

5.   WHICH OF THE FOLLOWING DID YOUR LIBRARY HAVE TO DO <u>IN ORDER TO MEET</u> REFERENCE STANDARDS? (of 64)

Write a reference policy	57 (89%)
Make plans to evaluate your reference service	46 (71.9%)
Purchase new titles to meet Core Reference List	32 (50%)
Adjust scheduling to provide time away for continuing education	31 (48.4%)
Make new efforts to acquire local government documents	23 (35.9%)
Make new efforts to acquire information on local organizations	21 (32.8%)
Acquire equipment to access online bibliographic databases (SWAN/IO)	15 (23.4%)
Retain longer runs of newspapers	13 (20.3%)
Change staffing in order to provide trained staff at all hours library is open	13 (20.3%)
Change job descriptions in order to meet formal education requirements of standards	9 (14%)
Acquire a typewriter or electronic equivalent	6 (9.4%)
Add a telephone to the reference area	3 (4.7%)
Get authority to make telephone calls within the Chicago metropolitan area	2 (3.1%)
Acquire or move a photocopy machine for easy access	1 (1.5%)

Only one of the 64 libraries had to do nothing in order to meet standards.

Of the 5 libraries which do not meet standards, 1 does not have online access to a bibliographic database (responded), 1 does not have trained staff on duty on Sunday (responded), 1 has not purchased all titles on Core List nor completed required workshops (no response), and 2 have not submitted any reports indicating whether or not they meet standards (no responses).

6.   PLEASE RATE THE IMPORTANCE OF EACH OF THE FOLLOWING REQUIREMENTS TO GOOD REFERENCE SERVICE IN YOUR LIBRARY. IT SHOULD MAKE NO DIFFERENCE IN YOUR RATING WHETHER YOU MET THOSE REQUIREMENTS BEFORE OR AFTER THE IMPLEMENTATION OF REFERENCE STANDARDS. (of 77)

Please note that the chart on the following page tallies answers in percentages only.

APPENDIX (Cont.)

ALL FIGURES = % OF TOTAL RESPONSES	Vitally Important +	Very Important +	=	Important +	=	No Effect +	Negative Effect +	=	No Answer
POLICY									
1. Process of development	13	44	57	32	89	6	-	6	5
2. Having written policy	38	31	69	25	94	3	-	3	3
3. Evaluation of reference service	22	39	61	31	92	3	-	3	5
STAFF									
1. Formal educ. requirement	30	39	69	19	88	5	3	8	4
2. SLS orientation session	16	49	65	27	92	3	-	3	5
3. Interview workshops, all staff	23	40	63	31	94	3	-	3	3
4. Four sources workshops, paraprofessional staff	22	38	60	31	91	5	1	6	3
5. SLS continuing educ. workshops, all staff	23	47	70	25	95	-	-	-	5
6. Cont. educ. requirement	21	34	55	36	91	1	1	2	7
7. Provision of in-house training	26	32	58	31	89	4	1	5	6
MATERIALS									
1. Acquisition of titles on core reference list	34	31	65	25	90	5	3	8	2
2. Acquisition of local govt. documents	13	30	43	47	90	5	-	5	5
3. Acquisition of info. on local organizations	13	42	55	36	91	5	-	5	4
4. Required retention of back files of newspapers	9	27	36	44	80	12	-	12	8
EQUIPMENT									
1. Easy access to telephone	71	17	88	5	93	4	-	4	3
2. Authority to make calls in metropolitan area	56	27	83	8	91	4	-	4	5
3. Easy access to typewriter	35	31	66	23	89	8	-	8	3
4. Easy access to photocopy	43	36	79	13	92	5	-	5	3
5. In-house access to bibliographic database (SWAN/IO)	56	26	82	14	96	1	1	2	2

APPENDIX *(Cont.)*

6. (cont.)

Additional Note to Chart: For some items, it seemed valuable to tally ratings of a subset of libraries which had to adjust scheduling, budgets, space, or procedures in order to meet the particular requirements (see Question #5).

Half of the ratings were surprisingly similar, using either the total responses or the subset as a base. Those which indicated more than a 10% difference in the "vitally/very important" rating are:

	Vitally/Very Important (%)	No/Negative Effect (%)
	Total/Subset	Total/Subset
Requirement for Formal Education	69/80	8/0
Interview Workshops	63/42	3/0
Reference Sources Workshops	60/42	6/0
Continuing Education Workshops	70/59	2/0
Local Government Documents	43/58	5/0
Information on Local Organizations	55/68	5/6
Retention of Newspapers	36/47	12/15

Most of the percentages unaccounted for above were rated in the "Important" column; a few had no opinion.

The numbers of libraries which had to acquire equipment were too small to make valid comparisons. The only exception was the 15 libraries which acquired equipment to access online databases. 82% of them rated that element as vitally or very important, exactly the same as the rating from total responses.

2 libraries which had to write a policy felt it had no effect on their services.

1 library which had to purchase titles on the Core List felt it had no effect on service; another felt it had a negative effect because of cost.

7.   OTHER COMMENTS WRITTEN ON SURVEYS:

In response to "Which of the following did your library have to do IN ORDER TO MEET reference standards?":

"We purchased a few titles to meet the standards but also used the list to expand our holdings further."

"The best method of evaluating reference service is yet to be decided. Do you plan to recommend something system-wide?"

"As a small suburban library, I appreciate having a standard to measure against our reference collection--even though it can be a juggling act to cover the cost."

APPENDIX *(Cont.)*

"We have always sent people to workshops, but now we are making more of an effort to make sure that everyone goes to at least 2 a year--and of course there are more available now."

"Writing a reference policy was very worthwhile in terms of deciding just what we will do and standardizing how we treat patrons. It was also a good cooperative project for the Adult and Young People's Services Department."

"Obtaining local documents has been far more difficult than we expected. It took nearly two years to receive current minutes of City Council meetings from XXXXXX, and we still don't have a complete set of ordinances from either XXXXXX or XXXXXX. Apparently, neither City Hall believes the library does more than just hand out Danielle Steel novels and host Story Hours for preschoolers."

"We don't do very much reference work at this library, but all the various steps the staff has gone through to meet the standards has made them more aware of the importance of reference service and more familiar with our reference collection."

"An essential aspect of reference to emphasize in continuing education is familiarity of electronic reference sources available, best utilization of such, budget concerns, management of such services and current display and information about such as electronic encyclopedias, video-audio technology, etc. Which is most cost effective? Which is the best to use to fulfill information requests? Update on a nationwide standard of information format. A budget plan to introduce electronic sources each year in a long range plan. Helping our youth to be aware of electronic availability of resources. When and how to use electronic information and critical decision making of which is best to use and digest at critical points of needs. Helping our youngsters become computer literate in knowing what to use, when, how?"

"We changed staffing and scheduling so that there is a more even distribution of those trained in reference."

"Writing the Reference Policy was the most difficult part. The whole staff contributed and it made us all more aware of our policies and able to be more consistent in our answers to patrons."

"Many of the books required have proven totally irrelevant to a library of our size and a community of our type."

"We held staff inservice training to use the new reference material and make better use of what we already had." (from a library which does not meet standards)

"We are always informally evaluating our reference service. The standards now make us do so formally."

"Since XXXXXX came aboard as our new director, we have added a reference desk complete with telephone, CLSI terminal with DIALOG compatability, increased our core reference collection substantially, added MLS trained librarians for around the clock coverage. I believe we have made enormous strides toward meeting reference standards in the past three years!"

"Frankly, I always fear something on the core reference list has gotten out of date with me forgetting to replace it. Chases's Annual Events remains for me the most delightful and important discovery on the list."

APPENDIX *(Cont.)*

In response to "Even if there were no reference standards, which of the following SLS-provided reference aids would you want continued?":

"This is a loaded question. All of the above are or have been helpful to a degree. But the 'Core List,' for example, as a requirement is different than a 'Suggested List,' that might be just as helpful."

"We have become increasingly aware of the depth of our own collection. With the new additions to our collection and the training of the staff we are able to answer the reference questions that are asked of us. Please keep in mind that the role we have chosen is a Popular Materials Library." (from a library which does not meet standards)

"Serving as a member of the 1990 Core Reference Committee was a pleasant and profitable experience for me. I learned so many things from my colleagues about reference sources and methods of service. It is an ideal way to up-date and develop one's own reference collection."

"Rather than just continue the requirements should be strengthened."

"Bibliographies in various subect fields of recommended titles to help small libraries in adding depth to their collection--the opinion of SLS peers would be more valuable to us than many printed bibliographies in books."

"Besides Core Reference Lists I would like to see suggestions for reference material that you have found useful, even though not required."

"This year's workshops had few of relevant value. Perhaps more on basic reference sources and tips and less on hi-tech and interviews."

"Evaluation of Reference Services for Youth Services Dept."

"We love all SLS-provided reference aids."

"Workshops are fine if they are on a subject you need--but to take a workshop for a requirement has a negative effect."

"The existence of written Reference Standards makes it easier to justify the Reference budget to library trustees; one can defend expenditures by arguing that 'we have these system reference standards to uphold...'"

"Reference workshops should be provided, but workshops should be offered IN SEVERAL SESSIONS for professional staff. So far, I've seen little of this."

"Even more meaningful than educational requirements is the hands on experience of staff--whether through SLS workshops or in house training."

"How often is a library visited? How is the schedule of visits decided?"

In response to "In general, do you think SLS reference standards have improved reference service in your library?":

"They keep us from losing sight of some basic things we need to maintain."

"Yes, but we were thinking along the same lines anyway. However, the workshops provide CE that we couldn't do on our own."

APPENDIX *(Cont.)*

"Found several good titles on core list."

"Seem to apply to small libraries."

"No, we have no SLS backup." (from a library which does not meet standards)

"Cannot evaluate, as very few changes were needed."

"If nothing else, just looking at and thinking about reference service is a great exercise. But the SLS standards have value beyond that. We're lucky to have them, even if we all do complain a little."

In response to "Whether you answered Yes or No to the above, would you recommend some type of reference standards as a good idea?":

"Guidelines yes/standards no!"

"Maybe called guidelines."

"Yes, I merely disagree with penalty. Knowing the norm is valuable; following like sheep is thoughtless." (from a library which does not meet standards)

In response to "How do you think SLS standards could be more effective?":

"By SLS helping (financially, if necessary) those libraries who do not meet standards. I strongly disagree with the process of denying service to any SLS library. SLS was founded to help libraries--not to punish them."

"Continue revisions of core list (two year intervals). Help libraries evaluate their reference service. A uniform method would be of greatest value."

"When I first dealt with the many pages of the core reference list I wished it could be published on interactive software for much greater ease of maintaining and upgrading the collection as well as budgeting! I still think it's a great idea..."

"The best way would be in terms of available consultation with SLS personnel so our standards could be better updated. Perhaps we could reserve at least 1 session annually of the Zone Reference Librarians' meetings for standards and one annual session (at least) for evaluation stats."

"Provide fewer workshops of higher quality and help the instructors by providing an outline of what to cover in workshops. There is an unevenness in the quality unfortunately."

"As long as member libraries are relatively autonomous, I doubt there is much more that can be done. I worry a bit about running out of new workshops for long-term SLS librarians, but continuing education (or just battery-recharging) is a real need. The fact that patrons are still being referred to us for help or materials they could have gotten in their own libraries bothers me, so may need to look at ways to reinforce training."

"They will be effective if they are enforced. Each library should assume its own responsibility in seeing that the SLS standards are met. Yet, we still need reminders that we are keeping in step with the standards."

APPENDIX *(Cont.)*

"Insist that academic libraries meet the same standards as the SLS public libraries."

"Standards should be re-evaluated for fairness to smaller libraries. Cutting them off from Reference Service assistance is a double punishment--they are the libraries who need it most. Also, the original concept was to set up standards to strive for and guidelines to good service--'what should we be doing?'--not what must we do."

"Sensitivity to the limitations in staff and reference materials of smaller, poorer libraries."

"Youth reference questions are a very important aspect of reference service. Consideration in training, input, etc. should always have a youth services librarian representative."

"The Head of Reference reports that the workshops are especially useful. She also recommends that workshops be offered on the subjects of business and legal resources, the two areas where staff have most expressed a need."

"Certain portions should be based on population and budget. The truly 'poor' library in a small population certainly doesn't require as much as a larger population needs."

"I think a workshop in 'writing winning proposals' would be valuable in helping us make our case with our boards."

"Basic Standards should be expanded. For example: long distance phone calls, large core list, immediate access to SWAN terminal, etc. It might be useful to have some standards cover the quality of the actual reference work, in addition to the collections and equipment."

"Divide standards by size of population served with varying degrees of standards."

"For those libraries that rely on Reference Service, the comments that I hear are that the service is slow and sometimes inadequate or nonexistent." (from a library which does not meet standards)

"They would be more effective if they took the conditions of the small libraries into consideration, e.g. Reference person on duty all open hours; on-line capability; and core reference."

"Reference standards currently require that the Reference Role be one of the top three roles for every library--it is not one of ours by action of the Board." (from a library which does not meet standards)

"I think continuing education for all professionals is a necessity. Technology is moving so rapidly--we all need help in keeping up-to-date."

"Perhaps if there were more distinction between the size of a library and the specific requirements."

"Provide more reference workshops pertaining to public libraries."

REFERENCES

Crawford, W. (1986). *Technical standards: An introduction for librarians.* White Plains, NY: Knowledge Industry.

Dubberly, R. (1988). Questioning public library accreditation. *Library Journal, 113*(9), 56-58.

Mackay, H. (1988). *Swim with the sharks without being eaten alive.* New York: William Morrow and Co.

Suburban Library System. (1989). Reference evaluation manual for public libraries. Oak Lawn, IL: SLS Reference Service.

White, H. S. (1989). The value-added process of librarianship. *Library Journal, 114*(1), 62-63.

BETTY J. TUROCK

Chair, Department of Library and Information Studies
Director, MLS Program
Rutgers University
School of Communication, Information and Library Studies
New Brunswick, New Jersey

Assessing Service to Special Populations

ABSTRACT

Over the past twenty years, librarianship has promulgated quantitative evaluation through the application of output measures to a goal-based model, even in the face of evidence that such an approach makes difficult the fair assessment of services to special populations. While outside librarianship the emphasis is on outcome measurement, we have failed to move into that realm, even when it is most appropriate. In the future, the way in which evaluation is conducted must be determined by the questions it seeks to answer, the model that will best supply the answers, and the design that will uncover an accurate reflection of the program. That requires a combination of qualitative and quantitative measurement rigorously applied. Eight models are suggested that can provide the valid, reliable evaluations that have to date eluded us.

INTRODUCTION

Not unlike other professions, librarianship has resisted evaluation. At the federal level, even with legislation like the Library Services and Construction Act (LSCA) Title I, which has as its major focus service to special populations—the aging, handicapped, disadvantaged minorities, the illiterate, and those for whom English is a second language—hard-hitting comments have become part of the record on library efforts (Shavitt, 1985, pp. 124-25). Although assessment is required to receive LSCA funding, the consensus of recent studies, including a 1989 meta-evaluation, is that library program evaluation stands now where educational program evaluation stood fifteen years ago (Roberts, 1985, p. 1; Turock, 1990, p. 50).

Why Is Evaluation Resisted?

Given this negativity, why do librarians continue to resist evaluation? Frequently, that question is answered by citing a tradition of limited interest which, in turn, is blamed on a limited knowledge and understanding of evaluation processes and techniques. But that supposition is not only condescending, it also reinforces the unrealistic expectation that minimal knowledge of the evaluative process will not harm the validity of the resulting product.

At a Midwinter Conference held during January, 1989 at the United States Department of Education's Office of Educational Research and Improvement, where eighty participants from forty-seven states analyzed the national status of evaluation in service programs funded by LSCA Title I, it became clear that ascribing resistance to lack of skill alone is too simplistic. Even when librarians are knowledgeable, they may not evaluate. Some of the conferees' reasons for abstinence had a philosophical basis, such as, "What we do can't be reduced to numbers"; others had an operational basis, such as, "Costs are too high and evaluation consumes more time than we have to give it." With some probing, however, two prevalent underlying reasons were brought forth. First, librarians have little faith in the usefulness of evaluations. For all of the effort assessment requires, they believe no one pays attention to the results. Second, all too frequently, evaluation militates against demonstrating the worth of nontraditional services for nontraditional populations. Taken together, these reasons pointed up the perceived lack of utility of evaluation, and the misinterpretation of evaluation as synonymous with currently practiced output measurement.

Expanded Options

In the last decade a shift has taken place in evaluation, from the dominance of numbers in quantitative assessments toward the addition of narratives in qualitative approaches. That shift is only now beginning to have an effect on library programs. Until twenty years ago, minimum standards for public libraries and public library systems issued by the Public Library Association (PLA) concentrated on the resources supplied to provide service, such as income, number of staff, volumes owned, and volumes added (Public Library Association, 1966). The major problem uncovered with these assessments was that putting standard inputs into a library did not necessarily assure standard levels of activities, such as circulation or the number of reference questions answered per questions asked, i.e., input and service did not necessarily go hand in hand (Chelton, 1987, pp. 463-84).

In the 1970s, with a grant from the U.S. Department of Education, Ernest DeProspo at Rutgers University began building the case for support from a more systematically developed and tested set of quantitative measures that emphasized outputs, i.e., measuring performance through services used, such as library visits, in-library materials circulation, and program attendance (DeProspo et al., 1973). By 1982, PLA had sponsored the publication of *Output Measures for Public Libraries* (Zweizig & Rodger, 1982), which was revised in 1987 (Van House et al., 1987).

As adoption grew, problems were uncovered. Today, although output measurement may be managerially necessary, stressing it without regard for its limitations has retarded the development of library program evaluation, especially with regard to demonstrating the worth of services for special populations. Studies over time have revealed that when measures of use are compared, the differences discovered may not be due so much to service performance as they are to the social and educational characteristics of the library's public (D'Elia, 1980, pp. 410-30; D'Elia & Walsh, 1983, pp. 109-33; D'Elia & Walsh, 1985, pp. 3-30; D'Elia & Rodger, 1987, pp. 5-20). Even in the face of evidence that applying output measures may make difficult the fair assessment of services to special populations, particularly those situated in economically disadvantaged communities, they are still the only approach widely recommended.

The use of input and output measurement has also been called into question because it does not reflect on the quality of service provided. It makes no distinction between technical quality—what is delivered—and functional quality—how it is delivered (Shaughnessy, 1987, pp. 5-10). While currently outside librarianship the emphasis is on outcome measurement, we have failed to move into that realm even where it is most appropriate. The focus of *output* measurement is the library, but the focus of *outcome* measurement is the library's users. The shift is to determining impacts, that is, what happens as a consequence of a program. This approach takes a marketing rather than an institutional stance by asking such questions as: How well did the service meet the magnitude of the need uncovered? Did it have the intended effects? Did it reach the target audience? What changes occurred in them? Were their skills enhanced? Were they able to reach a personal goal which improved the quality of their lives or the lives of their family members? What values did they derive from library use?

The answers to these questions give a better picture of the merit of services for special populations than traditional measures such as circulation per capita.

Common constraints put boundaries on the course undertaken in all evaluations. The aim is to conduct a credible assessment for affordable costs within the available time. Staff expertise also determines the design implemented; it cannot be more intricate or complex than staff can handle. When design demands a level of skill that is not available, options include hiring consultants, giving staff short, intensive training courses, or isolating complex or difficult portions of the design for performance under contract (United States General Accounting Office, 1984, pp. 12-13). The self-diagnostic approach to library evaluation currently in vogue has led to librarians assuming the role of evaluator in addition to other roles demanded of them. Indeed, that not only requires time unavailable, but it may not be worthwhile in the long run. A study of the U.S. Department of Education's National Diffusion Network (NDN), established to recognize and disseminate information and training on exemplary programs of educational innovation, has shown that most of the programs deemed outstanding were assessed by expert outside evaluators (Lynch, 1987, pp. 20-24). Librarians can stop the self-flagellation because they are not authorities in the craft of evaluation and realize that there are some things experts should be hired to do.

Measurement and measures have held the spotlight. But the application of measures alone does not ensure the systematic process that is a hallmark of rigorous evaluation. The demand for evidence that something good is happening can exert pressure to decide program merit on the basis of what is readily measured. This rush to quantify can damage progress in developing sound library programs for special populations aimed at long-term outcomes (Schorr, 1988). Ultimately, the way in which the evaluation of a program is conducted must be determined, not by the application of a few measures, but by the questions it seeks to answer, the model that will best supply the answers, and the design that will uncover an accurate reflection of the program under scrutiny. In some cases, qualitative data is needed first to better understand and measure what will adequately assess impact, particularly where services to special populations are concerned. But qualitative evaluation is rarely discussed and even more rarely implemented.

Two Perspectives on Rigor

Qualitative strategies frequently supply the only means to fairly and accurately assess what is occurring in services aimed at special populations. Perhaps they have largely been ignored because they are mistaken for a return to the conventional wisdom or because their rigor is questioned. But neither quantitative nor qualitative evaluations has a corner on rigor. They seek to answer different questions.

Qualitative strategies are directed toward descriptive questions. Quantitative strategies are directed toward normative and cause-and effect questions (United States General Accounting Office, 1984, pp. 1-2). Descriptive questions provide data on the condition of program participants, why they need the program undertaken, how to reach them and provide them with service. For example, an English-as-a-second language program for older adults will have limited access to previously gathered systematic data to guide program implementation. The first evaluative step, then, is to collect information that will lead to an understanding of what is going on in the lives of the elders and how that will affect the way in which the service is designed and delivered.

Normative questions provide data that compare what is observed to what was expected, a standard of performance, or a performance objective. For example, the influence of a homework hotline for disadvantaged youths may have been discovered by comparing scores on high school assignments before and after program participation. As the number of scores mounts up over time, the program will develop a standard for improvement by which continued program success can be measured and by which the effectiveness of this program can be compared to other similar programs. Cause-and-effect questions collect data that reveal whether an observed result can be attributed to the program's operation, for example, determining what part of the change observed in the quality of research papers submitted by disadvantaged high school students is attributable to the effects of the public library user instruction program they attended. The proof may be determined by comparing a group who participated in the program with a group who did not.

That is not to say quantitative strategies should be cast aside. Michael Quinn Patton (1987) has created a series of questions to guide the determination of the appropriate approach. Quantitative strategies are preferred when:

1. Standards exist by which to judge the merit and worth of a program.
2. Program goals are specific and measurable.
3. Concentration is on comparing participants of the program on standardized, uniform measures.
4. Instruments are available to measure important program results.
5. Instruments can be developed that measure important results.
6. Emphasis is on aggregating information so that uniformities are highlighted.
7. Causes of change in the target audience are the focus of the evaluation.

8. It is necessary to apply statistical tests of significance to the data.
9. Information is needed on the generalizability of the program's results.

But qualitative strategies are preferred when:

1. The evaluation will assist in developing standards where none currently exist.
2. The evaluation is intended for a new, innovative, or demonstration program.
3. No valid, reliable, and believable instruments are available or readily capable of being developed.
4. The program is at the formative evaluation stage, where goals and program content are still being developed.
5. The goals of the program are vague, general, and nonspecific.
6. The focus is on diversity among program participants or events, and their uniqueness.
7. Detailed, in-depth information is needed about unusual failures or other critically important instances for financial or political reasons.
8. Information is sought about the details of program implementation, such as what participants in the program experience, what services are provided, how the program is organized, what staff do, what is going on in the program, and how it has developed.
9. Descriptive information is needed about the quality of program activities.
10. It is possible that the program is affecting participants in unanticipated ways (pp. 41-42).

Figure 1 compares the ingredients set forth by Yvonne S. Lincoln and Egon G. Guba for a rigorous evaluation under the two strategies (1985, pp. 294-301).

Common Terms	Qualitative Evaluation	Quantitative Evaluation
Truth Value	Credibility	Internal Validity
Applicability	Transferability	External Validity
Consistency	Dependability	Reliability
Neutrality	Confirmability	Objectivity

Figure 1. Components of a rigorous evaluation

Truth Value

Quantitative strategies approach truth by safeguarding internal validity. When an evaluation has internal validity, change caused by the program can be distinguished from change resulting from other factors. Threats are avoided through controlling or randomizing sources of confusion.

Qualitative assessments approach truth through a determination of credibility, not a determination of causality. To establish credibility, the qualitative evaluator: (1) has extended contact with the program; (2) establishes review of the evaluation record as it is being created by a disinterested peer; (3) performs an active search for negative instances that may add insights to developing explanations; and (4) sets up checks during and at the close of the evaluation by a representative group of stakeholders to see if the reality which it presents is one that they agree represents the program.

Quantitative assessments approach applicability by safeguarding external validity. When an evaluation has external validity, the findings are generalizable, which is particularly important when results from current program participants will be used to make decisions affecting future participants, or when results are going to be applied elsewhere. Quantitative strategies ward off threats through random sampling which produces representative participants and allows precise statements about external validity. Within given confidence limits, the findings from the sample are considered to hold for the population represented. The results are said to extend to all environmental contexts within that population; they are generalizable.

Qualitative evaluators point out that the criteria of internal and external validity are in a trade-off situation by their definitions. If, for control, strenuous laboratory-like conditions are imposed on evaluations, then their results are not generalizable except in situations like the original laboratory. Threats to internal and external validity are a natural state of affairs for the qualitative evaluator, who must address them in making judgments of transferability. Here the evaluation sets out results with a description of the time and context in which they were found to hold. To be sure that the program and its success will transfer to other sites, it is not enough to know about the situation of the original program. Knowledge of the context to which it will be applied, and its similarity, is equally as important (Lincoln & Guba, 1985, p. 316).

Consistency

Quantitative assessments approach consistency by safeguarding reliability. The cornerstone on which reliability is built is replication. When an evaluation has consistency, two or more repetitions of essentially the same program under essentially similar conditions will yield similar findings. Qualitative assessments substitute proof of dependability for reliability. What happens in a program often varies over time because of changes in the program, or because of changes in participants or changes in the emergent design of the evaluation as insights grow.

To demonstrate dependability, the qualitative evaluation relies on the external audit. Detailed records are kept during the evaluation of process, procedures, and evaluator insights, which establish an audit trail. Then review of the record is carried out by a competent external, disinterested auditor or second evaluator. If an evaluation is dependable, the auditor's findings will agree with the original evaluator's.

Neutrality

Quantitative assessments approach neutrality by safeguarding objectivity. They attend to the question of the degree to which findings of an evaluation are determined by the participants and the conditions of the evaluation and not by the biases, motivations, interests, or perspectives of the evaluator. To avoid this bias, the quantitative evaluation relies on detailed design before the evaluation begins. Insulation of the evaluator is equally important to objectivity, since it is easy to be influenced by what is learned, and that is considered damaging.

Qualitative assessments establish neutrality through confirmability. The control device is agreement by multiple peers on findings as expressed by the program evaluation. The qualitative evaluation proceeds from the assumption that the evaluator cannot maintain an objective distance from the program being studied; rather, the relationship is one of mutual and simultaneous influence. Far from being value-free, all evaluations are value-bound.

Authenticity and Trustworthiness

To summarize the differences between the two approaches to evaluation: The qualitative approach is built on flexibility in deciding what data to collect, from whom, and under what circumstances, and in organizing the evaluation according to the meaning of events to participants; whereas the quantitative approach requires having to decide beforehand on a set of data elements or on an essentially immutable plan of action. Qualitative assessments seek understanding of the local situation, while quantitative assessments seek to prove that a program successful in one library would benefit other locations.

In practice, the two approaches are frequently combined. Indeed, there is often a flow from one to the other. After the exploratory work of finding out what the important questions are, completed in qualitative phases, the evaluations of similar programs may switch to quantitative testing aimed at confirming causality and then return to qualitative strategies to look for rival assumptions and unanticipated or unmeasured factors that may be influencing results.

Eight Models for Assessment

After the evaluation questions and strategy are decided, the model for assessment is selected. To date, the evaluation of programs for special populations has, in the main, relied on goals and objectives. But at least seven other approaches have been identified which can satisfy the underpinnings for rigorous evaluation and provide the trustworthy results that until now have eluded us in librarianship (House, 1978, pp. 4-12; & House, 1980, pp. 4-12, 21-43).

Quantitative strategies are represented in four models and qualitative strategies in an additional four. The Decision-making, Systems, Goal-Based and Goal-Free Models are all quantitative.

Decision-making Model

When utility is a hallmark of evaluation, program assessment is imbued with the Decision-making Model. The process is initiated by identifying stakeholders who have a share or an interest in the program under study from relevant constituencies and organizing them for input into the conduct of the evaluation. Three primary means that serve this purpose are stakeholder interviews, focus groups, and community forums (Rossi & Freeman, 1985, pp. 124-30). All provide an economical means of information gathering while developing support from community influentials.

For the evaluation of services for special populations, it is especially important to ensure that the stakeholders selected are: (1) knowledgeable about the community, its people, their needs, and the patterns of services already being delivered; (2) recognized leaders who are accessible; (3) representatives of the program's target population; and (4) consumers of the program in addition to program designers and staff. Stakeholder check sessions are built in so that judgments of the overall credibility of the evaluation, statements of major concerns and issues, and statements about factual or interpretation errors can be identified.

How does this model apply to services for special populations? Decision-makers should be part of every library program evaluation. For example, at the close of federal funding for an information and referral service targeted to older adults,the board of trustees will decide whether or not to continue the service initiated by a grant under LSCA Title I. At the same time, the president of the board of trustees wants a political career and one criterion affecting his or her decisions about library programs is whether or not they will increase visibility in a positive way among possible future constituents.

Interviews with board members and other stakeholders will form the basis for designing an evaluation that speaks to the information needed for decision-making. It is important to get below the surface and determine the real information sought. In evaluating the program serving older adults, information about the number of voters among elder participants, for example, would be as important as information about the number of elders who take part in the program.

The Systems Model

Typical questions addressed by the Systems Model include, "What impact did this program have? Can the results be produced more economically?" Library program evaluators who use this model collect data on a few well-defined outcome indicators deemed critical, for example, the per capita ratio of Information and Referral questions answered directly and by telephone to the total older adult target population. Variations in the measures are associated with differences in program outcomes, such as the improved ability of older adults to locate appropriate health caregivers. Generally, higher scores on measures are interpreted as meaning greater success. The relationship of outcome measures to program achievement is demonstrated via statistical techniques. The programs determined most effective have the highest possible activity measurement at the lowest possible cost. Many of these evaluations use test scores as the only measure of success. They are compared to normative data gathered on large numbers of similar cases over an extended period of time.

Application to Services for Special Populations: The Systems Model is appropriate for program evaluations that can compare participants' pre-program and post-program scores to standardized scores, empirically demonstrating the extent of the program's effects. One of the programs for special populations to which this model could be applied is literacy. Since there are numerous valid, reliable, standardized tests of reading achievement, *before* and *after* scores for literacy program participants provide strong evidence of program effectiveness. Unit cost measurement is added to demonstrate program efficiency.

For example, a library introducing two new methods of literacy tutoring might want to determine if one made more of a contribution than another to reading ability. Three groups of participants would be established and tested with standardized reading achievement tests before the new tutoring methods were begun. Then two of the three groups would be assigned to one of the two new methods; the third would continue with the earlier method. At the end of the program's funding, comparisons would be made among the achievement test scores of the three groups to determine whether there were significant differences in reading ability. The cost of the materials could be divided by the number of clients who used them, or the number of times each was used, for a unit cost figure.

Goal-Based Model

The most familiar approach and the most popular among evaluators, this model is also currently the most commonly advanced idea for evaluation. The primary question of the Goal-Based Model remains, "Is this program achieving what it intended?" Here, the identifying feature is the presence of goals and objectives. The object is to collect evidence to determine whether the program has achieved what it stated it would. The goals and objectives are the criteria by which the evaluator assesses what the program accomplished against what its developers started out to do. The discrepancy between the stated goals and the program's results is considered the measure of program success.

Proponents stress the accountability aspects of the model, since the program claims were the basis upon which the effort was mounted. Not unexpectedly, the Goal-Based Model has supplied most of the framework for the contemporary evaluation of public library performance. The extension course, "Are We There Yet?," developed by Jane Robbins and Douglas Zweizig, provides a step-by-step approach to the implementation of this model (1985, pp. 624-27).

Application to Services for Special Populations: The Goal-Based Model is a natural candidate for the evaluation of services for special populations. For example, a program might have as its goal improving services to the physically handicapped. An objective might be to locate and survey the needs of 10 percent of the physically handicapped population in the library's service areas in the first six months of operating a new Media Home Delivery Service. As one measure of success, the evaluation might compare the percentage located and the percentage surveyed against the target.

Goal-Free Model

Created in direct reaction to the ubiquity of the goal-determined evaluation, the Goal-Free Model was developed to reduce bias. It requires an outside expert or an internal evaluator unconnected to the program under review to carry it out. The major question it addresses is, "What are the intended and unintended effects of this program on its participants?" The evaluation is not based on program goals. In fact, the evaluator remains uninformed about them and searches for all program outcomes, many of which are side-effects or unintended results, both positive and negative. In this case, it is not intention that is sought, it is achievement.

Among the models presented to this point, the traditional notion of objectivity has been built on quantitative assessment alone, but the goal-free notion of objectivity developed first in the qualitative realm. It can combine both strategies. Consumers Union uses this model in focusing on product criteria that it thinks will benefit consumers.

Application to Services for Special Populations: The Goal-Free Model would be applicable to many types of programs for special audiences. For example, a program funded to provide materials to support after-school reading is meant to increase skills in the reading disabled by exposure to a wide range of high interest, low reading ability materials. A number of qualitative and quantitative indicators might point to the success of the program. Examining the pre-program and post-program test scores of the students, visiting the scheduled tutoring sessions, interviewing tutors and students, reading expert reviews, and examining the materials themselves would provide abundant data that could substantiate success or failure.

Qualitative strategies are represented in four models for assessment. They include the Art Criticism, Professional Review, Judicial, and Case Study Models.

Art Criticism Model

This approach relies on critical review, the major assessment tool of the arts. Evaluators draw on their own experiences and intuitive reasoning to judge what is happening in a program and to express their judgments in a way that nonexperts can understand. Some questions that the Art Criticism Model seeks to answer include: "Would an expert approve this program? Are the people for whom the program was designed being helped? Are they acquiring habits conducive to their further development?"

Like an art critic, the evaluator, who is an expert in the program's speciality, uses the critical review to render the essential qualities of the program and make judgements based on her or his own standards of excellence. The critic-evaluator presents feelings as well as facts about the program. Proper training and experience are necessary to make evaluative discriminations; the evaluator must have both in sufficient measure to be able to distinguish what is significant. The evaluative report will heighten the awareness of its readers as to what constitutes a good program and so improve future program standards.

Critical review is accomplished in a couple of fairly standard ways. Immersion in the program is vital. Notes, video tapes, and similar recording devices are used to retain observations and the qualitative procedure called Referential Adequacy is invoked. A portion of the data collected is archived and not included in the initial analysis. Later, it serves as a benchmark for comparison against a follow-up data analysis and interpretation to determine if features to which the critic pointed can be found in the archived data. The second data review also demonstrates whether different analyses reach similar conclusions.

Application to Services for Special Populations: This model would provide a good option for application to the evaluation of library programs for latchkey children. An evaluator using it would have been immersed in problems in the lives of latchkey children as well as in services that respond to those problems. She or he would be familiar with library programs considered exemplary across the country and the elements that led to success. The review of the specific program and the judgments expressed in the evaluative report would inform and educate those evaluated and/or less knowledgeable. The critical review would be based on extended observation, continuing over a period of at least a month. The narrative would establish the strengths and weaknesses of the program, offer comparisons to exemplary programs that might exist elsewhere, and make recommendations for improvement.

Professional Review Model
Conducted by a team of peers who have the qualifications to judge the merit of a program, this model culminates in a holistic assessment by other professionals (Dressel, 1971, pp. 277-87).

Before evaluators visit the site, the staff engages in self-evaluation. They are appointed to committees that review each of the program's functions and prepare a program profile. When turned over to the peer reviewing team, the self-study includes: definition and clarification of program purposes and goals; examination of the adequacy of resources; an appraisal of the quality and morale of the program staff; a review of the strengths and weaknesses of the current organization and delivery methods; consideration of the overall program climate and environment, including the role of clients and their satisfactions and dissatisfactions with the program and its services; and finally, a collection of evidence on the effectiveness of the program and the process of client development. Before they leave, in their evaluation members of the peer review panel indicate their differences from the staff review, give a brief oral report pointing out the strengths and weaknesses of the program, and make recommendations for change. After the visit, the program is expected to correct perceived weaknesses.

Application to Services for Special Populations: Using the Professional Review Model to evaluate an adult basic education program, one of the criteria established to determine excellence might be that "attention is given to improving study skills." The review panel, using a checklist, might find that item and mark the quality they believe existed on a five-point continuum from missing to excellent. Each of the major program functions would have similar checklists where criteria would be evaluated. The checklists would be totaled for a holistic appraisal of the program.

Judicial Model

Blue Ribbon Panels, like the Kerner Commission or the Warren Commission, fall within this approach. Presidentially appointed, members of these Panels heard evidence from witnesses, conducted their own investigations, and came to conclusions about probable occurrences in two momentous events in history.

The Judicial Model is based on the supposition that the facts in a case are uncovered best if each side strives as hard as it can, in partisan fashion, to bring the most favorable evidence for its view to the attention of the panel. The aim is to resolve the issue of how a program should develop in the future. Evidence is presented to demonstrate the program's strengths and weaknesses. The approach is patterned after the courtroom. Rules are formulated about who may testify and the conditions for testimony. Evidence includes not only facts, but also feelings, perceptions, opinions, biases, and speculations. The Judicial Model has four stages: issue generation, where sometimes as many as thirty or more interviews are conducted; issue selection, where surveys are undertaken to hone in on what is crucial; argument preparation; and a hearing. The major advantage of this model is that pressing issues can be addressed quickly by the panel who bring about an immediate resolution to future directions.

Application to Services for Special Populations: Clearly, the approach has promise for programs which may need revamping in midstream. For example, in a decision about whether or not to continue to fund the public programming elements of a library-based career center in a community where unemployment is high, members of the Blue Ribbon Panel, appointed perhaps by the State Library, would interview key members of the staff to ferret out the issues. To gather opinions, they would develop a questionnaire and send it to a broad number of stakeholders including administrators, persons served, and government officials, in addition to staff members. Arguments would be prepared for and against the continuation based on that data and the opinions of partisans. A hearing would take place before the panel and a decision would be made by the members following the hearing's conclusion.

Case Study Model
The final qualitative model provides a way of judging programs within the context of their environment. Rather than pushing for quantification, this model pushes for understanding. Its strength lies in its ability to assist us in determining how to create programs that are responsive to nontraditional audiences. Here stakeholders observe the program and assist in its evaluation.

Evaluators report on the perceptions of others as well as their own in giving their judgment of a program. Since this model attempts to improve the understanding of the audience, the program staff, and sponsoring agencies about the program is and what is going on in it, the aim is to collect data to demonstrate how the program is perceived by others, particularly by the audience it was intended to serve.

The case study is usually reported as a narrative with a great many quotes directly from the participants' own words. Actual instances are cited and observation is the primary data collection technique; it substitutes more objective experiences for anecdotes of unknown credibility (United States General Accounting Office, 1987, p. 59). This model concentrates on the description of program processes as well as outcomes. Program observers prepare and submit narratives, portrayals, and graphics to stakeholders for feedback. Evaluators find out what is of value to program audiences and gather expressions of worth from various individuals whose viewpoints differ. They check the quality of the records, get program personnel to react to the accuracy of their portrayals, and get stakeholders to react to the relevance of the findings.

Application to Services for Special Populations: There is no approach that gives better results for the evaluation of new or innovative programs than the Case Study. For example, an application might be to a program for high school dropouts that intends to provide nontraditional means to earn a high school diploma. Since the library has had little systematically evaluated experience in this area, the Case Study could bring a better understanding of what is needed to make such programs successful and to provide for their transportability to other library locations. In addition to gathering perceptions of program strengths and weaknesses, the study would provide extensive description of the context in which the program was conducted and how that context affected daily operations.

Although the models are separated into quantitative and qualitative strategies here, their actual differences are often not so cut-and-dry. Combinations frequently provide the basis for the best-case scenario to prove library programs for special populations work. They can and should be mixed and matched to meet the needs of the evaluation. Numbers can add authority to the Case Study; narratives create the context that adds authenticity to numbers. The combinations do not dilute the validity of the process as long as systematic procedures are followed in creating and implementing the evaluation design.

Rigorous evaluation shows a link among the major components of the evaluative process — questions, strategies, models, and measurement. The determination of the measures on which to collect data does not precede the process; it is a result of it.

Measuring Results

Input, output, impact, and cost measures are all useful when evaluating the worth and merit of a program of service to special populations. Figure 2 compares the definition, purpose, and elements on which program-related data are gathered for each of these measurements. *Output Measures for Public Libraries*, second edition (Van House et al., 1987) and *Cost Finding for Public Libraries: A Manager's Handbook* (Rosenberg, 1985) supply data collection techniques for output, and costs that can be adapted to evaluation. *Evaluation of Adult Literacy Programs* (Zweizig et al., 1990, pp. 39, 42) provides a few measures of impact which are amplified here. Once again, a most persuasive case can be made by creating combinations, this time of measures.

For example, in a community where no high school diploma is granted to students who read below the eighth grade level, the library set up a "Teens Top the Mark" program in cooperation with the local school system. In the application for LSCA funding, the problem statement clearly denoted the target population. Out of an annual graduating class of 400, about 10 percent failed to receive diplomas based on their inability to read at the appropriate level; that number had increased in each of the last five years. In the past, these students had not experienced success in traditional remedial reading classes established to help them improve their skills and graduate.

The "Teens Top the Mark" program was introduced by converting a little-used branch into a tutoring and homework facility staffed by teacher-librarians and stocked with young adult materials. The library's program incorporated a new approach modeled after adult literacy programs with confidential one-to-one tutoring. The tutors were volunteers who themselves learned to read proficiently as adults. All students who, at the beginning of their junior year, are in danger of not graduating because of lack of reading skills were recommended to the program.

The evaluation employed an interrupted time series design. Measurements were taken before and after participation in the program. Scores were recorded on a standardized reading test to show the impact on skills. A questionnaire captured data demonstrating the impact of the program on attitude and behavior related to reading, library use, and the program participants' views of themselves as self-learners. The questionnaire also measured participants' satisfaction with the quality of the program and facilities. Records of library use were kept for each student. Input and output data were gathered on the resources allocated to young adult services and on overall library use.

At the end of the year-long program, students had achieved an additional three years as determined by scores on a standardized reading achievement test taken before and after they participated in the program. They were no longer held back from reaching their personal goal of obtaining a high school diploma. The intent of the program was also met because the high school accepted the tutoring program as a valid means of gaining the level of competence needed, even though it did not contain all the elements prescribed by the high school's own remedial reading program. Attitudes on library use and reading showed significant improvement. Of the target population's forty students, thirty-five were eligible to graduate, 50 percent more than in previous years under other programs of remediation. The federally funded program had attained its intended impact.

Figures on output measures gathered one year after the program's initiation also showed that, for the target population, library visits quadrupled, the number of library cards issued had doubled, and circulation was three times larger. Input data documented that the library's expenditures for young adult programs from its locally supported budget had also doubled. When the per capita costs of running the seldom-used branch were compared to the per capita costs of running the branch once the program was up and running, a 25 percent decrease was calculated. At the time of graduation, nine months after the program's conclusion, there was no deterioration in reading skills. The proof of worth and merit was made.

CONCLUSION

The fact that evaluation results have led to so few action agendas is virtually a national scandal. A posture that includes stakeholders and empowers them to change the decision-making process holds promise for eliminating that lack of attention.

Diversity in design is incorporated into the models of evaluation recommended. While the Goal-Based Model currently embraced is worthy of consideration, it is not the only approach for evaluation to take. We have swung from assessment based on the conventional, collective wisdom to quantitative measurement without recognizing the

Population Measures
      Definition: Potential and actual number of program participants
      Purpose: Demonstrate the program reached its intended audience
      Gather Program Related Data On:
            Total Population in Service Area
            Number of Potential Program Participants
            Ratio of Potential Participants to Total Population
            Number of Actual Program Participants
            Ratio of Actual to Potential Participants
            Number of Program Participants Reaching Program
               Standard for Success

Input Measures
      Definition: Resources allocated to support a program
      Purpose: Demonstrate improve institutional practice
      Gather Program Related Data On:
            Income
               Local Taxes
               Capital Income
               Federal Funds
               State Funds
               Endowments
               Foundations

            Expenditures
               Salaries and Wages
               Materials
               Per Capita Expenditures
               Capital Expenditures

            Staff
               Librarians
               Volunteers
               Others
               Full Time Equivalents (FTE)

            Materials
               Owned
               Purchased During Program

            Facilities
               Square Feet of Building Space
               Number of Buildings or Sites

Output Measures
      Definition: Performance on services emanating from a program
      Purpose: Demonstrate improved institutional support
      Gather Program Related Data On:
            Circulation
            Turnover Rate
            In-library Use of Materials
            Library Visits
            Number of Library Cards Added
            Reference Transactions
            Attendance at Programming

Figure 2. Selected population, input, output, impact, and cost measures *(cont.)*

Impact Measures
>Definition: Outcome or Consequences of a Program
>Purpose: Demonstrate Enhanced Skills and Changes in Attitude and/or Behavior

Gather Program Related Data On:
>Enhanced Skills

>Behavior
>>Time Spent Reading
>>Comfortable Use of Other Libraries
>>Increased Visits to the Library
>>Borrowing More Materials from the Library

>Attitude
>>Desire to Read
>>Improved View of Self as Learner
>>Attitude Toward Reading Improved

>Satisfaction with Program

>Satisfaction with Program Facilities

>Perceived Match Between Program Expectations and Experience

>Achievement of Personal Goals

Cost Measures
>Definition: Funding Required to Finance a Program or its Components
>Purpose: Demonstrate Improved Institutional Practice

Gather Program Related Data On:
>Unit Cost, the Cost of Supplying One Unit of Service
>Cost Per Capita, the Cost of Supplying One Unit of Service to One Program Participant

Figure 2 *(cont.)*. Selected population, input, output, impact, and cost measures

---

many approaches available. The model pursued should fit the environment in which the evaluation is being conducted, mesh with the purpose and situation under assessment, and retain the rigor necessary for it to command the respect of evaluation experts. Given the constraints under which library programs operate and the little systematic evaluation undertaken, multiple models must be introduced and encouraged.

Since bad evaluations can irreparably damage programs and injure the constituents for whom they are intended, they must take into account more than measurement and measures. While in the past the emphasis in public librarianship has been on the performance of the library, it is time to focus on the special populations for whom the programs of service were developed. In such a shift, the institution recedes into the background and the library user becomes the focus of attention. Without that reversal in perspective, evaluations cannot measure impact and programs cannot fulfill their public service missions.

REFERENCES

Chelton, M. K. (1987). Evaluation of children's services. *Library Trends, 35*(3), 463-484.

D'Elia, G. (1980). The development and testing of a conceptual model of public library user behavior. *Library Quarterly, 50*(4), 410-430.

D'Elia, G., & Rodger, E. J. (1987). Comparative assessment of patrons' uses and evaluations across public libraries within a system: A replication. *Library and Information Science Research, 9*(1), 5-20.

D'Elia, G., & Walsh, S. (1983). User satisfaction with library service—A measure of public library performance? *Library Quarterly, 53*(2), 109-133.

D'Elia, G., & Walsh, S. (1985). Patrons' uses and evaluations of library services: A comparison across five public libraries. *Library and Information Science Research, 7*(1), 3-30.

De Prospo, E. R.; Altman, E.; & Beasley, K. E. (1973). *Performance measures for public libraries.* Chicago: American Library Association and Public Library Association.

Dressel, P. L. (1971). Accreditation and institutional self-study. *North Central Association Quarterly, 46*(2), 277-287.

House, E. R. (1978). Assumptions underlying evaluation models. *Educational Researcher, 7*(3), 4-12.

House, E. R. (1980). *Evaluating with validity.* Beverly Hills, CA: Sage.

Lincoln, Y. S., & Guba, E. G. (1985). *Naturalistic inquiry.* Beverly Hills, CA: Sage.

Lynch, K. B. (1987, April). *Practices in educational program evaluation, 1980-1983.* Paper presented at the annual meeting of the American Educational Research Association, Washington, DC.

Patton, M. Q. (1987). *How to use qualitative methods in evaluation.* Newbury Park, CA: Sage.

Public Library Association. (1967). *Minimum standards for public library systems, 1966.* Chicago: ALA.

Robbins-Carter, J., & Zweizig, D. L. (1985). Are we there yet? *American Libraries, 16*(9), 624-627.

Roberts, S. J. (1985). *Evaluating library programs for the NDN: A position paper.* Unpublished report, United States Department of Education, Washington, DC.

Rosenberg, P. (1985). *Cost finding for public libraries: A manager's handbook.* Chicago: ALA.

Rossi, P. H., & Freeman, H. E. (1985). *Evaluation: A systematic approach* (3rd ed.). Beverly Hills, CA: Sage.

Schorr, L. B., with Schorr, D. (1988). *Within our reach: Breaking the cycle of disadvantage.* New York: Doubleday.

Shaughnessy, T. (1987). The search for quality. *Journal of Library Administration, 8*(1), 5-10.

Shavitt, D. (1985). *Federal aid and state library agencies. Federal policy implementation.* (Contributions in librarianship and information science, number 52.) Westport, CT: Greenwood Press.

Turock, B. J. (1990). Assessing the evaluation of federally funded programs. *SCILS Research Report Series.* New Brunswick, NJ: Rutgers University, School of Communication, Information and Library Studies.

United States General Accounting Office, Program Evaluation and Methodology Division. (1987). *Case study evaluations: Transfer paper 9.* Washington, DC: USGPO.

United States General Accounting Office, Program Evaluation and Methodology Division. (1984). *Designing evaluations: Methodology transfer paper 4.* Washington, DC: USGPO.

Van House, N.; Lynch, M. J.; McClure, C. R.; Zweizig, D. L.; & Rodger, E. J. (1987). *Output measures for public libraries: A manual of standardized procedures* (2nd ed.). Chicago: ALA.

Zweizig, D. L., & Rodger, E. J. (1982). *Output measures for public libraries: A manual of standardized procedures.* Chicago: ALA.

Zweizig, D. L.; Johnson, D. W.; & Robbins, J. B. (1990). *Evaluation of adult library literacy programs: A structured approach.* Chicago: ALA.

RICHARD RUBIN

Assistant Professor
School of Library Science
Kent State University
Kent, Ohio

Evaluation of Reference Personnel

ABSTRACT

The evaluation of reference staff is a complex process involving important psychosocial as well as procedural factors. This article focuses on those aspects of performance evaluation that affect the motivation of reference workers to improve performance based on their performance evaluations. Factors such as rater-ratee interactions are explored as well as the motivational potential of various types of evaluation instruments.

INTRODUCTION

Reference service is a basic function in most libraries, and the evaluation of reference performance is a common subject in the library literature. Interestingly, however, the existing literature focuses primarily on departmental performance rather than on the performance of individual reference librarians. Departmental performance has been studied from a variety of perspectives including (a) the low accuracy of responses to reference queries (Hernon & McClure, 1987; Crowley, 1985; Childers, 1980; Roy, 1985); (b) the level of patron satisfaction with reference services (D'Elia & Walsh, 1983); and (c) methodological considerations in obtaining valid data on which to base departmental evaluation (Weech & Goldhor, 1982; Bunge, 1985; Westbrook, 1989; Hernon & McClure, 1987; Van House, 1990; Durrance, 1989). Discussions concerning the evaluation of individual performance tend to be anecdotal (Carter, 1985; Association of Research Libraries, 1987; Schwartz & Eakin, 1986). The issues raised concerning departmental performance are valuable, and it is logical to assume that such performance relies in large part on the performance of individual reference librarians and their ability to interact with library patrons and the library collection. If the evidence on departmental performance is correct, however, one can infer that individual reference librarians are performing poorly. In numerous studies, reference librarians are found to exhibit poor skills in the reference interview, make little effort to provide correct or complete answers, and have a limited knowledge of reference sources (Hernon & McClure, 1987). These findings underscore the need for library managers to develop techniques to assess individual reference performance and to improve it when necessary. If individual performance can be improved, increases in departmental performance are likely to follow.

One technique for measuring and promoting individual performance is the performance evaluation. (For the purposes of this paper, the terms *performance evaluation, performance appraisal,* and *performance review* will be used interchangeably.) Performance evaluation has many purposes and they are basically the same for reference librarians as for other employees: to improve communication between manager and employee, to ensure that employees know what is expected of them, to provide employees with an assessment of their work, and to provide documentation for promotions or disciplinary actions. The overriding goal of performance evaluation, however, is to improve human performance so that the goals of the organization can be fulfilled.

Regrettably, positive outcomes to performance reviews of librarians do not occur as often as we would like. There is considerable evidence, even when ratings are satisfactory, that performance evaluations result in reductions in organizational commitment, demotivation, and increases in job dissatisfaction, alienation, demoralization, and negative feelings toward the organization (Pearce & Porter, 1986). Fortunately, because of the interest in individual motivation and productivity manifested over the years by business and industry, there is a large and ever-expanding body of psychosocial and management research from which library managers can draw to improve their evaluation techniques. The focus of this article is on those aspects of the performance evaluation process that can promote positive outcomes to the review process and increase the motivation and productivity of reference librarians.

Problems with performance evaluations derive from many sources but a prominent one is a reluctance to see the evaluation as a constructive process. Supervisors and employees alike often approach evaluation with trepidation and find it unfulfilling. Such feelings are not without a rational foundation; the stakes are high because the process deals with fundamental emotional, professional, and psychological factors. Among the characteristics that are involved are the following (Rubin, 1991):

Feelings of Self Worth: When a reference librarian participates in a review, it is as a person as well as a professional. Criticisms of performance may well be interpreted as deficiencies in character or intelligence or as an attack on self-esteem.

Feelings of Professional Worth: Obviously, performance evaluations are primarily about work performance. If employees fear that the review will involve criticism of their work, they are bound to have trepidations and be defensive.

Threats to Fiscal Security: The evaluation process has a direct effect on the employee's job security. An employee may believe that an unspectacular review will result in no merit increase. At worst, a poor evaluation could lead to termination and consequent loss of income to the employee, spouse, and family.

Threats to Status: It is not uncommon that employees become aware of the evaluations given to others. No matter how this information becomes known, librarians who receive low performance ratings may believe that they are perceived as poor workers by their colleagues.

It is not surprising, then, that few situations in the library have as great a potential for emotional distress and argument. This highlights the need for a systematic approach that considers not only the need to measure objectively the performance of the reference librarian, but also takes into account the uniquely human factors that permeate this process. The performance evaluation system must be so structured that it provides important organizational information and concomitantly stimulates human motivation and performance.

GENERAL ISSUES IN THE EVALUATION PROCESS

The pitfalls of performance evaluation are numerous, and they deal with both structural aspects and with the characteristics of the participants and their interaction. Among the key factors that affect review outcomes are the following:

1. *Characteristics and attitudes of the individual doing the rating.* Usually, when one thinks of performance evaluation, one thinks first of the individual being evaluated. In theory, the evaluation is based simply on an objective assessment of the employee's performance. In fact, however, the same performance may bring substantially different evaluations from different raters. This is referred to as rater subjectivity. Not all subjective judgments on the part of raters are wrong, but the possibility of inaccurate assessment based on subjectivity can be a troubling problem—a problem that could subject the rater and the organization to legal

liabilities. Among the factors that have been shown to affect evaluations are the rater's level of education, intelligence, attention to detail, knowledge of the job to be rated, and implicit beliefs about human performance (Bailey, 1983). The latter issue is especially important in the library field because it includes different attitudes toward the successful work performance of men and women, and will be discussed later.

When rater subjectivity occurs, a variety of common rating errors may persist:

Halo and horn effects: A *halo* effect occurs when an individual is given a high rating in one performance area which leads the rater to give inappropriately high ratings in other areas as well; the opposite condition, the *horn* effect occurs when the individual receives inappropriately low ratings overall because of poor performance in one area.

Central tendency: This error involves the propensity of raters to assign ratings near the midpoint of the rating scales.

Leniency or strictness error: This involves giving ratings either higher or lower than the individual deserves.

Recency errors: This involves basing a rating on only the most recent occurrences rather than those over the entire rating period. An associated error involves allowing atypical performances to outweigh the more common performances.

Bias: This involves the imposition of personal prejudices or stereotypes on the ratings.

Spillover error: This involves permitting previous performance ratings to affect current ratings.

2. *Characteristics and attitudes of the individual being rated.* As with raters, a variety of factors related to the individual can affect the review outcome. Obviously, the knowledge, skill, and ability of the person to perform the job will affect the evaluation profoundly. But other factors also play a role. For example, the race and sex of the employee have been found to have significant impact on performance evaluation (Bailey, 1983). Similarly, an individual's attitude toward the evaluation process itself may affect the outcome. For example, if the employee believes the process is unfair, the supervisor lacks important knowledge, or that no rewards or punishments follow from the process, then the motivation to improve performance based on the review is significantly diminished.

3. *Rater-employee interaction.* Although both the rater and employee possess individual characteristics that can affect the review, the interaction of these characteristics may also have a substantial impact. For example, the degree to which the rater and employee

possess similar characteristics, attitudes, gender, personalities, or the degree of personal attraction or liking between the participants have been shown to affect evaluation results (Bailey, 1983). An additional aspect of this interaction involves the perceived credibility of the rater in the eyes of the employee. If the employee believes that the supervisor understands the job, then the chances of a successful outcome to the review are increased (Cederblom, 1982).

4. *The type and quality of the evaluation instrument.* Different types of instruments are more appropriate than others for different types of jobs and organizational philosophies. Organizations that emphasize evaluation for promotion and merit might well use quantitative standards or graphic rating scales, while systems that emphasize employee development and goal setting might use management-by-objectives or some other collaborative system (Taylor & Zawacki, 1984). Of course, even if the type of instrument used is appropriate, it is still necessary that the measures of performance accurately reflect the job being evaluated. A high quality evaluation instrument increases the chances of good results no matter what system is used.

5. *The manner and accuracy of the reviews conducted.* The efficacy of a performance review is substantially affected by the way in which it is conducted and the perceived accuracy of the review by the employee. In this regard, the ability of the employee to participate in the review process has been shown to be a significant contributor to the review's success. No matter what type of system is used, the supervisor who invites comments and observations from the employee is more likely to create a sense of ownership in the review and improve the chances for a more beneficial outcome (Geller, 1978).

The motivational potential of a review may be diminished if the rater is stingy with credit due the employee, or if the rater attributes the employee's success to luck, circumstances, or the actions of others. Similarly, if the environmental circumstances of the review are poor, for example, if there are many disruptions, the employee is not likely to perceive that the review is taken seriously. The motivational potential of reviews can also be lost if the employee believes that the rater's evaluation is not fair. Employees are not likely to accept new goals or performance targets from supervisors if they believe that the evaluation did not accurately reflect their work.

6. *The manner in which results are used.* An employee's subsequent performance based on an evaluation may reflect her or his belief that rewards or punishments will follow. Administrative conviction toward the review process is vital. The impact of performance evaluation is tempered by the employee's perceptions of the seriousness with which reviews are perceived, the willingness of

the administration to invest time and money in training and education, and management's willingness to base the system of rewards and punishment on the review process. Employees who believe that promotions or merit increases are closely connected to their performance evaluation are more likely to alter and improve their performance based on the evaluation. In contrast, if an employee believes that there are no organizational consequences that follow from performance evaluations, or that the consequences that follow are not rationally related to the evaluation system, then the employee is not likely to take the review seriously (Kopelman & Reinharth, 1982).

Gender and Evaluation

Because psychosocial factors play such a crucial role in determining the outcome of reviews, it is important to consider possible gender-related problems that affect evaluations. This consideration is especially important in librarianship given the numerical dominance of women in the profession. Although there are little substantial data to support the view that gender discrimination occurs during library performance evaluations, there are reasonable grounds for suspicion. It is well documented, for example, that although females comprise between 70 to 80 percent of the library workforce, they hold a disproportionately low number of administrative positions and receive disproportionately lower salaries (Heim & Estabrook, 1983). Although some of these differences can be explained in part due to differences in length of job tenure and level of education, not all of the disparity can be explained by these factors alone.

There is ample evidence in the general management literature to suggest that women are evaluated differently than men and usually to their detriment (Deaux & Emswiller, 1974; Heilman & Guzzo, 1978; Lott, 1985). Women's attractiveness, for example, appears to affect their evaluation. Attractiveness appears to help women when they are applying for nonmanagerial positions, but hurts them when applying for managerial jobs (Heilman & Stopeck, 1985). This highlights an important point: that discriminatory evaluation may sometimes work in favor of women. Some management research suggests that women in professional positions receive unduly high evaluations because evaluators are surprised that they perform well on traditionally male tasks (Nieva & Gutek, 1981). Nonetheless, as a rule, being a woman is disadvantageous when it comes to the evaluation process.

One possible explanation for gender differences in the evaluation process is based on *attribution theory*. This psychological theory was developed in the 1970s as an attempt to explain possible differences in the performance of boys and girls in school and was subsequently adapted to the business setting (Weiner et al., 1971). Attribution theory suggests that an evaluator may attribute different reasons to an employee's success or failure. Broadly speaking, there are four possible attributions: ability, effort, luck, and task difficulty. These four attributions can be further combined into two groups: internal attributions (ability and effort) and external attributions (luck and task difficulty). The internal attributions are characteristics of the individuals, while the external attributions are characteristics of the environment and lie outside the control of the individual.

One might better understand how attribution theory can be applied to library evaluation by using the example of a reference librarian who is performing well at the reference desk. Four possible explanations could be advanced to explain this performance: (1) the librarian is highly intelligent and talented at reference work (ability); (2) the librarian puts considerable energy and hard work into locating the right information (effort); (3) the reference librarian is just lucky to locate the right sources of information (luck); and (4) the questions the librarian receives are easy to answer (task difficulty).

If the evaluator believes that the successful performance is due primarily to luck or easy questions, the employee is not likely to receive substantial pay increases or opportunity for promotion. If, on the other hand, the employee's success is perceived to be a result of talent and hard work, then pay raises and promotions are much more likely to follow. Disturbingly, when this theory is tested, the results usually indicate that successful female performance is more likely to be attributed to luck and task difficulty in contrast to successful male performance which is more often seen as a result of ability and effort (Heilman & Guzzo, 1978; Deaux & Emswiller, 1974). Interestingly, failure tends to be more risky for males than females; men receive harsher evaluations than females when their performance is unsuccessful (Nieva & Gutek, 1981). This is not a particularly happy finding for women because it suggests that women are not expected to perform as well as men. This lowered expectation for performance appears to arise even if the evaluator is a woman. Women appear to have a lower evaluation of their own talents and skills than their male counterparts (McCarty, 1986; Heilman et al., 1987). Overall, women are not as likely to receive credit when they are successful but not as likely to be blamed when they fail.

EVALUATIVE TECHNIQUES FOR REFERENCE LIBRARIAN

Given the complex psychosocial environment in which evaluation operates, what evaluation techniques are best? The selection of an evaluation technique depends in great part on the attitude of the organization toward the purpose and importance of the process, the willingness to invest time and money in training evaluators, the purpose to which the evaluation system will be put, and the types of jobs to be evaluated. This last point is of particular importance when considering evaluation techniques for reference librarians. Reference work tends to be thought of as an easily identifiable process. In reality, reference activity consists of a wide variety of possible tasks which vary considerably as to the knowledge, skills, and abilities required; and the degree of autonomy, creativity, and routinization involved. For example, a reference librarian's duties may consist of any one or combination of the following: answering simple directional questions, answering complex research questions, conducting automated searches, providing bibliographic instruction, selecting and evaluating the reference collection, providing liaison activities, supervising employees, and managing reference departments. The level of cooperation required for the accomplishment of these tasks may also vary. Some tasks require considerable group cooperation and these tasks are more difficult to evaluate at the individual level (Bailey, 1983). For activities requiring cooperation, departmental standards may be needed in addition to individual ones and supervisors must realize that when evaluating an individual on such activities, the discussion must include external factors that may be affecting individual performance.

Because the range of reference tasks varies so widely, it is not possible to recommend one evaluation system; different types of evaluation approaches might be taken for different types of positions and organizations. Nonetheless, there are a variety of techniques that can be used for reference librarians. In assessing these techniques, it is important to examine them from at least two perspectives: (1) Does the system accurately measure worker performance?, and (2) Does the system provide motivation to improve performance?

Generally, there are three types of performance evaluation approaches that would be useful in evaluating reference librarians: trait-based, behaviorally anchored, and goal-oriented.

Trait-Anchored Systems

Suppose, for example, that the organization does not wish to spend a great deal of time on the evaluation process. This may be due to lack of evaluation expertise, lack of time and money, or because the organization believes that time is better spent in other types of activities. Under such circumstances, a trait-based system may be recommended.

Trait-based systems are the most common form of evaluation in business and industry. In this system, the employee is rated on the basis of general characteristics or traits (see Figure 1). These might include dependability, adaptability, honesty, judgment, knowledge of the job,

Characteristics	Unsatisfactory	Needs Improvement	Satisfactory	Excellent	Superior	Comments
Quality of Work						
Productivity						
Work Habits						
Knowledge of Job						
Initiative						
Relations with People						
Judgment						
Attendance and Punctuality						
Adaptability						
OVERALL RATING						

COMMENTS _____

Figure 1. Sample graphic rating scales

leadership, appearance, approachability, cooperativeness, and initiative. In order to promote objectivity, these traits are often measured using a graphic rating scale on which some categorical or numerical value can be assigned. In some of the newer systems, the traits are weighted so that the employee can determine which traits are more important than others. In addition, recognizing the ever-increasing need for greater specificity in performance evaluation, some trait-based forms include spaces for narrative comments and examples.

In the case of reference librarians, it is possible that some traits would be important for one type of reference librarian and not another. For example, reference librarians who exercise managerial responsibilities might be assessed on administrative traits such as problem-solving ability, leadership, planning or delegating skills, as well as other common traits for reference workers. For reference librarians whose duties are exclusively patron services, such traits as knowledge of the job, appearance, initiative, and approachability might play a greater role.

Trait-based systems have the distinct advantage of being relatively inexpensive. The forms are usually short and easy to use so there is little training required for supervisors, and it usually takes little time to administer. Given the busy schedules that many reference managers and their employees experience, and given the trepidation that most employees and supervisors feel toward the evaluation process, a quick and easy method is often met with relief by reference employees and supervisors alike.

In addition, there is some, albeit limited, evidence that workers prefer trait-based to other types of systems. One study of county government workers indicated that the employees preferred trait-oriented evaluation over more specific performance standards and felt that the trait-based system was actually more helpful in improving their performance (Harris, 1988). One should not, however, overstate the meaning of this evidence. The same study cites other research suggesting that other workers prefer more specific performance standards (pp. 443-44). Interestingly, the workers in the government study felt better about the trait-anchored system because more employees received similar evaluation scores; that is, in the system with performance standards there was much wider disparity in the evaluations. In effect, the performance standards instrument was more sensitive in detecting differences in performance among employees than the trait-based system. This ability to differentiate performance increased resentment and decreased motivation among many workers. Ironically, *increased accuracy decreased motivation.* Of course, if an important purpose of performance evaluation is accuracy in order to make decisions for merit and promotion, then the system using performance standards allows the manager to make more discriminating judgments. One hopes, of course, that both motivation and accuracy can be increased in an evaluation process, but one is not necessarily present with the other.

Despite some of the advantages of trait-based systems, there are also significant disadvantages. Among the deficiencies are the following:

Decreased Validity and Reliability: The validity and reliability of the system is threatened by several factors. Most notably, the system is vulnerable to rater bias. Concepts such as appearance, approachability, and adaptability are very difficult to define and measure. As such, it is easy for the rater to impose personal judgments on the reference librarian. Similarly, it is difficult to determine a standard of comparison when assigning a rating on an abstract trait. For example, what does it mean to say that a person is a "3" in adaptability?

Legal Problems: The system is more vulnerable to legal challenges. Evidence concerning court decisions indicates that trait-based systems are more likely to be challenged successfully than other types of systems (Feild & Holley, 1982).

Lowered Motivation: The system has little motivational potential because it is not goal-oriented, nor does it provide substantial feedback on the employee's performance. Rather, the system focuses on characteristics of the individual rather than on actual job performance. Emphasizing traits is not likely to stimulate discussion of the job tasks and a valuable opportunity to focus on future performance goals is lost.

The trait-based system can be efficient, but it is not primarily designed to motivate employees or to provide substantial information to the organization or the employee. Organizations that perceive formal evaluation as burdensome, unnecessary, or unproductive may find this the best choice. Insofar as supervisors are scrupulous about their judgements, the system may work, but it is vulnerable to attack if employees become unhappy.

Behaviorally Based Systems

In contrast to the trait-based system, behaviorally based systems focus on specific behaviors that are directly related to the performance of the employee on the essential activities of a job (see Figure 2). Given the wide range of duties for the reference librarian, the number and variety of behaviors to be measured can be substantial. Reference desk tasks could be supplemented with management behaviors or those related to bibliographic instruction and online searching. Fortunately, because many of these library activities can be accurately described in behavioral terms and observed by a supervisor, this evaluation approach is sensible for many reference positions.

The advantages of behavioral measures are considerable. The standards focus on specific job behaviors rather than on vaguely defined traits. This increases the chance that the review will be a valid measure of employee performance. It also increases defensibility of the system if challenged in court. Similarly, the propensity of raters to impose bias or stereotyping common to trait-anchored systems is reduced because tasks are described specifically (Bailey, 1983). In addition, as mentioned above, there is evidence suggesting that some employees are more satisfied with systems which focus on specific standards of performance rather than general traits (Harris, 1988). From a motivational perspective, behavioral systems are of value because they provide employee feedback and they can be rationally tied to an incentive system. They are not, however, future-oriented. Emphasis is not on future goals but on past performance.

A special type of behaviorally based system not commonly used in libraries is called BARS (Behaviorally Anchored Rating Scales). In this system, a job is broken down into several essential categories. For

I. COMMUNICATION STYLE (Verbal & Nonverbal)	SELDOM	NOT FREQUENTLY ENOUGH	SOMETIMES	MOST OF THE TIME	COMMENTS (examples)
2. Communicates well (uses clear, concise English)					
3. Uses good telephone etiquette					
4. Speaks with proper volume (voice not too loud or soft)					
5. Is verbose					
6. Uses appropriate facial expressions (smiles, looks concerned, as appropriate)					
7. Uses nonverbal communication as appropriate (head nod, eye contact)					
8. Points vaguely to where information can be found					
II. USER INTERACTION AT DESK					
1. Lets patron shape question					
2. Assumes too quickly what patron wants					
3. Treats all users with courtesy and consideration					
4. Determines what level of help is needed					
5. Displays calm when working with difficult users					

Figure 2. CRD Reference Desk Performance Standards (Evaluation Form)

a reference position, this might include such categories as answering reference questions, conducting reference interviews, maintaining files, selecting reference materials, and preparing reports. For each category, a range of behaviors is identified from those representing poor performance to those representing average and superior performance. Each of these behaviors is assigned a specified number of points, with higher levels of performance receiving more points. An example of one set of BARS scales currently in use in a public library is provided in Figure 3. Weights can be assigned for various categories to indicate that certain duties are more important than others. An employee's performance evaluation is based on the total number of points accumulated.

The advantages to BARS are the same as those mentioned for other behavioral systems. The numerical ratings are especially useful in making rational decisions concerning wage increases and merit awards. There are, however, some problems with BARS. Most notably, the initial process of identifying representative examples of performance requires considerable time and organizational effort. Generally, the process requires establishing three work groups: those who identify and categorize the range of behaviors from poor to outstanding; those who reexamine the behaviors and categories to ensure that they are accurate and correctly grouped; and those who assign points to the various behaviors. The skills required to administer this process are considerable, and it should be undertaken only with a serious commitment on the part of staff and administration. Problems with BARS also include difficulties some supervisors have in recording a sufficient number of examples to determine the level at which the employee is performing, and trying to fit observed behaviors into the sample behaviors provided (Latham & Wexley, 1981). Finally, at least some studies suggest that BARS is no better or worse than other evaluation methods (Jacobs et al., 1980).

I. Answering or Referring Questions

Points	Behavior
1	Is not able to answer or refer reference questions.
2	Has difficulty answering and referring reference questions.
3	Is generally able to answer or refer most reference questions. Has knowledge of and ability to use sources. Chooses sources appropriate to the level of the patron. Learns about new sources as they are published.
4	Shows above average skill in answering questions. Makes proper use of local sources before referring. Continually works to improve knowledge of reference sources.
5	Has command of reference sources and is always able to answer or refer questions. Shows creativity and tenacity when answering questions. Questions are referred to this person by other staff because of his or her knowledge of sources.

Figure 3. Behavioral anchors for a reference librarian

Goal-Oriented Standards

Another option for the library is to use mutual goal setting as part of the evaluation process. A goals-based system emphasizes the establishment of agreed-upon performance targets. It is a collaborative and developmental technique as much as it is an evaluative one. Although a review of past performance related to previous goals is essential, the focus of the evaluation is on the setting of future goals and on a discussion of how to meet them. During such a discussion it is expected that the employee, in conjunction with the supervisor, will not only establish goals but will prepare a developmental plan which details specific actions the employee may take to improve their ability to meet their goals. For example, an employee might state an intent to take additional courses or training programs during the next review period. Generally, performance goals should meet several criteria. They should be measurable, mutually agreeable, realistic, clearly stated, attainable, reflective of the essential functions of the job, and complimentary to broader departmental and organizational goals.

Libraries that use performance evaluation as a motivator should seriously consider goal setting when appropriate. There is a substantial body of research in the management literature that suggests that goal setting can be a strong motivator toward higher levels of productivity, especially if difficult and challenging goals are set (Locke & Somers, 1987). In addition, the fact that the goal setting is mutual, that is, the employee participates in the goal-setting process, has been shown to increase the effectiveness of the performance evaluation (Cederblom, 1982; Burke et al., 1978).

Despite these advantages, goal setting should only be used for certain job tasks. For example, when a job requires programmatic activities, e.g., developing a bibliographic instruction program, developing an online searching unit, or creating a training program for reference assistants, then goal setting would be appropriate. Similarly, for activities that are easily quantified, e.g., increasing the use of interlibrary loan by 25 percent in the next year or increasing the number of automated searches by 10 percent in the next year, then goal setting is useful. However, when activities are not easily quantified, depend on qualitative judgments, or are highly structured or routine, then behavioral standards may be more appropriate. For this reason, goal setting may be inappropriate for many basic reference desk activities such as interviewing and interacting with patrons.

Although there are definite motivational advantages to goal setting, there are also problems. First, goal setting is usually time-consuming in terms of administering the review, training supervisors, orienting staff, and preparing evaluation materials. Second, goal setting requires good negotiation and communication skills, especially on the part of the supervisor. Autocratic and uncommunicative managers are not likely to stimulate an atmosphere of participation among employees, and this will reduce the employee's commitment to the goals that are set. Similarly, uncommunicative or uncooperative employees may not like the negotiation process, hence reducing commitment to the goals created.

Recent trends indicate that businesses which had turned to goal setting as a form of evaluation are coming back to behavioral and quantitative standards coupled with graphic rating scales (Taylor & Zawacki, 1984). This trend is important because it reveals that business has not been satisfied with the results of "collaborative systems" which emphasize mutual goal setting and employee development; instead, they are reemphasizing the measurement of past performance so that job decisions such as pay increases and promotion can be accomplished with maximum documentation.

RECOMMENDATIONS TO LIBRARY MANAGERS

If the library is to maximize the motivational potential of the performance evaluation system, there are certain recommendations that are important no matter what type of system is employed. These include the following:

1. *Encourage employee participation in the development of job standards and in the evaluation process.* No matter whether the standards are behavioral or goal-oriented, employees should play a part in their creation. Participation on the part of the employee creates a stake in the process that would not otherwise be present. In addition, employees must be comfortable participating in their review. It is useful, for example, to give reference employees a copy of the review form several days before the actual review. In this way, they can prepare their own evaluations. Do not, however, expect that employees will be harder on their own performance than supervisors; 70 to 80 percent of employees put their performance in the top 25 percent (Meyer, 1986)!

2. *Attach concrete monetary incentives to the evaluation process.* It is a basic behavioralist premise that if a behavior is rewarded it will be repeated and if it is punished it will stop. Although human behavior cannot be explained so simply, the evidence is clear that attaching pay to worker performance increases worker productivity from 29 percent to 63 percent (Nash & Carroll, 1983). Employees who perceive that high levels of performance will be rewarded are more likely to maintain and improve their performance.

3. *Ensure that all standards and expectations for performance are clear and specific.* Goal specificity and clarity are directly related to employee satisfaction. It is particularly important that the supervisor and employee agree on which job tasks are most important. There is disturbing evidence that supervisors actually weight criteria differently than they think they do and that subordinates are unable to assess accurately what their supervisors expect of them and how they are rated (Hobson & Gibson, 1984). A concerted effort must therefore be made to communicate clearly what is important and to employ these valuations in the review process.

4. *Provide for timely and frequent reviews.* To some extent, the frequency of reviews depends on the purposes set by the organization. If the purpose is to have a documented record for promotion, demotion, or merit, then semiannual or annual reviews are all that are generally needed. If motivational and counselling effects are desired, then reviews should be more frequent: the more frequent the reviews, the more effective the evaluation (Kane & Lawler, 1979; Gleuck, 1974).

Of course, it is neither possible nor desirable to conduct formal performance evaluations all the time; this emphasizes the need to give employees informal evaluations of their performance often.

For motivational purposes, it is critical that employees receive feedback from their supervisors on both a formal and informal basis. Some research suggests that when feedback is combined with difficult goals, output can be increased by as much as 13-15 percent (Das, 1986). However, it is also important to realize that the *type* of feedback has a significant effect on the outcome of the evaluation. If criticism is part of the feedback, it must be done sparingly. As the amount of criticism increases in an evaluation, the less likely it is that performance behavior will improve. Even when the feedback appears to be positive, it may have unanticipated consequences. For example, one study revealed that employees who received "satisfactory" in comparison to those who received "outstanding" ratings suffered declines in their organizational commitment (Pearce & Porter, 1986).

5. *Set high and realistic standards of performance.* When goals are realistic and challenging, employees will increase their productivity. It is not sufficient to tell employees to "do their best." They must have unambiguous goals that challenge them (Locke & Somers, 1987; Latham & Locke, 1983). It is important, however, that the employee perceive that these goals can in fact be realized, and that the organization will provide the necessary resources to accomplish them. Otherwise, frustration will result.

6. *Make sure that supervisors are adequately trained.* This involves training in the purpose and implementation of the process. Supervisors must be skillful in communicating the evaluation process to the employee, and in making frequent observations of employee performance. Careful observation serves several purposes: first, frequent contacts to observe performance decrease the likelihood of the use of negative stereotypes (Bailey, 1983); second, well-trained supervisors are less likely to make procedural and substantive errors, hence decreasing the chance of legal liabilities if challenged.

7. *Make sure that supervisors are knowledgeable concerning the jobs they are evaluating.* The effectiveness of a review depends in part on the employee's perception that the supervisor understands the work of the employee (Cederblom, 1982).

CONCLUSION

The evaluation process is much more than a set of forms and written procedures. Its success depends on the complex interaction between the supervisor, the employee, and the organizational philosophy concerning the purposes of evaluation. Evaluating individuals who perform reference work is further complicated by the variety and nature of the tasks performed. For jobs with highly varied tasks requiring considerable flexibility in decision-making and high need for professional development and achievement, collaborative approaches such as goal setting may be desirable. For jobs that are more structured, behavioral approaches may be best (Taylor & Zawacki, 1984). The disparities in the nature of reference jobs suggest that the type of evaluation used may vary, and that combinations of different evaluation strategies may be advisable. Ultimately, the success of evaluations depends on the human aspects. Although performance evaluation is an essential process, the risks are easily as great as the benefits. By minimizing the risk, one inevitably will reap the benefit: a more effective reference staff.

REFERENCES

Association of Research Libraries, Office of Management Studies. (1987). *Performance evaluation in reference services in ARL libraries: Kit #139.* Washington, DC: ARL.

Bailey, C. T. (1983). *The measurement of job performance.* Aldershot, UK: Gower.

Bunge, C. A. (1985). Factors related to reference question answering success: The development of a data-gathering form. *RQ, 24*(4), 482-486.

Burke, R. J.; Weitzel, W.; & Weir, T. (1978). Characteristics of effective employee performance review and development interviews: Replication and extension. *Personnel Psychology, 31*(4), 903-919.

Carter, T. (1985). Performance appraisal for reference librarians. *Reference Services Review, 13*(3), 95-98.

Cederblom, D. (1982). The performance appraisal interview: A review, implications, and suggestions. *Academy of Management Review, 7*(2), 219-227.

Childers, T. (1980). The test of reference. *Library Journal, 105*(8), 924-928.

Crowley, T. (1985). Half-right reference: Is it true? *RQ, 5*(1), 59-68.

Das, B. (1986). Production feedback and standards as determinants of worker productivity, satisfaction and job attitudes. *Journal of Human Ergology, 15*(2), 113-122.

Deaux, K., & Emswiller, T. (1974). Explanations of successful performance on sex-linked traits: What is skill for the male is luck for the female. *Journal of Personality and Social Psychology, 29*(January), 80-85.

D'Elia, G., & Walsh, S. (1983). User satisfaction with library service—A measure of public library performance. *The Library Quarterly, 53*(2), 109-133.

Durrance, J. C. (1989). Reference success: Does the 55 percent rule tell the whole story? *Library Journal, 114*(7), 31-36.

Feild, H. S., & Holley, W. H. (1982). The relationship of performance appraisal system characteristics to verdicts in selected employment discrimination cases. *Academy of Management Journal, 25*(2), 392-406.

Gleuck, W. F. (1974). *Personnel: A diagnostic approach.* Dallas, TX: Business Publications.

Greller, M. M. (1978). The nature of subordinate participation in the appraisal interview. *Academy of Management Journal, 21*(4), 646-658.

Harris, C. (1988). A comparison of employee attitudes toward two performance appraisal systems. *Public Personnel Management, 17*(4), 443-456.

Heilman, M. E., & Guzzo, R. A. (1978). The perceived cause of work success as a mediator of sex discrimination in organizations. *Organizational Behavior and Human Performance, 21*(3), 346-357.

Heilman, M. E.; Simon, M. C.; & Repper, D. P. (1987). Intentionally favored, unintentionally harmed? Impact of sex-based preferential selection on self-perceptions and self-evaluations. *Journal of Applied Psychology, 72*(1), 62-68.

Heilman, M. E., & Stopeck, M. H. (1985). Being attractive: Advantage or disadvantage?: Performance based evaluations and recommended personnel actions as a function of appearance, sex, and job type. *Organizational Behavior and Human Decision Processes, 35*(April), 202-215.

Hernon, P., & McClure, C. R. (1987). Library reference service: An unrecognized crisis— A symposium. *Journal of Academic Librarianship, 13*(2), 69-80.

Hernon, P., & McClure, C. R. (1987). Quality of data issue in unobtrusive testing of library reference service: Recommendations and strategies. *Library & Information Science Research, 9*(2), 77-93.

Hobson, C. J., & Gibson, F. W. (1984). Capturing supervisor rating policies: A way to improve performance appraisal effectiveness. *Personnel Administrator, 24*(3), 59-68.

Jacobs, R.; Kafry, D.; & Zedeck, S. (1980). Expectations of behaviorally anchored rating scales. *Personnel Psychology, 33*(3), 595-640.

Kane, J. S., & Lawler, E. E., III. (1979). Performance appraisal effectiveness: Its assessment and determinants. In B. M. Staw (Ed.), *Research in organizational behavior* (Vol. 1, pp. 425-78). Greenwich, CT: Jai Press.

Kopelman, R. E., & Reinharth, L. (1982). Research results: The effect of merit-pay practices on white collar performance. *Compensation Review, 14*(4), 30-40.

Latham, G. P., & Locke, E. A. (1979). Goal setting—A motivational technique that works. *Organizational Dynamics, 8*(2), 68-80.

Latham, G. P., & Wexley, K. N. (1981). *Increasing productivity through performance appraisal.* Reading, MA: Addison-Wesley.

Locke, E. A., & Somers, R. L. (1987). The effects of goal emphasis on performance on a complex task. *Journal of Management Studies, 24*(4), 405-411.

Lott, B. (1985). The devaluation of women's competence. *Journal of Social Issues, 41*(4), 43-60.

McCarty, P. A. (1986). Effects of feedback on the self-confidence of men and women. *Academy of Management Journal, 29*(4), 840-847.

Meyer, H. H. (1986). The pay for performance dilemma. Cited in Pearce, J. L., & Porter, L. W. (1986). Employee responses to formal performance appraisal feedback. *Journal of Applied Psychology, 71*(2), 211-218.

Nash, A. N., & Carroll, S. J., Jr. (1983). *The management of compensation.* Monterey, CA: Brooks/Cole.

Nieva, V. F., & Gutek, B. A. (1981). *Women and work: A psychological perspective.* New York: Praeger.

Pearce, J. L., & Porter, L. W. (1986). Employee responses to formal performance appraisal feedback. *Journal of Applied Psychology, 71*(2), 211-218.

Roy, L. (1985). Sources of books for adults in eight Illinois communities. *Illinois Library Statistical Report #15*, 1-42. Urbana, IL: University of Illinois Library Research Center.

Rubin, R. (1991). *Human resource management in libraries: Theory and practice.* New York: Neal-Schuman.

Schwartz, D. G., & Eakin, D. (1986). Reference service standards, performance criteria, and evaluation. *The Journal of Academic Librarianship, 12*(1), 4-8.

Taylor, R. L., & Zawacki, R. A. (1984). Trends in performance appraisal: Guidelines for managers. *Personnel Administrator* (March), 71-80.

Van House, N. A.; Weil, B. T.; & McClure, C. R. (1990). *Measuring academic library performance: A practical approach.* Chicago: American Library Association.

Wallace, D. P. (1983). An index of quality of Illinois public library service. *Illinois Library Statistical Report #10*, 1-46. Urbana, IL: University of Illinois Library Research Center.

Weech, T., & Goldhor, H. (1982). Obtrusive versus unobtrusive evaluation of reference service in five Illinois public libraries: A pilot study. *Library Quarterly, 52*(4), 305-324.

Weiner, B.; Frieze, I. H.; Kukla, A.; Reed, L.; Rest, S.; & Rosenbaum, R. M. (1971). *Perceiving the causes of success and failure.* Morristown, NJ: General Learning Press.

Westbrook, L. (1989). *Qualitative evaluation methods for reference services.* Washington, DC: Association of Research Libraries.

GERALDINE B. KING

Associate Director
Ramsey County Public Library
Roseville, Minnesota

SUZANNE H. MAHMOODI

Continuing Education and Research Specialist
Library Development and Services
St. Paul, Minnesota

Peer Performance Appraisal of Reference Librarians in a Public Library

ABSTRACT

The reference librarians at Ramsey County Public Library, a suburban Twin Cities public library, developed an innovative performance appraisal system that includes self-evaluation and a peer group discussion. Each librarian rates her/himself on a thirteen-page list of reference librarian competencies and assesses the effect of other factors on his/her ability to do the job. A summary of these two parts plus a report on past objectives, a draft of future objectives, and a list of prioritized duties are given to each member of the reference department prior to a one-hour group discussion. Initial evaluations of the process were primarily positive; all twelve participants wished to continue its use. Relating competencies to objectives resulted in a specific self-development plan. Relating self-development needs and job duties facilitated priority setting. The process has now been expanded to include nonprofessional public services personnel, technical services staff, and branch libraries.

INTRODUCTION

The past ten years have seen a publication explosion in the subjects of management theory and organizational structure. Phrases like participatory management, democratic management, matrix management structure, horizontal organization, etc. are used to describe the "new management." This new management is characterized by greater individual responsibility, authority, and control over one's job, as well as by recognition that many jobs are now being accomplished by groups or teams of people working together. Studies of job satisfaction and motivation indicate greater individual responsibility, involvement in projects, and commitment; and the opportunity to change, to learn, and to develop on the job results in higher levels of satisfaction.

Stanley Davis (1987) proposes the theory that the organization and structure within which people work is the last element to change when revolutionary developments happen in the workplace. Davis' theory is that we are now in the early stages of the organizational changes brought about by the "post-industrial" workplace (p. 6).

One area which has particularly lagged behind even in organizations adopting much of the "new management" is performance appraisal. Most performance appraisal is still implemented in an authoritarian style and is based on a theoretical structure which is suited to a hierarchial management style and organizational structure. That is, it is a one-on-one judgment by the supervisor ("boss") of the worker ("employee")—more akin to the roles of the king and the feudal vassal than to the coach and team or to the members of a group of co-equals working together.

A recognition of this lack of congruity between their performance appraisal system and the kind of management structure they had developed led the twelve librarians in the Ramsey County Public Library reference department to experiment with peer performance appraisal. For ten years, the reference staff had been involved in increasing collegial and participatory management practices in the department. Starting in the early 1970s, they began referring to themselves as a "team" with a manager. Regular weekly departmental meetings, at which matters needing decisions were discussed and decided on by vote, were initiated. Management duties such as scheduling the desk, coordinating selection of reference materials, training of new staff, etc., were gradually allocated among the various staff members, partly on the basis of who was good at doing a particular task and partly on a rotating basis so that each person could experience and learn several tasks. As time went on, the person in the department head position was handling no more administrative duties than any other member of the department. In the fall of 1983, the department head transferred to a branch library. The vacancy was filled so the reference group had the same number of people, but no department head was named. Instead, the department adopted the term *project manager* to describe the duties of the several staff members who were in charge of the various management tasks. Developing a peer performance appraisal system seemed a logical next step for a group of professionals working as a team.

During this same ten-year period, another component of a participatory management system was established. The reference department began writing annual departmental objectives, and staff members were required to write individual annual objectives. By the time the peer performance appraisal experiment was initiated, all librarians wrote six-month objectives as well. Although the staff members were clearly involved in collegial management practices, the department was still using the standard performance appraisal form and the supervisor interview required by the county civil service. The Associate Director of the Library was acting as the supervisor for this purpose.

Over the years, the department members talked about the inadequacy of the civil service check-list and discussed trying other systems. Twice during the ten-year period, the county brought in outside consultants and held workshops on performance appraisal. The county system was acknowledged as unsatisfactory yet remained in place.

In writing their departmental objectives for 1984, the reference department included an objective to experiment with peer performance appraisal. A task force of department members was formed to work out a proposal. The Library Director consulted with the County Director of Civil Service, who agreed that the experiment could be undertaken provided that interim reports were made to the Library Director.

The peer performance task force proposed guidelines which were subsequently agreed to by the entire reference department staff. Those guidelines were:

- A competency checklist would be developed and used to aid reference personnel in judging themselves.
- Each staff person would draft his/her own professional objectives.
- The approach to evaluation would be constructive rather than critical.
- Each staff member could expect help and suggestions from their colleagues on projects and problems.

The task force reviewed the literature on peer performance appraisal in librarianship and found that the systems described involved a committee and/or departmental chairperson and not the entire staff. To the Ramsey County task force, a "peer" system meant that each person would have equal weight or status in the process. They concluded that a peer system appropriate to the Ramsey County situation did not exist and that they would have to develop their own system. At this point, the task force contacted the state library agency consultant in library research, one of whose areas of expertise was librarian competency research, who agreed to work with the task force.

The task force and consultant met and refined the criteria for the system. Two additional important concerns were identified. Because many of the tasks and projects in the reference department were accomplished by two or more librarians working together, an individual's achievements were affected by their colleagues' work. An individual's performance was also dependent in part on other factors over which they had little or no control, such as library funding.

Thus, the amended criteria for peer evaluation included the individual's competencies; a "committee-of-the-whole" approach to peer appraisal; evaluation of the team and of projects as well as of individuals; a consideration of other factors relevant to performance such as budget, equipment, etc.; and individual objective setting. To meet the criteria, a system was developed which included the following parts:

• a self-assessment based on competencies,
• a self-assessment of factors affecting performance other than competencies,
• a listing of past and future objectives, and
• a one-hour group discussion for each individual based on the self-assessment and individual objectives.

Developing the Competencies

The consultant agreed to develop an initial comprehensive, reference librarian competency list which the group would tailor to their particular department.

Two competency identification studies had been conducted in Minnesota with public library personnel. In those studies, the competencies had been identified by those performing the functions and by observers, such as supervisors, familiar with the job. Both studies used the job element method to identify and rate the elements, i.e., knowledge, abilities (including skills), attitudes, and personal traits required by a worker to perform a job and included both observable and unobservable elements. The terminology used was consistent with Bloom's (1956) taxonomies which describe the precise levels of knowledge and attitudes required by a job. One study identified competencies for performance at the entry level, the other at a superior level (Office of Public Libraries and Interlibrary Co-operation, 1980; Mahmoodi, 1978.) The authors were involved in both studies.

The consultant used the competencies identified by these two studies as the basis for the list compiled for the Ramsey County Library reference staff. The King Study (1984) competencies for the reference function in public libraries had been tested for validity by the Ramsey County Library staff, and were compared with the compiled list. Managerial and automation-related competencies were developed by staff members based on their own experience and a literature search. The compilation of competencies from these sources was then tested by the staff for its validity in the Ramsey County Library setting. The edited list was used by the participants, in preparation for their peer appraisal discussions, to self-assess their most outstanding or significant competencies and those competencies which were their top priority for improvement.

Related Factors

As noted by the task force, an individual's job performance was affected by other factors in addition to personal competencies. Factors within the workplace, within the individual's personal life, and from the environment may have a positive or a negative effect on performance.

The factors, identified through a literature search and developed by the consultant, are listed in Appendix C, "Factors Affecting the Level of Performance." This listing of factors became the second part of each individual's preparation for the peer appraisal. Each individual listed those factors which affected his/her performance and summarized the effect.

Objectives

The individual's preparation for the peer appraisal also included objective setting. Prior to adopting the peer appraisal system, each librarian had been developing six-month objectives using the system outlined in M. Scott Myers' *Every Employee a Manager* (1981, p. 240). For each performance appraisal with the department head or Associate Director, they had summarized, on one sheet of paper, their responses to Myers' questions:

1. What were your major achievements during the past six months?
2. What are your goals for the next six months?
3. What are your long-term goals?

Each person's objectives had been modified by negotiation with the department head. For the peer performance appraisal, this practice was continued with the person listing her/his previous six-month objectives, briefly reporting on their current status and adding a draft of the next six-months objectives for consideration by the group.

These four parts prepared by the individual—competency assessment, other performance factors, previous objectives, and new objectives—were summarized on one side of an 8 1/2 x 11 sheet in a standard format. Once they had experienced the first two peer appraisal discussions, the group expressed a need to add priorities and job functions to the information provided to the group so that competencies and objectives could be discussed within those parameters. As a result, a section requesting a listing of job functions (duties, responsibilities, etc.) in a self-determined priority order (time, importance, etc.) was added to the form (see Appendix A). This revised self appraisal form replaced the official civil service form for library and county use. Individuals, as they were upcoming subjects of the peer appraisal discussions, distributed copies of their completed form to their colleagues. The individual's responses would be the basis for the peer discussion. Following the group appraisal discussion, the individual revised the responses as agreed upon within the group. This revised self-appraisal form was then placed in the individual's personnel file.

Peer Discussion

The procedure agreed upon by the group for the initial round of appraisals was that each person's discussion was to last for one hour. These discussions were scheduled one per week. Members of the peer performance task force agreed to be the first and second subjects for the process. Objectives for the peer discussion were: honest assessment; constructive criticism; problem solving for the individual and the group; and clarification of functions, objectives, and priorities.

To participate in and be comfortable in a group without an assigned leader, each individual had to have group process skills and be willing to assume various group member responsibilities. The consultant provided the group with a discussion skills outline, "Tips for Peer Evaluation Participants" (see Appendix D). Since the majority of the participants had worked together for more than five years and had participated in various team efforts, their group process skills and trust in each other in a group problem-solving setting were already highly developed.

At the beginning of the one-hour group session, a few minutes were allowed for reading the individual's written responses to the items on the self appraisal form. Then the first subject for discussion was the competencies the individual had listed as those five she/he considered to be outstanding and those five that were top priority for improvement. The initiator of the discussion could be any member of the group, including the individual whose performance was being evaluated. The individual might volunteer or be asked to give specific examples of his/her strengths or needs for improvement. A member of the group might begin by giving specific examples of an identified strength he/

she had observed in the person. Another member might ask for clarification of something listed as needing improvement by requesting specific reasons why the individual considered it a deficiency.

After discussing the individual's strengths and needs for improvement, the group would discuss the "factors affecting level of performance." On the self-appraisal form, the individual was asked to identify those factors which most hindered performance and those which most influenced good performance. For each factor, the group would elicit specific instances and examples of how the person was affected. They then turned to group problem solving and identified solutions or strategies. The group often identified hindrances to good performance they had in common with the individual and would spend some time sharing similar experiences. These shared problems would then be referred to the regularly scheduled departmental meetings for problem solving.

As the group turned to the topic of objectives, they acknowledged accomplishments, analyzed progress towards previous six-month objectives, and did problem solving on how the unmet objectives might be accomplished. They also accepted or rejected objectives proposed for the next six months. The group often used the job functions for understanding objectives.

When discussing objectives the person was proposing for the following six months, the group used all items on the self-appraisal form—competencies, factors, job functions and priorities, and objectives—as well as their knowledge of departmental and library goals and objectives to help the individual set realistic objectives. They would suggest objectives and strategies for using personal strengths as well as improving the abilities of the individual; they would also suggest options and resources for meeting personal developmental objectives.

At times, honest co-assessment could only be achieved through use of confrontation and conflict resolution techniques. When there were conflicts, the consultant reminded the group that peer discussion offered such an opportunity for resolution of conflict and obligated them to handle conflict openly and in a non-threatening manner. Suggestions for revising the individual's responses on the form were made throughout the discussion, and agreement was negotiated between the individual and the group.

The closing questions of the discussion were, "Has everything been discussed that you think should have been?" and "Are there ways in which we could help you further?" Following the discussion, the self-appraisal form was modified by the individual on the basis of the discussion, then checked by a member of the group to verify that it truly reflected changes agreed upon in the discussion. This form was then turned in as the official evaluation form to the Library Administrative Office and, subsequently, to the County Civil Service Department.

PROJECT EVALUATION

The project was evaluated by the state library agency consultant. Evaluation procedures used included a telephone interview with each person following her/his individual peer discussion and a questionnaire distributed four months after the first round of appraisal discussions. Following the second round of appraisals, another telephone interview was conducted with each person. Process observation of the discussions was also part of the evaluation.

The first telephone interviews took place within two days of the individual's performance appraisal peer discussion. Nearly all participants reported experiencing feelings ranging from uncertainty to apprehension and anxiety prior to their appraisal discussion. However, half of the participants noted that their feelings of nervousness and uneasiness were mixed with feelings of trust and of being secure, open, and confident. After their individual appraisal discussions, all but one noted positive feelings, including feeling reinforced, supported, a member of the group, appreciated, and more self-confident as a result of the experience. One third added they felt relieved and satisfied. One person expressed feeling let down and disappointed because of having a personal incident aired.

All but one considered the peer appraisal process worthwhile. Two had had doubts about the process prior to participating but had found it beneficial. All but the one person expressing disappointment were willing to participate in the process again.

The participants were asked about the self-assessment exercise used prior to the group discussion. They considered the exercise helpful because it gave them the opportunity to organize their thoughts, a vocabulary for communicating about themselves to others, concrete examples to use, and an awareness of their own and others' personal priorities and objectives. Some considered the self-assessment exercise as valuable as the peer performance discussion because of the self knowledge and understanding they gained. One considered the self-assessment part of the process only somewhat helpful.

Each person was asked several questions concerning the group discussion:

1. Did you participate fully?
2. Were you heard?
3. Did the participation of the others help/hinder?

4. Was what was said of you accurate/inaccurate? Helpful/useless? Vague/specific?
5. Were you satisfied?
6. Were important issues aired?
7. What was helpful, not helpful?

All felt they had participated fully, had been heard, that important issues had been aired, and that the discussion had been helpful. Two-thirds of the participants considered what was said of them to be accurate, helpful, and specific. One reported that the suggestions given were too vague to be helpful, another reported being uncomfortable about a confrontation, and a third wanted more direction for personal improvement.

When asked what was most useful about the discussion, one half of the participants identified the problem-solving aspect. Some mentioned the opportunity to clarify their specific job duties and others considered receiving support, appreciation, and feedback from their colleagues as most useful to them. Only four responded to what aspect of the discussion was least useful. They identified as not useful both lack of concrete suggestions and descriptions of specific situations.

Participants were asked whether their knowledge of themselves and others had changed and whether they anticipated making any personal changes based upon the experience. One half learned more about themselves; one half, more about others. Half expected to be making personal changes as a result of the experience; half did not.

Written Survey

Four months after the first round of peer appraisal discussions, participants were asked to respond to a survey on whether any personal changes had occurred as a result of the experience and whether the process fulfilled functions usually associated with performance appraisal. Ten of the eleven respondents (the twelfth had retired during this period) had experienced personal change they considered attributable to use of the technique. They reported improved ability in setting personal objectives and priorities, increased sense of responsibility, and self-identification as a committed professional. An increased willingness to share with other team members and to learn from and problem-solve with others was also attributed to the peer appraisal experience. Other changes reported were being more at ease in making decisions and expressing ideas, being more confident about abilities, and being more tolerant of others. Eight of the eleven also experienced change in others. They reported as examples of this change an increase in the team approach to problem-solving among their colleagues, an increase in mutual understanding, improved communication, and openness. They also reported less stress, higher morale, and more accommodation of requests for specialized duties.

Survey respondents acknowledged some of these changes reported could be attributed to other factors as well. They identified as other possible contributors to the changes: committee assignments, added experience, influence of project manager and associate director; personnel rotation, stability of the reference work force, other problem-solving techniques tried, and personal observation and motivation. Those reporting little or no change resulting from the use of peer appraisal identified increased workload, lack of time, and preoccupation with personal problems as factors which may have contributed to their not experiencing change during this period.

FUNCTIONS OF PERFORMANCE APPRAISAL

Fifteen functions of performance appraisal were listed. Respondents were asked to rate the effectiveness of the peer appraisal process for fulfilling each function on a scale of 1-7. (1 = very effective, 4 = not different from other evaluation processes, 6 = not effective at all, 7 = have not observed.) Of the functions which are listed below, the majority of the respondents rated the peer appraisal process as effective to very effective in serving each function with the exception of making employment decisions. For this function, three had not observed a relationship and two others rated peer appraisal as no more effective than other evaluation processes in making employment decisions.

The fifteen performance appraisal functions which the respondents used to rate the effectiveness of the peer appraisal were:
1. learning about others with whom one works,
2. providing performance feedback to colleagues,
3. eliciting feedback from colleagues,
4. supporting job development,
5. providing ideas about learning and personal development needs,
6. improving work relationships,
7. acknowledging work that was done well,
8. creating a base for modification of behavior,
9. improving work focus,
10. putting fears to rest,
11. facilitating personnel planning,
12. improving communication skills,
13. improving productivity,
14. identifying work that could have been done better, and

15. making employment decisions, i.e.,identifying candidates for branch and project management, etc.

They were also asked for further comments on the process. They identified being better able to co-assess personal plans, understanding the relationship of their and others' individual goals and objectives and their day-to-day activities, being able to relate better with coworkers by giving and receiving feedback and support, and being able to benefit from group problem-solving through the peer appraisal process.

Two individuals reported, however, that they remained hesitant about participating in peer appraisal, one giving as a reason a personal crisis and the other, the possibility of "group think." Some noted that the group could improve in identifying needed changes, in confronting one another about problem behavior, and in being critical about each other's work. They added that more experience with the peer appraisal process might increase open communication.

Second Interviews

After a second round of peer appraisal discussions, the participants were also interviewed by phone. Once again, they expressed positive reactions to the process. They identified the following as benefits:

- a positive change in relationships related to increased understanding of one another;
- being able to use personal strengths, identified through the process, in facing new challenges such as the implementation of an automated system;
- greater and more accurate self-knowledge;
- willingness to be more open;
- peer evaluation of personal accomplishments;
- solving problems productively and with quality, e.g., developing strategies for working with staff shortages and being overworked;
- seeing the wholeness of one's job and of one's role in the institution;
- identifying personal needs, e.g., for additional training in supervisory skills;
- understanding nonverbal expressions;
- understanding that compensating for others' shortcomings is more stressful than confrontation;
- learning to whom to speak to get things done;
- reorganizing work in own area of responsibility;
- becoming positive about the process, especially because of its problem-solving potential; and
- learning how to compensate for personal uneasiness in confrontations.

When asked about changes needed in the process, the majority saw no change needed at that time but were open to the idea of possible future change. Two suggested that other procedures to provide one-on-one feedback, such as coaching and mentoring, should be used in conjunction with peer appraisal. When asked about scheduling of the process, some wanted the rounds of discussions to be scheduled every six months. Having the benefit of group problem-solving focused on their own problems and objectives, they wished that opportunity to be made available more often than once a year.

CONSULTANT OBSERVATIONS

The consultant observed both the first and second rounds of peer discussion. She and the group discussed her observations on content and process at the end of each individual peer discussion. The group learned from this evaluation to recognize and interpret nonverbal gestures, to gain confidence in situations which demanded confrontation, to assign problems to appropriate groups for solving, and to assume various group process roles as needed.

In her evaluation of a group without a designated leader, the consultant observed various leadership behaviors. The discussions were led by the interviewee or any other member of the group. If the interviewee appeared to want to be in control of the discussion, he or she would lead the discussion. In this case, other group members would assure that all sections of the self-assessment form were covered by intervening when needed. If the interviewee seemed to not want to initiate the discussion, another group member, usually self-selected, would take the lead by asking the first question. By the second round, interviewees tended to lead their own discussions.

As they became more experienced in the process, all became more skilled in isolating problems, working through conflict, giving specific examples of an individual's strengths and needs for improvement, and understanding when certain personal traits needed to be accommodated.

Members of the group were supportive of one another. They helped those lacking self-confidence to make statements about themselves; they were empathetic about problems and frustrations shared; they helped one another analyze problems; they offered options for solutions; they listened; they reminded one another that the five competencies needing improvement were to be provided for in the objectives; they cajoled, if needed. Phrases that became part of each discussion included "What could help you?" and "How could we help you improve?" Each discussion ended with "Have we discussed everything you wanted to discuss?"

CONCLUSION

The peer evaluation technique met all four objectives: honest co-assessment, constructive criticism, problem-solving for individual and group, and clarification of functions, objectives, and priorities. The technique offered both self and group assessment of factors that affected an individual's performance. Participants voiced satisfaction with both their self-assessment, which involved responding to the questions on the self-appraisal sheet, and the group discussion, which assessed, validated, and corrected the individual's responses. Two-thirds considered what was said of them to be accurate and specific. Both parts—the self-appraisal and the group discussion—were necessary to achieve this objective. As the group accepted and used confrontation and conflict resolution, they reported even more openness and satisfaction with their personal appraisals by others and their appraisals of others. The technique met the objective of constructive criticism. The participants viewed the criticism of themselves as accurate, helpful, and specific. A few wished for even more specific comments. The group adopted the practice of helping individuals incorporate changes which needed to be made into the following six months' objectives.

The problem-solving portion of peer evaluation is one of its outstanding features. The group problem solving for the individual with its clarification of issues, examples of specific situations, and suggestions of strategies and resources the individual may use led to evaluative comments such as the following:

> Changes in technology are accompanied with changing relationships and procedures. Peer evaluation makes us aware of how to use our strengths in such situations.

> We need peer evaluation every six months for problem solving.

> I have everyone's attention on me and my problems for an hour—wonderful!

> Alleviates feeling of being overworked when we know we will have an opportunity to problem-solve.

The clarification of functions, objectives and priorities were achieved by use of the self-appraisal form as well as within the discussion. The individual was asked to self-identify these on the form, and the group used these self-identified items as a basis for their discussion. Perceptions were clarified and changed by the discussion.

The peer evaluation process as used by the Ramsey County staff accomplished the objectives set by the group as well as fulfilled the functions of performance appraisal identified in the literature. Its success might be attributable in part to the Ramsey County staff's having experience with various participative techniques, trusting in their leader, being accustomed to innovative approaches used in the library, and having other experiences with team organization. However, the use of this technique clearly improved the problem solving of the group, the self-knowledge of the individual, and the clarification of functions, objectives, priorities and perceptions.

This system of employee performance evaluation strengthens and fits in with participatory management in two valuable ways: (1) the process contributes to establishing an environment of trust, and (2) the process provides the opportunity for the communication and discussion needed for coordination and setting of priorities. The work of individual professionals and the various group projects involving some but not all of the group can be integrated into a logical departmental plan.

Trust is established and fostered by the repeated experience of discussing their individual jobs and objectives and their commitment to providing information for people. The individuals' self-esteem is enhanced by seeing themselves as their colleagues see them and by having their colleagues validate their self-assessment. They are "empowered" by this enhanced self-esteem, by the support of and the help given them by their colleagues, and by their acknowledged commitment to the projects each manages. They and their colleagues benefit from reaching mutual agreement on each person's objectives and priorities. As an additional benefit, the clarification of objectives and functions and agreement upon priorities allow the individual to ask for and receive help without worrying about personal image and status as perceived by others.

Discussing activities and projects as they relate to each individual and that person's work objectives allows for continual readjustment of priorities and refinement of projects as each person's perspective is taken into account by the group. A work group such as the Ramsey County reference department can truly become a team which minimizes the effect of individual shortcomings, which benefits from the strengths of each individual, and which creates a whole greater than the sum of its parts through using management techniques that recognize coworkers as co-equals, such as the peer appraisal process described herein.

Subsequent Experience with the Peer Appraisal Process

Five years after the initial experience with peer appraisal, the Ramsey County reference librarians are still using this process. In the intervening five years, the process has been expanded so that the majority of Ramsey County Library employees are evaluated in this way.

Five years have resulted in few changes in the way the reference department practices peer appraisal. The list of competencies has proved remarkably stable. Twice in five years, a formal process of revision of the list has been carried out. The first revision resulted from the introduction of an integrated automated system into the library. Changes and expansion were needed in the Information Technology section of the list; changes in database searching procedures also provided some new competencies for this section. An example of an added competency is "is able to teach users to do computerized searching." At the time these changes were made, the entire list was reviewed by all the reference librarians but no other changes were made.

The second revision was handled with the assistance of the state library consultant. She provided the librarians with some readings about the future of library service and then met with them to brainstorm new or revised competencies. Except for some editorial changes to clarify meaning, the established list was not changed. A carefully prepared list of competencies appears to need little revision except for the changing terminology of new technologies; the Information Technology section seems to need revision about every two years.

Working out the optimum scheduling and timing of the appraisals has been a continuous tension between what would make the process work best, how much time can be devoted to the formal process, and the annual requirements of the County. During the first year and a half, the feeling was that individual objectives needed to be monitored by the group about every nine months. Since the nine-month interval did not fit the County's requirements, in 1988, a midterm process was skipped. However, letting a whole year go by made it too easy to forget one's objectives and priorities, whereas a six-month interval seemed too onerous on the work schedule.

An alternate midyear process was tried in 1989 in which each librarian did a one-page written report on his/her personal objectives. Copies of these reports were handed out to each person in advance and then a one-hour group planning conference was held. Group planning and priority-setting were accomplished in this session, but there was not time to deal with each individual. And the kind of trusting atmosphere necessary for individual concerns could not be established in so short a time period. Again in 1990, no midyear formal review has been held. What seems to be the best compromise between the needs of the library and the annual requirement of the County is for each individual to monitor her/his own objectives. He/she can then request informal feedback from the group or other individuals as desired.

The most significant aspect of long-term use of the appraisal process is dealing with new librarians coming into the group, both transfers and job rotations from other Ramsey County Library branches and newly hired reference librarians. While the reference librarian group had been quite stable prior to the introduction of peer appraisal and for the first two years of its use, approximately one-half the work group changed as a result of the introduction of a job-rotation plan near the end of 1987.

Integration of these new group members was handled in two ways. New employees were eased into the peer appraisal process. The County requires a six-month probationary period for them and they must be evaluated on the County form at three months and at six months. During their first six months, new employees participated in the discussion periods for their colleagues but were not evaluated by that process themselves.

For those coming from other branches, individual educational meetings were held where the background and rationale for the process were explained, the experience with it and its evaluation were described, and the various forms were studied. These transfers were scheduled for their evaluations after they had participated in the peer appraisal sessions for the "veterans." This caused only the usual initial apprehension at the first time one is the subject of the peer discussion.

Another effect of job rotation was that those former members of the reference group wanted to expand peer appraisal to the Ramsey County branch libraries.

The change in group composition had some effect on the openness and trusting atmosphere of the group discussion sessions. A person's initial appraisal by this process is often primarily an informative or educational process for one's peers. The second time that person is evaluated in this way, more help is usually provided for solving one's problems. As the individuals get to know each other better, more trust is established and confrontation of difficult issues is easier to do. To some extent, changing the group membership temporarily sets back the effectiveness of the peer appraisal process for team building and individual development. However, as the process has expanded to other branches, individuals who have had experience with it in one location transfer their understanding of the process and tolerance for stress in the group discussion to the new location. In the long run, the rotation plan strengthens the process throughout the Ramsey County Library system.

Expansion of the Peer Appraisal Process to Less Homogeneous Groups

The first attempts at using this peer appraisal process by work groups composed of professional, paraprofessional, and clerical employees took place at about the same time in a local college library and in a branch library of Ramsey County. The staffs of both of these libraries were about the same size. The branch library had acquired some of the original reference librarian group as a result of job rotation. They were eager to continue using peer appraisal but wanted to expand it to include the paraprofessional and clerical branch staff; the nature of branch library work is such that the various types of employees work more closely together and their roles overlap more than in a larger or headquarters library. To have a group of a reasonable size for discussion—eight to twelve rather than three to five—it was necessary to include more than the librarians. This same rationale applies to the college library.

The major piece of work which needed to be done before the process could be expanded was to provide competency lists for other levels of staff. The college library asked the state library consultant to work with them in setting up their process. The consultant met with them and presented an overview of the process and the steps needed to start using it. They were able to begin their construction of competency lists with the King Study (1984) lists which were compiled for academic libraries.

The branch public library needed to go back to some of the competency lists from the earlier Minnesota studies (1980) which included public library competencies in addition to the reference ones already mentioned such as "Staff-Patron Relations" or "Staff Communications."

At the same time as these experiments were getting underway, the authors were also working with other public library assistant and associate directors to draft a "top management team" competency list for public libraries. This project started with generic management competencies as well as selecting the management competencies from the various librarian lists already mentioned.

Part of this list of library management competencies, combined with some of the competencies from the Minnesota studies mentioned above, formed the basis for expanding the peer appraisal process to the management team of the headquarters library, which includes the nonlibrarian supervisors of the circulation services. This became the basis for developing lists for branch library managers by including the reference librarian competency list. This list also was used as a starting point for other circulation clerical workers at both the headquarters and branch libraries.

It was possible to begin using the process with draft lists, refining them in use and combining them with training and orientation checklists which were also being developed for the library system.

Another kind of job rotation plan led to the technical services staff adopting the peer appraisal process. Each librarian and paraprofessional and all full-time clerical workers in technical services work one day each week in public services. As a result of their public service day in the various libraries, some of them were participating in the peer appraisal processes in those public service libraries. They requested that the technical services department adopt the process. In 1989, the technical services staff was divided into two- to three-member subcommittees to work on the parts of competency lists for their work. Some of the subdivisions such, as management, had many ready-compiled lists. Others, such as processing, had to start from the very beginning, modelling their lists on the style of those already completed and using their training manuals as guides to the competency content. They developed lists for five competency areas which were used for their 1989 evaluations: acquisitions, cataloging, processing, management and communications, and computer/automation skills.

The process is now sufficiently well-developed at Ramsey County Public Library that it can be carried on with only a little more time than a traditional appraisal system. Beginning in October each year, each week someone in the work unit is scheduled for an appraisal-discussion period to precede the weekly work-unit meeting. The group discussions often cover topics that would need to be discussed in the work-unit meetings. By the end of the year, most units have completed the individual appraisals and developed and prioritized their list of unit objectives for the coming year. They have a clearer understanding of how the unit and the individual objectives fit together than they would had they had traditional individual appraisals.

APPENDIX A
Self-Appraisal Form

RAMSEY COUNTY PUBLIC LIBRARY
Peer Performance Appraisal Summary Form

Name _____ Date _____

I. <u>Competencies.</u> List the five that you think are your outstanding competencies or the five most significant competencies on which you rate yourself highly. Also list the five that are your top priority for improvement.

<u>Outstanding competencies</u>

<u>Needs improvement</u>

II. List factors, both positive and negative, which affect your level of performance, and which you would like to discuss with the group.

III. List your previous year's objectives. Write one or two sentences about your achievement for each one.

IV. List your next 12 months objectives as suggestions for consideration by the group.

IVb. List your long-range objectives.

V. List your present duties and try to put them in priority order.

SIGNATURE _____

DEPT.
HEAD'S
SIGNATURE _____

APPENDIX B
Reference Librarian Competency List

O = Outstanding
S = Superior (above average)
A = Acceptable (average/moderate)
NI - Needs improvement
NET = No experience or training

	O	S	A	NI	NET

A.   RESEARCH SKILLS
Of critical importance (essential)

Is able to analyze information needs
with careful attention to detail.

Understands how library materials and
information sources are organized.

Is able to match the best available
information resource to the information
need.

Is able to use various search strategies.

Is able to decide whether a manual or an
on-line search is more appropriate.

Is able to use information networks as
appropriate.

Is able to interpret information sources as
appropriate

Very important (should)

Is able to use Boolean logic in
conducting on-line searches.

Is able to use print thesauri and on-line
indexes to develp search strategies
for on-line searches.

Is able to compile bibliographies.

B.   COMMUNICATION SKILLS
Of critical importance (essential)

Is able to accurately comprehend the oral
communications of others.

Is able to remember, evaluate and
use data obtained through listening.

APPENDIX B *(Cont.)*

O = Outstanding
S = Superior (above average)
A = Acceptable (average/moderate)
NI Needs improvement
NET = No experience or training

B. COMMUNICATION SKILLS
Of critical importance (essential)(cont'd)

	O	S	A	NI	NET
Is able to orally express or present ideas and factual information clearly and effectively.					
Is able to use interviewing techniques to determine the individual's information needs.					
Is able to teach individuals how to use information sources.					
Is able to use bibliographic instruction techniques appropriate for groups.					
Is able to interpret library policy, goals, services, and procedures for individuals or groups.					
Is able to give directions clearly.					
Is able to translate between users, their needs, and information sources, translating information into terms used by both.					
Is able to work with users of all ages appropriately and fairly.					
Is able to convey to the public knowledge of materials and services.					
Establishes initial climate that facilitates open communication.					
Is able to balance the need for efficiency and friendliness in telephone reference transactions.					

APPENDIX B *(Cont.)*

O = Outstanding
S = Superior (above average)
A = Acceptable (average/moderate)
NI = Needs improvement
NET = No experience or training

	O	S	A	NI	NET
B. COMMUNICATION SKILLS (con't) Very important (should) (cont'd)					
Is able to interpret and/or summarize information accurately for telephone reference transactions.					
Is able to perceive and react to the feelings and needs of others.					
Is objective in perceiving own impact on others.					
Is able to clearly express concepts and information, in writing, in well-organized and good grammatical form.					
Is able to use non-verbal communication effectively.					
Is able to evaluate the individual user's response to information provided.					
Of moderate importance					
Is able to work with individuals, local media and other groups using appropriate techniques to promote reference service.					
Is able to use questionnaires and discussion techniques.					
Is able to conduct meetings with individuals and groups both within and outside the library.					
Is able to convey the image of friendly, professional library service in contacts with others.					

APPENDIX B *(Cont.)*

O = Outstanding
S = Superior (above average)
A = Acceptable (average/moderate)
NI = Needs improvement
NET = No experience or training

	O	S	A	NI	NET
C. KNOWLEDGE OF COMMUNITY Very important (should)					
Is familiar with community demographic, social, economic, and political information.					
Is able to identify specific needs of clientele groups.					
Is able to anticipate future needs based on knowledge of the community.					
Knows current events in the community.					
Is familiar with institutions, organizations, agencies and industries within a community.					
Knows history of the community.					
Is aware of the relation of a community's political structure to a library.					
Participates in community organizations.					
Is able to work with community groups and agencies on cooperative projects.					
D. MANAGING SKILLS AND KNOWLEDGE Of critical importance (essential)					
Knows when to accept or delegate responsibility.					
Is able to identify problems, research relevant information, identify possible causes of problems, and suggest workable solutions.					
Is able to set, modify and follow through priorities.					

APPENDIX B *(Cont.)*

O = Outstanding
S = Superior (above average)
A = Acceptable (average/moderate)
NI = Needs improvement
NET = No experience or training

	O	S	A	NI	NET
D. MANAGING SKILLS & KNOWLEDGE Of critical importance (essential) (cont'd)					
Is able to develop and maintain good working relationships with personnel in other library areas.					
Knowledge of the operation of other sections in the library and how they work.					
Is able to perform effectively under pressure with frequent interruptions, and when faced with difficult tasks.					
Is able to manage personal and task time effectively.					
Has political skills, e.g., planning strategies for accomplishing objectives.					
Very important (should)					
Formulates and interprets reference policies.					
Is able to organize the available personnel resources to optimize strengths and compensate for weaknesses.					
Is able to utilize appropriate inter-personal styles or methods in order to effectively guide individuals (sub-ordinates, peers, supervisors) or groups toward task accomplishment.					
Is able to train and develop staff.					
Is able to establish procedures to monitor and/or regulate processes, tasks, or job activities and responsibilities of subordinates.					

APPENDIX B *(Cont.)*

O = Outstanding
S = Superior (above average)
A = Acceptable (average/moderate)
NI = Needs improvement
NET = No experience or training

	O	S	A	NI	NET
D. MANAGING SKILLS AND KNOWLEDGE (cont'd) **Very important (should) (cont'd)**					
Is able to evaluate personnel, using appropriate standards, measures and methods.					
Is able to develop alternative and appropriate courses of action based on logical assumptions and which reflect factual information and rational and realistic thinking.					
Is able to develop new and innovative services.					
Is able to measure and evaluate reference service.					
Knowledge of evaluation methods and techniques to evaluate systems, services and products.					
Is able to collect, analyze and interpret data.					
Is able to manage a budget.					
Is able to anticipate long-range needs of the library.					
Is able to design systems and procedures to improve library operations.					
Is able to arbitrate and negotiate among staff.					
Has knowledge of statistical description, analysis, interpretation and presentation.					
Has knowledge of standards, measures and methods for evaluating personnel.					

APPENDIX B *(Cont.)*

O = Outstanding
S = Superior (above average)
A = Acceptable (average/moderate)
NI = Needs improvement
NET = No experience or training

	O	S	A	NI	NET
D. MANAGING SKILLS AND KNOWLEDGE (cont'd) Very important (should) (cont'd)					
Has knowledge of alternative management structures and their implications for the operation of the library.					
Encourages innovation and new ideas of others					
Is able to work as a member of a group to reach decisions & accomplish tasks.					
Has knowledge of the costs associated with library resources (materials, personnel, space, etc.)					
Has knowledge of cost analysis and interpretation methods.					
E. KNOWLEDGE OF INFORMATION RESOURCES Of critical importance (essential)					
Is familiar with the mission, goals and objectives of the library.					
Knows the policies and procedures relevant to the library.					
Is able to use the expertise of the entire staff.					
Is able to identify and use community information or referral sources.					
Has a broad generation knowledge in order to interpret patrons' questions and information sources.					
Is familiar with the expanding information community, its participants and their interrelationships (social, economic technical, etc.)					

APPENDIX B *(Cont.)*

O = Outstanding
S = Superior (above average)
A = Acceptable (average/moderate)
NI = Needs improvement
NET = No experience or training

	O	S	A	NI	NET
E. KNOWLEDGE OF INFORMATION RESOURCES Of critical importance (essential) (cont'd)					
Knows the characteristics & use of the most commonly used information resources.					
Very important (should)					
Is familiar with the entire library collection.					
Is familiar with alternative approaches to the organization of information, e.g., classification schemes.					
Is familiar with the literature of various subject areas, both fiction and non-fiction, especially those of primary interest to users.					
Is familiar with authors and titles, both current and standard.					
Knows the arrangement (structure) of information resources in all formats.					
Is able to identify appropriate resources of other libraries.					
Is familiar with the operations of other sections of the library and how they relate to reference.					
Of moderate importance					
Understands the relation of the publishing industry to libraries.					
Is familiar with the contracting process.					

APPENDIX B *(Cont.)*

O = Outstanding
S = Superior (above average)
A = Acceptable (average/moderate)
NI = Needs improvement
NET = No experience or training

	O	S	A	NI	NET
F. **ATTITUDES** Of critical importance (essential)					
Is aware of the purpose of library service in society.					
Is committed to promoting libraries and library services.					
Is committed to equal service for all patrons.					
Willingness to draw upon and share knowledge and experience with others.					
Maintains a nonjudgmental attitude toward patron questions.					
Has the persistence to obtain requested information or to locate a correct source for information.					
Is alert toward recognizing and responding to patron needs.					
Is committed to maintaining a high standard of personal and professional ethics.					
Is tolerant of individual differences.					
Is sensitive to others' feelings in dealing with people.					
Participates in educational activities to improve her/his job performance.					
Is committed to protecting the patron's right to privacy in his search for information.					
Is willing to learn to use equipment necessary for library service.					

APPENDIX B *(Cont.)*

O = Outstanding
S = Superior (above average)
A = Acceptable (average/moderate)
NI = Needs improvement
NET = No experience or training

	O	S	A	NI	NET

F. ATTITUDES
Of critical importance (essential) (cont'd)

Is committed to defending the right of patrons to intellectual freedom in their pursuit of knowledge.

Listens objectively to other people's ideas and suggestions.

Accepts responsibility for decisions and their consequences.

Is committed to participating in professional organizations.

Is receptive and adaptable to change.

Is committed to achieving user satisfaction.

Very important (should)

Is interested in and seeks to become better educated in a wide variety of subjects.

G. PERSONAL TRAITS
Of critical importance (essential)

Respects others.

Is tactful.

Is cheerful.

Shows self-confidence.

Has a sense of humor.

Has self-control.

APPENDIX B *(Cont.)*

O = Outstanding
S = Superior (above average)
A = Acceptable (average/moderate)
NI = Needs improvement
NET = No experience or training

	O	S	A	NI	NET

G.   PERSONAL TRAITS
Of critical importance (essential) (cont'd)

Is imaginative and resourceful in
meeting patrons needs.

Is able to use calm, logical approaches
to library problems.

Projects a friendly, pleasant manner.

Admits the need to confer with, or
refer the patron to another person
or agency.

Very important (should)

Has poise.

Is committed to maintaining good physical
and mental health.

Is committed to maintaining appropriate
appearance/grooming.

H.   KNOWLEDGE AND SKILLS FOR
INFORMATION TECHNOLOGY
Of critical importance (essential)

Understands basic information technology
(e.g., computer, telecommunications) terms.

Is able to use protocol and command terms
of two or three major database vendors.

Is familiar with the contents and
characteristics of the most commonly used
on-line databases.

Very Important (should)

Is familiar with the keyboarding functions
of commonly available cathode ray terminals,
(CRTs).

APPENDIX B *(Cont.)*

O = Outstanding
S = Superior (above average)
A = Acceptable (average/moderate)
NI = needs improvement
NET = No experience or training

	O	S	A	NI	NET

H. KNOWLEDGE AND SKILLS FOR
    INFORMATION TECHNOLOGY (cont'd)
    Very important (should) (cont'd)

Keeps up with trends in hardware and
software which relate to reference work.

Understands how various hardware parts fit
together and can do simple trouble-shooting
to determine which part failed.

Is able to train other staff   to do on-line
searching.

Is informed about available and emerging
information technologies and their
application.

Is able to teach users to do computerized
searching.

Understands MARC fields in order to
effectively search &/or evaluate on-line
catalogs.

Is able to use command terms of all
modules of in-house integrated automated
system.

Of moderate importance

Is able to communicate with analysts or
programmers to facilitate development
of new programs.

Can apply knowledge of command languages
to obtain results in such various
applications as information and retrieval
file creation and word processing.

Of minimal importance

Is familiar with one programming
language.

APPENDIX C
Factors Affecting Level of Performance

FACTORS	Discussion of each factor as it affected my job for the past 12 months—why this factor has a positive (or negative) effect on my performance, how this factor could be improved, etc.
1. Personal	
Physical condition/ Health Emotional stability	
2. Motivation	
Personal interest in work satisfaction with job assignment Incentives and rewards feedback recognition salary	
3. Resources	
Equipment Facilities Availability of resources	
4. Work group	
Cohesion Leadership Co-workers competencies interpersonal	
5. Work environment	
Conditions Space allotment Arrangements	
6. Staffing	
Sufficient Scheduling	

APPENDIX C *(Cont.)*

7. Users

    Competencies,
        especially attitudes

8. Organization

    Climate
    Structure
    Size
    Management
        levels
        type
    Policies and
        practices

9. Funding

    Sufficient

10. New Technology Impact

11. Cooperative efforts

    Intralibrary
    Interlibrary

SUMMARY: a 2 or 3 sentence summary highlighting the worst and the best (to be transferred to summary sheet #2)

APPENDIX D
Tips for Peer Evaluation Participants

Participants in peer evaluation should:
  Understand agenda: setting, keeping on
  Have listening skills, i.e.,
    Adopt attitude of I can always learn something new
    Withhold judgment & action until meaning is clear, i.e., don't jump to conclusions
    Listen for meaning
    Ask questions
    Concentrate on ideas & information; avoid becoming defensive
    Avoid preconceptions, i.e., avoid putting a label on someone (job or position)
  Be able to communicate feelings and understand the communication of feeling
  Be able to gather data by:
    Interview
    Observation
      Look for accomplishments, skills, and style
      Manage your biases, i.e., be cognizant of your personal values and stereotypes
      Observe specifics, i.e., what person does, how he/she works, what the effects are on others, what is accomplished
      Have a broad enough perspective, i.e., recognize
      factors which might affect performance
  Understand group process by demonstrating responsible group membership, voluntary expression, and mutual acceptance of other persons involved
  Understand the principles of working as a group (team)

During the evaluation:
1. LISTEN; let interviewee talk
2. DIALOGUE, do not pronounce
3. Acknowledge all bring feelings, emotions, values, needs and opinions to discussion. Realize interviewee comes in with emotions, such as being on edge, apprehensive, defensive, or with guilt, fear, pleasure, regret, hope. Participants may fail to hear clear messages, may distort.
4. DON'T BE JUDGMENTAL
5. TAKE other person's feelings into account
6. BE CLEAR, be sure the other person knows what you mean
7. DON'T TALK ABOUT ISSUES other person can do nothing about, or are beyond his control
8. BE SPECIFIC, talk in concrete terms, etc.
9. EXPLAIN, but not how to do it your way
10. REASSURE, but do not undermine evaluation
11. CRITICIZE CONSTRUCTIVELY; negative criticism may blunt initiative & encourage mindless conformity.
    a. Avoid terms "always", "never"
    b. Criticize actions, not the person
    c. Be specific, not ambiguous
    d. Make criticism objective
    e. Be clear, non-threatening

APPENDIX D: *(Cont.)*

12. Use attending skills
    a. Set tone for interview
       Nonverbally
       1) A slight, but comfortable forward lean of upper body trunk (leaning back can encourage or discourage participation)
       2) Maintain eye contact (you are paying attention; breaking eye contact indicates your disinterest)
       3) Speak in a warm, but natural voice
          Verbally
          1) Use minimal encouragers: head nods, "I see's" "Uh-huhs" and simple repetition of key words: "Policy?" "Budget problems"
          2) Encourage interviewee to go on with explanations
          3) Stay on a topic—exhaust topic to your satisfaction; don't topic-hop; don't propose solutions before problem is thoroughly discussed

    b. Feedback
       1) Feedback should contain clear, concrete data; statements should be precise, not vague, e.g., vague: "Your work with patrons has been very good this year"; concrete: "This year you've increased responses by 20%, while cutting complaints in half."
       2) Adopt a non-judgmental attitude, i.e., be factual, matter-of-fact, analytical, e.g., judgmental: "You're terrible in meetings with other people. Every time I take you, you foul it up." Non-judgmental: "You seem too eager to me in meetings. Your behavior could be misinterpreted as pushiness, and be turning people off."
       3) Timely/present-tense statement: use recent problems, e.g., Distant Past Feedback: "You've screwed up the budget for the past three years, and this time I've had enough of it." Recent Past Feedback: "In reviewing the annual budgets last week, I found yours to be fouled up the worst. As usual." Timely/Present-Tense Feedback: "Hurry, I've just made some suggestions to you on how you can improve your budget. But you don't sound too enthusiastic about them. How can I help you become more effective in your budget preparation?"
       4) Deal with correctable items over which the subordinate has some control
    c. Paraphrase: A concise statement in your own words of the essence of what interviewee has just said. Should be non-judgmental, matter of fact, e.g., "If I heard you correctly...," "You're saying that ...," "It seems that what you're telling me is..." To check for accuracy of your paraphrase at end "Is that close?" or "Is that what I hear you saying?" e.g., Interviewee: "...So the headquarters problem is why our requests filled are down." Interviewer: "You're saying that the new Director's staff shakeups have lowered their productivity. And that now it's spilled over to your desk: Is that about right?" Interviewee: "Yeah. And what's more..."

APPENDIX D *(Cont.)*

d. Reflect Feelings; empathize
   Similar to paraphrase
   Literal, matter-of-fact, timely statement or question with a structure
   First use interviewee's first name or pronoun "you"; then, "It sounds like you feel..." or "I hear you expressing some..."
Next comes the label for the emotion, concentrating always upon the person seated in front of you.
Third, mention the context in which the emotion occurs.
Finally, if you wish, check with "Am I right?" "Is that so?" e.g., "Hank, I sense that you're really anxious about this interview. Would you like to talk about it?" e.g., "Jane, you seem to be feeling frustrated right now about your performance in this area. Perhaps we could talk about it for a few minutes?" Share your own similar experiences to illustrate that you "know what it's like..."

e. Use Open & Closed Questions
   Open: "Could..., Would..., Why... Tell me..., How..." Encourage interviewee to talk, to share. An open question offers an invitation to respond in more than just one or a few words. Good at beginning of interview, to promote understanding. Closed: "Did, Is, Are, How Many?", to speed up interview, to clarify, to be specific, e.g., Open question: "How is that new budget coming along?" e.g., Closed question: "Is your new budget in?"

f. Establish Focus; helps us identify five potential areas of organizational problems and possible direction to take: person, problem, other, context, self.

   —A person focus concentrates upon the person. Using the person's first name, or the pronoun "you" can help, e.g., "John, you sound frustrated about this performance appraisal system."
   —A problem focus deals with the issue at hand while trying to gain more information about it. A major concern could be the technical aspects to the problem. e.g., "John, could you tell me of your complaint with the appraisal instrument we used this year?"
   —Another person or other people become the highlight in another focus, e.g., "John, do you realize that every civil servant in this state is evaluated using the instrument you object to?"
   —In a self focus, attention is concentrated upon you. Here, you seek information from another about the impact of your actions upon her/him, e.g., "John, I'd like to know if I said or did anything in this performance appraisal process to upset you so much?"

Sources:
Kikoski, J. F., & Litterer, J. A. (1983). Effective communication in the performance appraisal interview. *Public Personnel Management Journal*, *12*(Spring), 33-42.
McLagan, P., & Krembs, P. (1983). *On the level: Tips to help managers and employees communicate about performance*. St. Paul, MN: M & A Press.

REFERENCES

Davis, S. (1987). *Future perfect.* Reading, MA: Addison-Wesley.

Bloom, B. (1956). *Taxonomy of educational objectives: The classification of educational goals, handbook I: Cognitive domain.* New York: D. McKay.

Mahmoodi, S. H. (1978). *Identification of competencies for librarians performing public services functions in public libraries.* Unpublished doctoral dissertation, University of Minnesota, Minneapolis, MN.

Minnesota Office of Public Libraries and Interlibrary Co-operation. (1980). *Self-assessment guide for reference.* St. Paul, MN: OPLIC.

Griffiths, J.-M. (1984). *Public librarian competencies: Validation package.* Rockville, MD: King Research, Inc.

Myers, M. S. (1981). *Every employee a manager.* (2d ed.). New York: McGraw-Hill.

Contributors

BRYCE ALLEN is Assistant Professor in the Graduate School of Library and Information Science, University of Illinois at Urbana-Champaign. He received his Ph.D. from the University of Western Ontario and worked in a variety of public service settings as a professional librarian. He currently teaches courses in reference, library administration, and library automation.

CHARLES A. BUNGE is Professor in the School of Library and Information Studies, University of Wisconsin-Madison, where he teaches in the areas of reference and information services, library cooperation and networking, and collection development. He is the author of numerous articles in the professional literature, especially in the area of evaluation of reference services. He is active in professional associations, including having served as President of the Reference and Adult Services Division of the American Library Association, and has provided consulting and continuing education services for reference staffs and library organizations throughout the country.

THOMAS CHILDERS is Professor in the College of Information Studies at Drexel University, Philadelphia and holds a Ph.D. in Library and Information Science from Rutgers University. His teaching, research, consultation, and writing have embraced the broad topics of the management of information organizations; adult information environments, information service provision, the effectiveness of libraries, and the quality of library services. Over twenty years, he has authored three books and numerous journal publications and technical reports, and is currently at work on a book about library effectiveness. His major awards include a British Library fellowship and the American Library Association's Isadora Gilbert Mudge Citation.

PRUDENCE WARD DALRYMPLE is a member of the faculty of the Graduate School of Library and Information Science at the University of Illinois at Urbana-Champaign. She received her Ph.D. in Library and Information Studies from the University of Wisconsin-Madison. She has published several articles in her fields of interest which include information retrieval, particularly studies of end-user access to electronic information systems, and health sciences librarianship. Her experience prior to joining the faculty at UIUC includes more than ten years as a reference librarian, search analyst, and manager in health sciences libraries.

CHERYL ASPER ELZY is Assistant Professor and Head of the Education/Psychology/Teaching Materials Center Division of Milner Library at Illinois State University in Normal, Illinois. She holds a master's degree and Certificate of Advanced Study from the University of Illinois at Urbana-Champaign. Her fields of interest include all aspects of reference service; collection evaluation; and children's and young adult materials.

MARY GOULDING is the Director of Reference Service for the Suburban Library System, a multitype cooperative of 178 libraries in the southern and western suburbs of Chicago. She received her M.L.S. degree from Rosary College and has worked as Head of Adult Services at Elmhurst Public Library and Administrator at Berkeley Public Library, both in the Chicago area. During her seven years with the System, Goulding has presented workshops in Illinois, Ohio, Wisconsin, Michigan, Minnesota, and Florida, spoken at state and national meetings, and published articles in *RQ* and *Illinois Libraries*. She currently serves as a member of the ALA/RASD Evaluation of Reference Services Committee and the Dartmouth Medal Committee.

GERALDINE B. KING is the Associate Director of the Ramsey County Public Library, a suburban Twin Cities public library. She holds a Ph.D. in Library Science from the University of Minnesota and has worked in both academic and public libraries and taught in library and information management programs. She has been president of the Minnesota Library Association and the Reference and Adult Services Division of ALA, and was editor of *RQ*. In addition to consulting, workshops, and writing, primarily in the areas of reference service and library personnel management, Dr. King has authored publications on performance evaluation for librarians.

F. W. LANCASTER has been a professor in the Graduate School of Library and Information Science at the University of Illinois at Urbana-Champaign since 1970, and is the editor of *Library Trends*. He is the author of eight previous books on various facets of library and information science, several of which have been translated into Russian, Chinese, Japanese, Arabic, and Spanish. Three of them received the Best Information Science Book award of the American Society for Information Science. His most recent book is *Indexing and Abstracting in Theory and Practice* (1991).

SUZANNE H. MAHMOODI, as Continuing Education Specialist for the Minnesota State Library Agency, specializes in needs assessment and self-assessment; competencies identification; and facilitating planning, decision-making, and problem-solving groups. She received a Ph.D. in Library Science from the University of Minnesota. She is currently a participant in the National Leadership Institute in Adult and Continuing Education at the University of Georgia, Athens. Her Institute project involves working with health services librarians in Minnesota to redesign their professional associations, consortia, etc., to meet current and emerging needs.

ALAN R. NOURIE is Professor and Associate University Librarian for Public Services and Collection Development at Milner Library, Illinois State University. He was formerly head of the Humanities Division at Ralph Brown Draughon Library of Auburn University. He received his M.S. in Library Science from the University of Illinois and also holds a Ph.D. in Modern British Literature from Southern Illinois University. He is co-editor of *American Mass-Market Magazines,* which was published in 1990.

JAMES RETTIG is Assistant University Librarian for Reference and Information Services at Swem Library of the College of William & Mary. He holds both B.A. and M.A. degrees in English from Marquette University and received an M.A.L.S. from the University of Wisconsin-Madison. Since 1981, he has been author and editor of the 'Current Reference Books' column in the *Wilson Library Bulletin.* In 1988, ALA's Reference and Adult Services Division awarded him the Isadora Gilbert Mudge Citation for 'distinguished contributions to reference librarianship.'

RICHARD RUBIN is Assistant Professor at the School of Library Science at Kent State University. He received his Ph.D. in Library and Information Science from the University of Illinois at Urbana-Champaign, and his MLS from Kent State University. He is author of *Human Resource Management: Theory and Practice* and was formerly Personnel Director of the Akron-Summit County Public Library.

BETTY J. TUROCK is Chair of Library and Information Studies and Director of the M.L.S. Program at Rutgers University, where she received her M.L.S. and Ph.D. degrees. Prior to her career in library education, she was Assistant Director, then Director of the Montclair (NJ) Public Library and Assistant Director of the Rochester and Monroe County (NY) Library System. During the 1988-89 academic year, she served as a Senior Associate in the United States Department of Education, Office of Educational Research and Improvement, Library Programs. She is the author of more than sixty publications centering on public libraries.

Evaluating Federally Funded Public Library Programs, the result of
her year at the U.S. Department of Education, was recently released.
Another publication, *Proving Library Programs Work,* is also
forthcoming from the Department of Education.

INDEX

Affective measures of information retrieval effectiveness, 89, 96-97. *See also* User-centered evaluation of information retrieval: user satisfaction

Atherton, Pauline, 95

Automation, effect on reference service, 14-18. *See also* Library use instruction

Bannister, Roger, 111

Bates, Marcia, 92

Bawden, David, 88, 99

Behaviorally Anchored Rating Scales (BARS). *See* Evaluation of reference staff

Berry, Rachel, 21

Bessler, J., 18

Bibliographic instruction (BI): and InfoTrac, 12-13; and library reference, 7-8; behavioral objectives of, 17; emphasis on document retrieval, 9, 12, 16; lack of data on, 86; limitations of universal search strategy model, 10-12; manifesto, 12; movement, 3, 10; shift from instruction to information provision, 7, 18, 19, 20. *See also* Library use instruction

Bibliographic Instruction Think Tank, Association of College and Research Libraries, 7

Bunge, Charles A., 23

Catalogs: facilitating access to library resources, 6; performance measures of, 96

Child, William B., 6, 20

Congressional Research Service (CRS), 19

Cost Finding for Public Libraries: A Manager's Handbook, 140

Council on Library Resources (CLR), 44

Cranfield studies. *See* User-centered evaluation of information retrieval

Crawford, Walt, 104

Crews, Kenneth D., 31

Cronbach's alpha statistic, 64

Crouch, Wayne, 95

Crowley, Terence, 27

Dalrymple, Prudence, 96

Daugherty, Robert, 92

Davis, Stanley, 168

DeProspo, Ernest, 127

Dervin, Brenda, 88, 93-94

DeVinney, Gemma, 9

Disney World computerized information system, 15

Drake, Miriam, 9, 18

Drucker, Peter, 35, 39

Durrance, Joan C., 31

Eliot, T. S., 15

Elzy, Cheryl, 31, 51

End-user searching studies, 86-87

Evaluation: qualitative, 126-27, 129-33, 136-40; qualitative/quantitative comparisons, 129-33; resistance to, 126

Evaluation of Adult Literacy Programs, 140

Evaluation of reference staff: 147-65; behaviorally anchored rating scales (BARS), 158-59; behaviorally based system, 157-59; factors affecting review outcomes, 149-52; gender differences and attribution theory, 152-53; goals-based system, 159-60; performance evaluation technique and problems, 148; rating errors, 150; recommendations to managers, 161-62; review of research, 147-48; trait-based system, 154-57

Evaluation of services: surveys, problems with, 21; unobtrusive testing, 21, 22, 23; necessity of faculty/practitioner collaboration, 23-24. *See also* Unobtrusive study of reference

Every Employee a Manager, 171

Fenichel, Carol, 95

Goldhor, Herbert, 38

Goodwin, Jane, 38

Guba, Egon G., 130

Hallman, Clark N., 17-18

Unobtrusive study of reference service:
27-42, 43-57; application of method
to other fields, 28; application of
method to other library services, 28-
29; at Brigham Young University,
32, 36, 38; at Illinois State University, 31, 35, 36, 43-57; at Memphis
and Shelby County Library, 32;
dependent variables, 30-32; dominant findings, 29-30; factors com-
promising validity of, 33-35; hierarchy of reference products, 36-37;
history of, 27-29, 37, 38; independent variables, 32-33; lack of experimental and qualitative studies, 40,
56; managerial aspects of, 38;
method, 37-39; nature of queries,
33-35; nature of reference product,
35-37; short factual unambiguous
queries (*sfus*), 34; State of California's reference referral hierarchy, 38.
See also Evaluation of services
User-centered evaluation of information retrieval: 86-102; context and
impact, 97-98; cost, 92-93; Cranfield
studies, 90; history of, 90-94; information need, 93-94; novelty, 93;
precision and recall, 90-92; qualitative methods, 99; relevance and
pertinence, 90-92; system goals, 86;
use studies, 88; user satisfaction, 94-
97; user-centered studies, 89-90. *See
also* Affective measures of information retrieval effectiveness, Information retrieval systems goals

VTLS integrated system, 18

Weaver, 89
Webb, Eugene, 28
Weech, Terry L., 38
White, Herbert S., 21
Whitlach, Jo Bell, 22
Wiberly, Stephen, 92
Wilson, Patrick, 98
Wilson, T. D., 89
Wisconsin-Ohio Reference Evaluation
Program: 62-75; demographics, 65-
67; objectives, 62-63. *See also* Ref-
erence question-answering effec-
tiveness, evaluation of

Wyer, James I., 36
Zweizig, Douglas, 88, 96, 135